IMAGES
of America

ROSEBUD SIOUX

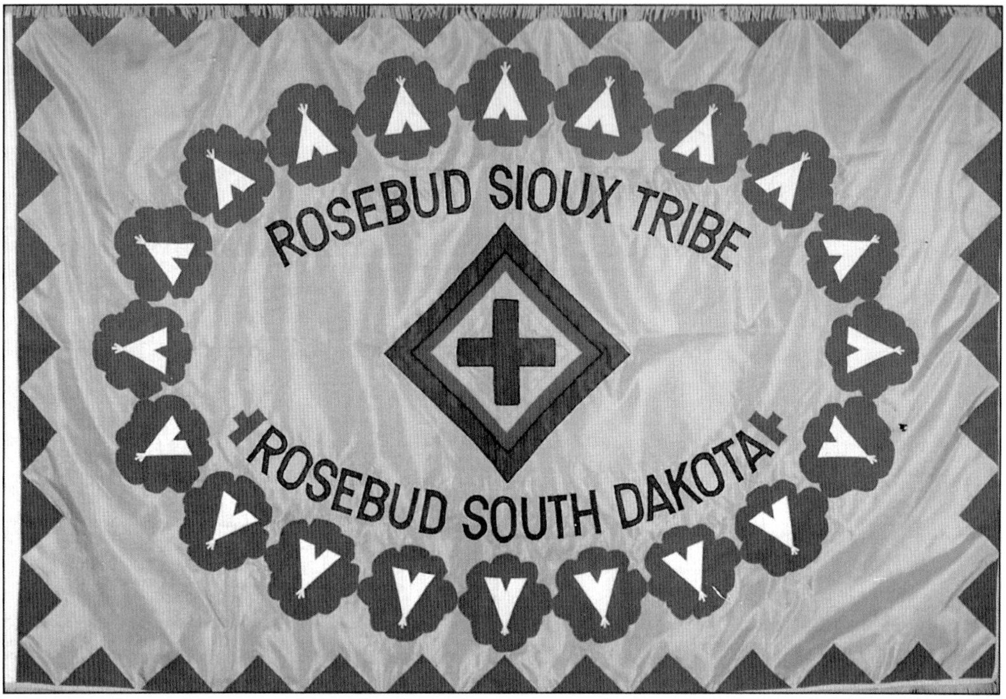

ROSEBUD SIOUX TRIBAL FLAG. The flag of the Sicangu has 20 red roses in an oval ring which represent the 20 Rosebud Sioux communities. Each rose bears a white Lakota tipi in its center. The ring of roses encircles a three-layered rainbow colored diamond, or "god's eye" figure, that stands for the reservation itself. A blue cross in the center of the diamond symbolizes the pipe of peace and the extension of friendship to all who come to the reservation. The two crossed lines of the cross also represent the number four. The colors in the diamond are blue, red, and yellow, on white. Arching over the diamond is "Rosebud Sioux Tribe" in blue, and at the bottom is "Rosebud South Dakota." On each side of "Rosebud South Dakota" are pipe bowls in red which represent peaceful relations between the tribe and the United States. Around the outer edge of the flag is a red border of small triangles, representing tipis whose lodge welcomed visitors seeking food and shelter.

The colors all have meaning: white stands for purity and the direction north from which the snows come; Red is a ceremonial color for thunder, lightning, and forms of plant and animal life, and refers to the sunrise and the direction of east; Yellow represents the land of sunshine, a nickname for South Dakota, and the south direction; Blue represents water, wind, the sky, clouds, the moon, the day, and the west direction; Black stands for the night and the mysteries of life. The fringe around the edge is yellow.

The Rosebud Lakota claim one of the oldest tribal flags, designed in the early 1960s by Lloyd One Star and sewed by Julie Peneaux.

The Sicangu (burnt thigh) received their name when some of their men's thighs burned in a prairie fire. Bands within the Sicangu evolved over the years, but Josephine Waggoner recorded 13 Sicangu sub-bands in her book *My Land, My People, My Story*. These included: Canupaskopayuka, Wagmizayuha, Askekapemni, Waglure, Warpesa, Okaga, Itecangugu, Hinhansunwapaha, Sunkahawanju, Wannawega, Wajaje, Wara, and Miniskuyakicun.

The letter 'r' is not used in Lakota.

IMAGES
of America

ROSEBUD SIOUX

Donovin Arleigh Sprague

ARCADIA
PUBLISHING

ISBN 978-0-7385-3447-3

Published by Arcadia Publishing
Charleston, South Carolina

Printed in the United States of America

Library of Congress Catalog Card Number: 2005924980

For all general information contact Arcadia Publishing at:
Telephone 843-853-2070
Fax 843-853-0044
E-mail sales@arcadiapublishing.com
For customer service and orders:
Toll-Free 1-888-313-2665

Visit us on the Internet at www.arcadiapublishing.com

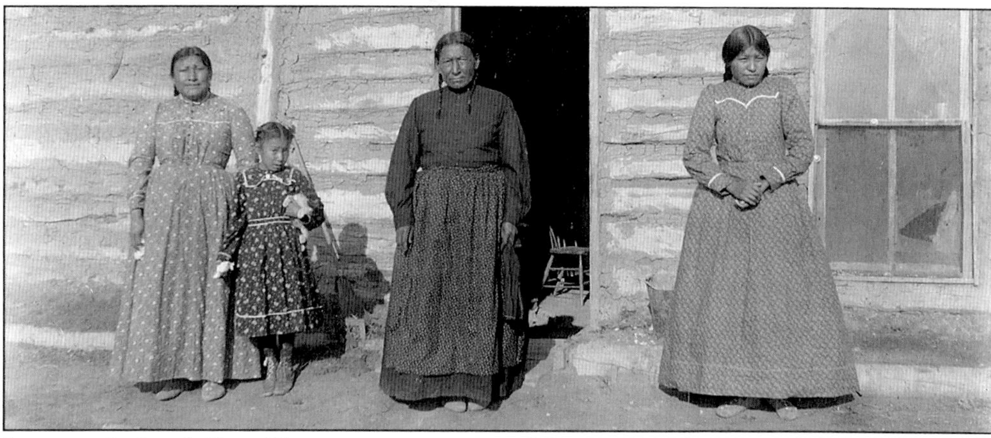

(cover and above) **KATE HUNTER AND OTHERS (MINNICOUJOU).** Pictured, from left to right, are Kate Hunter-Kills Plenty-Garreau-Randall-Blue Legs-Hall-Poor Elk-Mcgras, Ollie Eastman, Frances Hunter (Four Horses), and Irene Hunter. This photograph is undated. Kate Hunter had several marriages. Her Lakota name was Kills Plenty. Kate's grandparents were One Horn/Lone Horn and his wife Wind. Four Horses was the daughter of One Horn and Wind, and Kate's mother. Four Horses became known as Frances Hunter and this photograph is believed by family members to be her. Next to her was written "Grandma." The grandfather of Four Horses was the Itancan (leader) Black Buffalo. Black Buffalo was also the father of One Horn/Lone Horn and High Back Bone (Hump). Four Horses married Thunder Buffalo, and One Horn/Lone Horn and Wind were her parents. One Horn/Lone Horn had seven wives and three of them were sisters: Wind, Little Old Woman/Stands On Ground, and Stiff Leg. Spotted Elk, also called Chief Big Foot (Si Tanka), is related to Wind, Stiff Leg, and the One Horns. Wind's aunt was Rattling Blanket Woman (Minnicoujou), biological mother of the well-known Crazy Horse. It was written: "Wind killed at Wounded Knee at age 78 in 1890 with grandson Big Foot," however she would only have been about 14 years older than him. In Lakota kinship, Wind may have called him son, due to him being a son of One Horn and one of his wives. Some family tie Si Tanka (Big Foot) to Wind, or to her sister Stiff Leg. Kate Hunter has family and residential ties to Cheyenne River, Pine Ridge, and Rosebud. (Photograph courtesy of Alvera Wise.)

Contents

ACKNOWLEDGMENTS

Thank you to my friends past and present who provided conversation, friendship, kindness, or assistance to me:

Father Phillip Allen and family, Bill and Geraldine Anderson, Paula Anderson Family, Lou Ann Barton, Mildred Benway, Elgene Black Lance, Lorenzo Black Lance, Jim and Virginia Blevins, Chris Bordeaux, Doyle Bramhall, Cleveland Brave Bird, Eddie Brigati, Darren Brings Plenty, Virginia Broncho Bill-Broken Leg, Clarence Gatemouth Brown, Anthony Castaway, Dallas Chief Eagle, Jay Citron, Eddy Clearwater, Johnnie Clifford, Crazy Horse Memorial, Crazy Horse Tiwahe, Charlie Daniels Band, Velma DeVries, Tom Domek, Tinsley Ellis, Fabulous Thunderbirds, Roy Forgets Nothing, Chester Fuhrman Jr., Todd Gabry, William Gerry, Billy Gibbons, Renee Greenman, Bill Groethe, Merle Haggard, Ted Harvey, Francis He Crow, Michael He Crow, Darlene Helper, Pete Helper Sr., Jane Henry, Duane Hollow Horn Bear, Jemma Horse Looking-Brave-MacKichan-Moccasin, Donald Hudson, Jim and Lenora Hudson, Hump Tiwahe, Waylon Jennings and Jessi, Lenova Kills Enemy, Albert King, B.B. King, Freddie King, "Lakota Nation Journal," Marie Yellow Bird Lange, Ernie and Sonja LaPointe, Claes-Hakan Jacobson, Bob Lee, David and Joanie Lindley, Edna Little Elk, Lisa Little Chief-Bryan and family, Rosalie Little Thunder, Barbara Logan, Lone Horn Tiwahe, Margaret MacKichan, Erma Maldonado, Ed McGaa, JoDee Messina, Rita Metcalf, Berneita Miller and family, Joel Minor, Donnie Moccasin, Jack Moore, Michael Martin Murphey, Willie Nelson, Oglala Lakota College Archives, Julie Peneaux, Bob and Nell Pearson, Pooley Family, Marilyn Pourier, Scott Pourier, Marcie, Todd, and Dylan Pudwill, Red Cloud Indian School and Heritage Center, Lula Red Cloud, Jimmy Rogers, Junior Rousseau, Alvina Lucille Runs After, Kurt Schweigman, Grover Scott, Seven Council Fires, Howard Sharp Butte, Ben Sherman, Mark Shillingstad, Short Bull Family, Harold Shunk, Brother Simon S.J., Nancy Sinatra, Mildred Thoede Sleep, Vance Sneve and Virginia Driving Hawk Sneve, Soldier Woman Gallery, Skip Spotted War Bonnet, Brandon Sprague Band, Rylan Sprague, Theresa Stands, Ed Stover, Karen Swan, Rose Two Strike Stenstrom, Ken Stewart at S.D. State Archives, Arlene Swift Hawk, Paul and Linda Szabo, Ben Trent, Mike Trent Family, Tanya Tucker, Mel and Evelyn Utterback, Joe Valandra, Wanda Valandra, Vance Family, Jimmie Vaughan, Stevie Ray Vaughan, Wakan Tanka, Luke Warm Water, Tim Whirlwind Soldier, Francis White Lance, White River Health Care Center, Tony White Thunder, Kim Wilson, Tom and Joanne Winter Chaser, Alvera Wise, Wounded Knee Survivors, Vere Wright, Jim Young, ZZ Top, and to my high school and college classmates.

This book is dedicated with love to my family
Darrel, Velda, Lila, Sis, Deb, Marcie, Brandon, and Rylan Sprague

Introduction

Rosebud Sioux tribal members are descendants of the Sicangu Oyate (Burnt Thighs Nation/people) of the Tetonwan division of the Great Sioux Nation. The Great Sioux Nation is also called the Lakota/Dakota/Nakota Nation, by language dialect. The Rosebud Sioux Tribe is home to the Sicangu tribe, called the Brule by the French. The Sicangu were further divided into the Heyata Wicasa (Upper Brule) and the Kul Wicasa Oyate (Lower Brule Nation). The people of the Lower Brule Reservation are today separated geographically from the Rosebud Sioux Reservation. Although there are family ties between these two reservations, this book will focus on the people of the Rosebud Sioux.

The name Sioux is part of the Ojibwe/Ojibway/Chippewa/Anishinabe word "Nadoweisiw-eg," which the French shortened to Sioux. The original word meant "little or lesser snakes/enemies." Lakota means "friend or ally." There are seven groups of Lakota and the Sicangu are the second largest by population. The Sicangu are located at Rosebud Reservation in south central South Dakota, and the smaller group of Sicangu resides at Lower Brule Reservation in central South Dakota on the west bank of the Missouri River. The other six Lakota groups are the Oglala on Pine Ridge Reservation just west of Rosebud Reservation in southwestern South Dakota; the Minnicoujou, Itazipco, Siha Sapa, and Oohenumpa at Cheyenne River Reservation in north central South Dakota; and the Hunkpapa at Standing Rock Reservation in northern South Dakota and south-central North Dakota. Some of the Lakota also settled in the Wood Mountain Reserve area in Saskatchewan prior to the reservation era.

The Lakota knew no boundaries and traveled in search of the buffalo for food, and buffalo hides provided shelter and clothing. Chief Conquering Bear was a Sicangu leader and was appointed by the U.S. as a "Chief" to represent much of the Lakota nation that the government was dealing with at that time. This was the signing of the 1851 Fort Laramie Treaty and was the first time the U.S. interfered with Lakota decision making. The treaty set a land base which extended from the Big Horn Mountains in the west to eastern Wisconsin. The northern boundary stretched to Canada and the Republican River near present-day Kansas was the southern boundary. The nation of the Lakota was reduced by the 1868 Treaty of Fort Laramie, from the Big Horn Mountains in the west to the east bank of the Missouri River. The Heart River in North Dakota was the new northern boundary and the Platte River in Nebraska was the southern boundary. In the summer of 1868, an agency was built on the Missouri River at Whetstone Creek to accommodate the Sicangu and some Oglala, 23 miles above Fort Randall in South Dakota. Congress had given the military control of Whetstone and other new agencies. The Sicangu were forced to leave their hunting camps south of the Platte River by military threats that they would be attacked if they did not leave for the Missouri. At Whetstone, most of the Lakota were unhappy living at that site which could not sustain them in hunting and put them next to white traders, although the fort Indians who had intermarried with the traders liked the area. Spotted Tail warned the people not to leave Whetstone but some of them tried to return south to the area of the Republican River where they were attacked by Pawnees and driven back to Whetstone. Some were killed and their camps were destroyed. The Pawnee were now scouts for the U.S. military, and the government appropriated money to change the Lakota into farmers. Chief Swift Bear and his Corn band adopted farming and seemed content with the Whetstone location. The government built a small house for Swift Bear as a reward. During this era, Lakota leaders from their agencies took their first trip to Washington, D.C. Spotted Tail told the Commissioner of Indian Affairs that the Lakota must choose their own agency on the White River. Upon their return the Lakota had succeeded in getting their agency moved west from Whetstone. The new, but temporary, Whetstone Agency would be on Upper White River in 1870-71. It moved in 1872, and by 1874 it was in Nebraska, with brief locations on Big White Clay Creek below the Red Cloud Agency and on Beaver Creek.

The Rosebud Sioux lands were again reduced to a reservation with boundaries by the U.S. Congress in the Act of March 2, 1889. South Dakota then became a state in November of 1889. The Lakota reservations of today are about one half their original size from the Act of 1889. Rosebud Reservation was established in 1878 for the Sicangu and its headquarters was located at the town of Rosebud, which was the only town of note. The land was allotted to enrollees of the tribe and districts were created and named for physical features, creeks, and tribal leaders. Later food and supply issue stations started with an agent, "boss farmers," and missionary schools. Around 1895 the districts or communities in the north along the south side of the White River included: Black Pipe "Canumpa Sapa," Red Leaf, Corn Creek "Wagmiza Wakpala," Swift Bear's "Mato Ohanko" Camp, Bad Nation "Oyate Sica," Whirlwind Soldier, and Bull Creek "Tatanka Wakpala." The Little White River flows south across the reservation and the communities in that area include: Pine Creek, White Thunder Camp, Ring Thunder "Cangleska Wakinyan" Camp, Rosebud "Onjinjintka Oyanke" Agency, Cut Meat "Wosose," He Dog's "Sung Bloka" Camp, Two Strike's "Numpkahpa" Camp, St. Francis Mission "Sapunti," and Spring Creek "Wiwila Wakpala." In the central part of the reservation Oak Creek flows south from the White River and in this area was the home of Little Crow's "Kangi Cikala" Camp, and Butte Creek "Paha Wakpala." Also in the central part of Rosebud Reservation is The Mission (where Mission, South Dakota is today), and Antelope "Tatoka or Nigesanla." Both were on Keya Paha River. The original eastern boundary of Rosebud Reservation was the east bank of the Missouri River. Eastern communities were known as Rosebud Landing, Pond Creek, and Milk's Camp "Asanpi Tawicoti." On the south end of Rosebud Reservation were Fort Niobrara, Sparks, and Valentine, all in Nebraska. Fort Niobrara was established in 1880 to protect Nebraska settlers from the Sicangu and other bands. It was just northeast of Valentine, Nebraska.

Later, 21 districts were listed (today they have been combined to 13): Antelope "Tatoka or Nigesanla," Bad Nation "Oyate Sica," Black Pipe "Canumpa Sapa," Bull Creek "Tatanka Wakpala," Butte Creek "Paha Wakpala," Corn Creek "Wagmiza Wakpala," Grass Mountain "Peji Paha," He Dog "Sung Bloka," Horse Creek "Sunkakan Wakpala," Ideal "Waste," Milk's Camp "Asanpi Tawicoti," Okreek (Oak Creek) "Utahu Can Wakpala," Parmelee (named for David Parmelee), Ring Thunder "Cangleska Wakinyan," Rosebud "Onjinjintka Oyanke," Soldier Creek "Akicita Wakpala," Spring Creek "Wiwila Wakpala," St. Francis "Sapunti" (Where The Black Robes Live), Swift Bear "Mato Oh'anko," Two Strike "Numpkahpa," Upper Cut Meat "Wosose."

George Catlin, early artist, made his trip west and came up the Missouri River in present day South Dakota in 1832 and made early portraits of the Lakota at that time. A premier photographer from Sweden, John A. Anderson, moved to the Fort Niobrara area in the mid-1880s, and by 1885 was commissioned as a civilian photographer for the U.S. Army at the fort to record life on Rosebud. Another important photographer, William R. Cross, had a studio at Fort Niobrara, and Anderson first served as an apprentice under Cross. By 1889 Anderson served as the official photographer of the Crook Treaty Commission. Anderson returned to the East and married but in 1891 would return to Valentine, Nebraska, to run Shaw's Art Gallery and lived on Rosebud Reservation. He also worked as a clerk at Jordan's Trading Post which was nearby. In the 1930s the Anderson's moved to Rapid City to manage the Sioux Indian Museum.

Many Lakota's were photographed at the Trans-Mississippi and International Exposition held at Omaha, Nebraska, June 1-October 31, 1898. President McKinley opened the ceremonies on land formerly occupied by the Omaha Indians and it was now called "Magic City." Frank A. Rinehart was once a partner in photography of William Henry Jackson and Rinehart was given his own small studio on the grounds of the large Exposition at Omaha. In the last week of the Exposition, Rinehart's photographs were taken by Adolph F. Muhr. Muhr would later work with photographer Edward S. Curtis. The Gerhard sisters, Mamie and Emma also worked as photographers at the Omaha Exposition.

Donovin Sprague
Cankahu Wankatuya/Canhahake
High Back Bone/Hump

One

SICANGU OYATE (BURNT THIGH PEOPLE/NATION)

Early recorded history among the Sicangu started with oral story telling, though important events were recorded upon buffalo, elk, and deer hides called winter counts. Winter counts often recorded the most important event of the year on the hide.

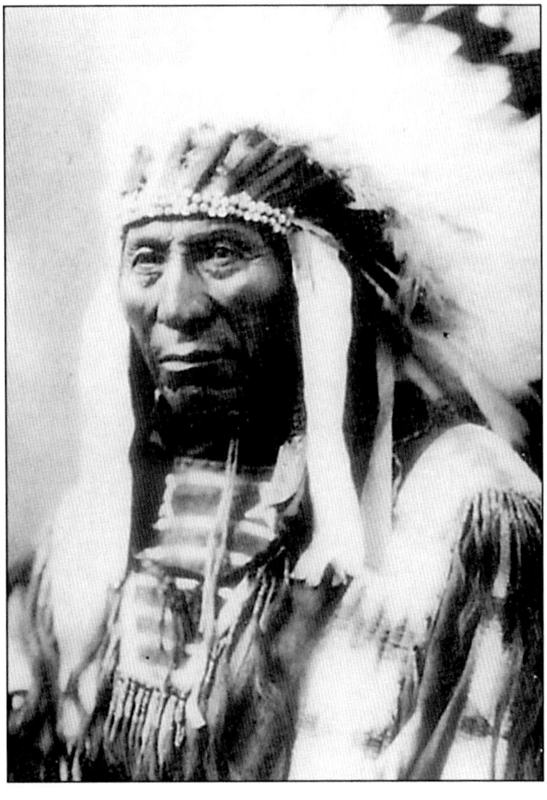

CONQUERING BEAR "MATO WAYUHI" (SICANGU). This photograph is undated. This is the younger son of Chief Conquering Bear. The elder Conquering Bear was appointed Chief of the Lakota nation at the 1851 Treaty of Fort Laramie gathering there on Horse Creek, 35 miles southeast of Fort Laramie in present Wyoming. His appointment was an unrealistic position which no man could fulfill. He was called in to intercede and settle an incident where a Mormon cow had strayed and then been butchered by a Minnicoujou Lakota. Lt. Grattan brought troops into a tense situation in which a battle erupted on Aug. 19, 1854 with the Lakota and Conquering Bear died nine days later of wounds he received. Lt. Grattan and all of his men were killed and this is referred to as the Grattan Incident/Grattan Affair/ Mormon Cow Incident. This event would mark the beginning of many battles between the U.S. and the Lakota. A relative of Conquering Bear whom the author spoke with is Tim Standing Soldier, who is also a descendant of Chief Bad Wound (Oglala) and Lakota artist Andrew Standing Soldier (Oglala). (Bureau of Ethnology photograph. Postcard courtesy of Donovin Sprague).

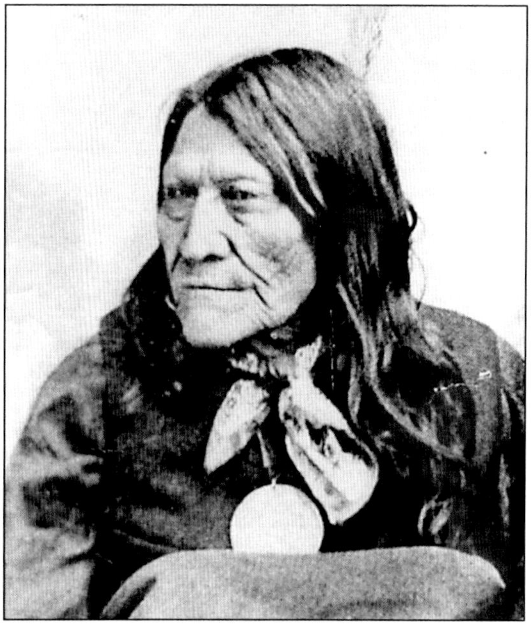

(left) **CHIEF TWO STRIKE "NUMPKAHAPA" (SICANGU).** This photograph is undated. Two Strike was born in 1815 near the White River Valley of northwest Nebraska. His three wives were Bear Heart (Oglala), Standing/Her Good Horse (Oglala), and Brown Eyes. The son of Two Strike and Her Good Horse was Arthur Two Strike (1865-1909). Arthur married Maggie "Blue Eyes" Metcalf and their son was Louis Two Strike (1899-1937). The son of Arthur and Maggie is Floyd Two Strike. Floyd married Harriet Blue Thunder-Two Strike. Rose Two Strike Stenstrom is the great-great granddaughter of Chief Two Strike and provided information on the Two Strike family. Chief Two Strike settled near Spring Creek in the late 1870s and moved to the present site of Two Strike community in 1879, after the last great Sun Dance was held with relatives from other bands. During the Bozeman Trail wars Chief Two Strike and Chief Crow Dog were in the Powder River country of present day Wyoming and allied themselves with bands such as Chief Crazy Horse. Two Strike and his band were present at the Battle of Summit Springs in Colorado on July 11, 1869, allied with the southern Cheyenne in which a force of 244 members of the U.S. 5th Cavalry along with 50 Pawnee scouts made a surprise attack upon their camp. William F. "Buffalo Bill" Cody was also there as Chief Scout for the Cavalry. Chief Tall Bull of the Cheyenne's and 51 other Cheyenne-Lakota were killed. The soldiers tried to block off escape routes but surprisingly the vast majority of Indians escaped while a smaller group held off the soldiers. 17 women and children were taken prisoners. The cavalry started 150 fires, burning items belonging to the Indians, including 84 tipis. (Photograph courtesy of Rose Two Strike Stenstrom.)

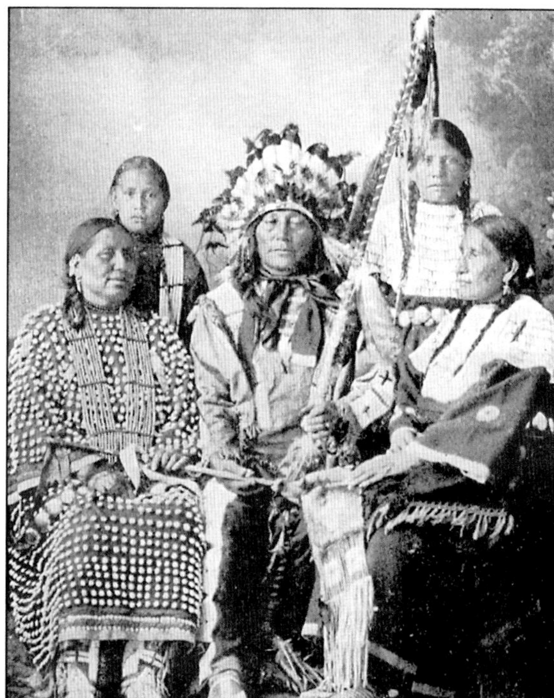

***(right)* CHIEF HOLLOW HORN BEAR AND HIS FAMILY.** Pictured from left to right are: (front row) Laura Hollow Horn Bear, Chief Hollow Horn Bear, andGood Bed; (back row) Jenny Hollow Horn Bear and Jennifer Hollow Horn Bear (Sicangu). This photograph was taken by Captain Clark. Emily Hollow Horn Bear was his youngest daughter, born in 1893, and she was the mother of Albert White Hat. (Photograph courtesy of Donovin Sprague.)

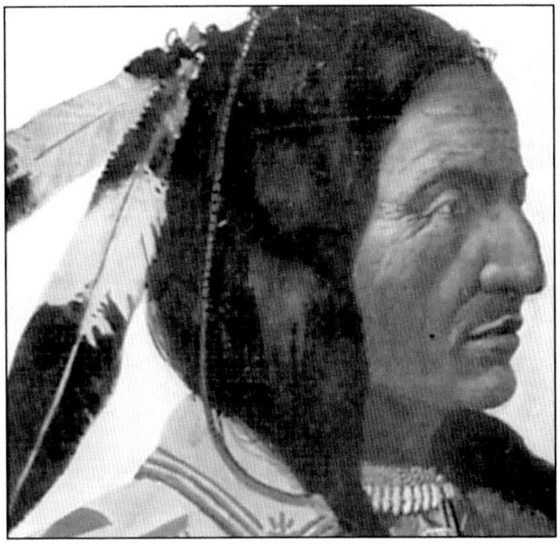

CHIEF HOLLOW HORN BEAR "MATO HE OKLOGECA" (SICANGU). Undated postcard. On June 25, 1876, Hollow Horn Bear was in the area where the Battle of the Little Bighorn took place, but he missed the fight because he had left prior to the battle on an excursion, possibly scouting and hunting. The author visited with Duane Hollow Horn Bear, a great grandson of Chief Hollow Horn Bear. Duane works at Sinte Gleska University. (Postcard courtesy of Donovin Sprague.)

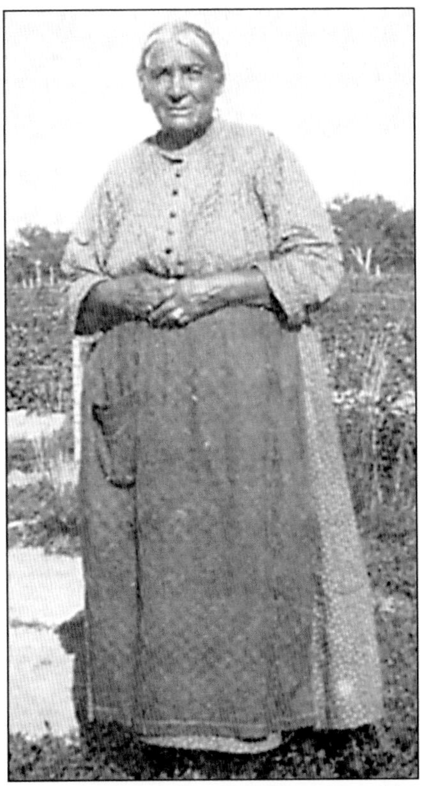

ZOE "GEO" UTTERBACK. Photo undated. Zoe Larrabee/Laravie/Larvie was born in 1862 and married James E. "Cornie" Utterback in 1879. Various family use different spellings for Zoe's last name but her sister was Nellie/Helen Larrabee who moved in with Chief Crazy Horse when he surrendered at Fort Robinson in 1877. J.E. Utterback came west from Virginia and was a blacksmith at the fort at that time and Zoe's father Long Joe Larrabee was also a civilian working at the fort. Zoe's mother was Chi-Chi aka Cheyenne Woman of the Cheyenne Tribe. Everyone spoke about the beauty of the four Larrabee sisters. Nellie/Helen married Greasing Hand after the killing of Crazy Horse and he took the name of Albert Crazy Horse and they moved into the Wanblee area. There were no children from Chief Crazy Horse and Nellie/Helen and no blood relatives to Crazy Horse even though Albert and Nellie/Helen kept the name Crazy Horse as their last name and all their children used it as their last name. James E. Utterback witnessed the killing of Crazy Horse at Fort Robinson and also was a witness of the Wounded Knee Massacre of 1890. Zoe was also at Fort Robinson when Crazy Horse was killed, and was at Wounded Knee in 1890, treating the wounded at the church for many days following the massacre. Zoe had been escorted into the agency with her 3 children by soldiers. Zoe recalled that she hid her sewing machine and valuables in a deep well before the soldiers took her. At this time James and Zoe moved southeast of Belvidere on the Big White River where Zoe received a 320 acre allotment from the Rosebud Agency. James lived to the age of 87 and both are buried in the Belvidere Cemetery. (Photograph courtesy of Donovin Sprague.)

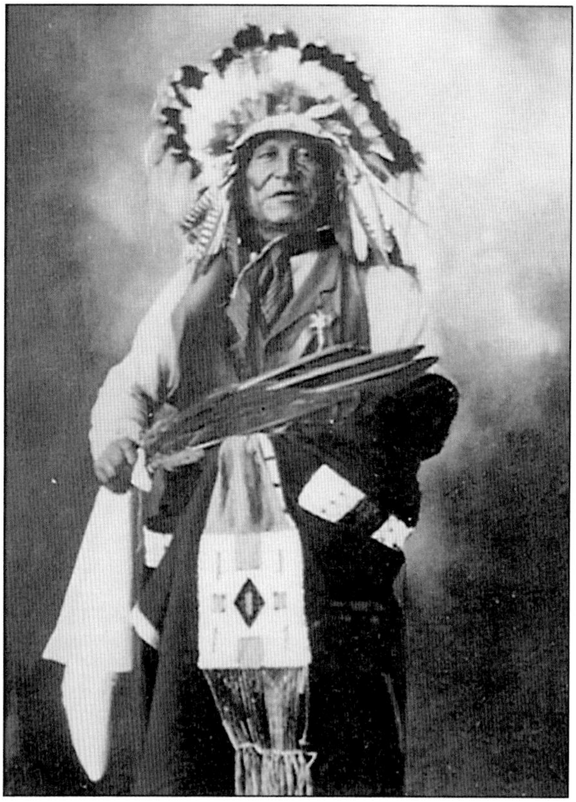

TURNING EAGLE (LAKOTA). This photograph was taken in 1898 by F.A. Rinehart. One of the Turning Eagles married a woman named Give Pay and two of their children were Kate Turning Eagle (b. 1882) and Benjamin Turning Eagle (b. 1889). All were from Rosebud. (Photograph courtesy of Donovin Sprague.)

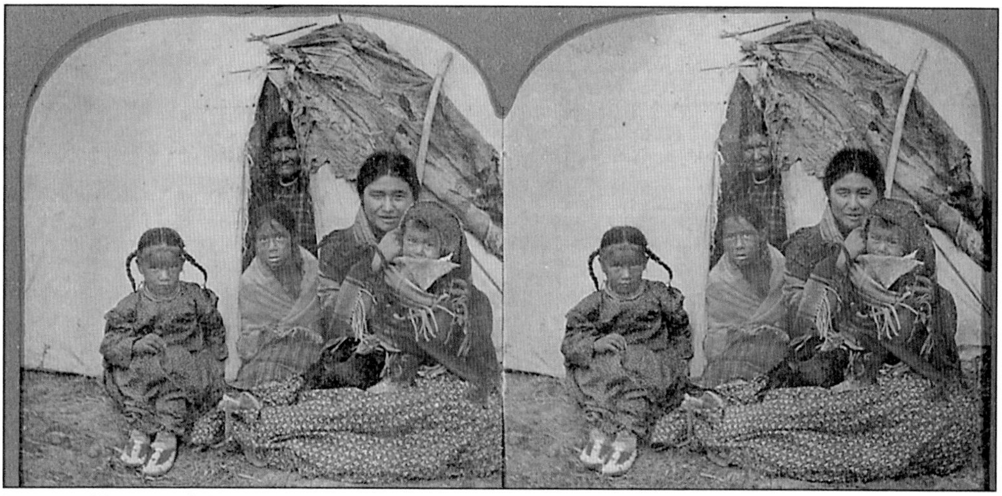

LAKOTA/DAKOTA/NAKOTA FAMILY. This photograph was taken in 1899. This family group is pictured by their lodge in this stereoview card taken by T.W. Ingersoll. (Stereoview card courtesy of Donovin Sprague.)

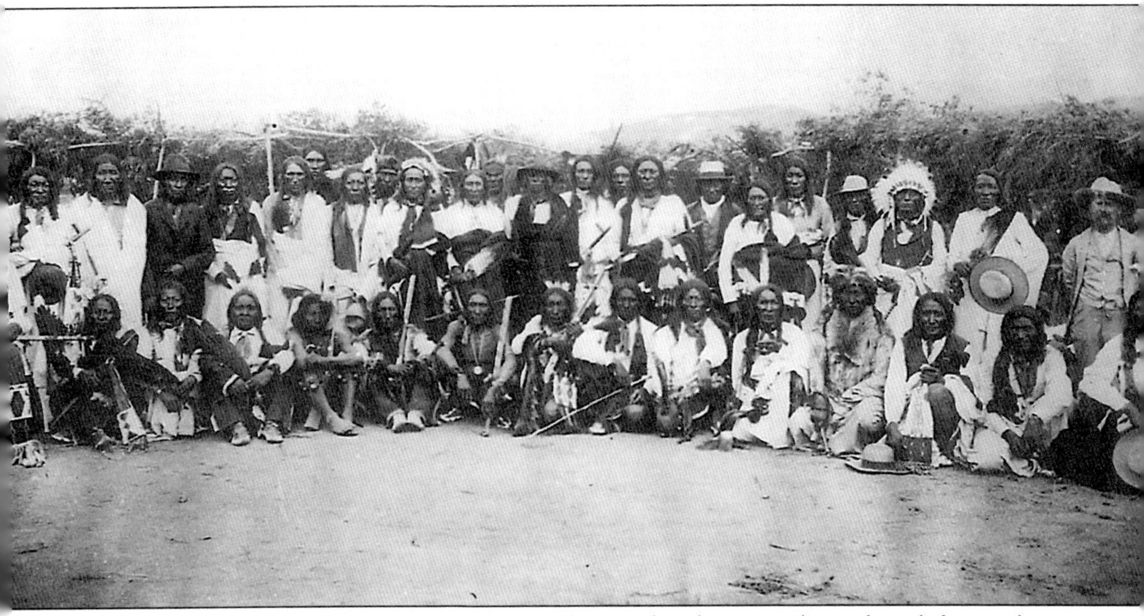

Itancan (Headmen/Leaders). This photograph is undated. Pictured are, from left to right: (front row) Tall Mandan, Turning Eagle, Thin Elk, Big Head, Picket Pin, Turning Bear, High Beart, Lance, High Pipe, High Hawk, Yellow Hair, Little Thunder, Bear Head, He Dog, and Black Bull; (second row) Louis Roubideaux (interpreter), Whirlwind Soldier, Yellow Horse, Good Voice, White Crane Walking, Pretty Eagle, Ring Thunder, Stranger Horse, Quick Bear, Swift Bear, Poor Dog, Hollow Horn Bear, Crow Dog, Two Strike, Milk, Sky Bull, Stands and Looks Back, Bears Looks Behind, and Colonel Charles P. Jordan; (third row) Blue Eyes, Big Horse, and Joe Good Voice. These men are prominent leaders of the Sicangu Lakota. (Photograph courtesy of Rose Two Strike Stenstrom.)

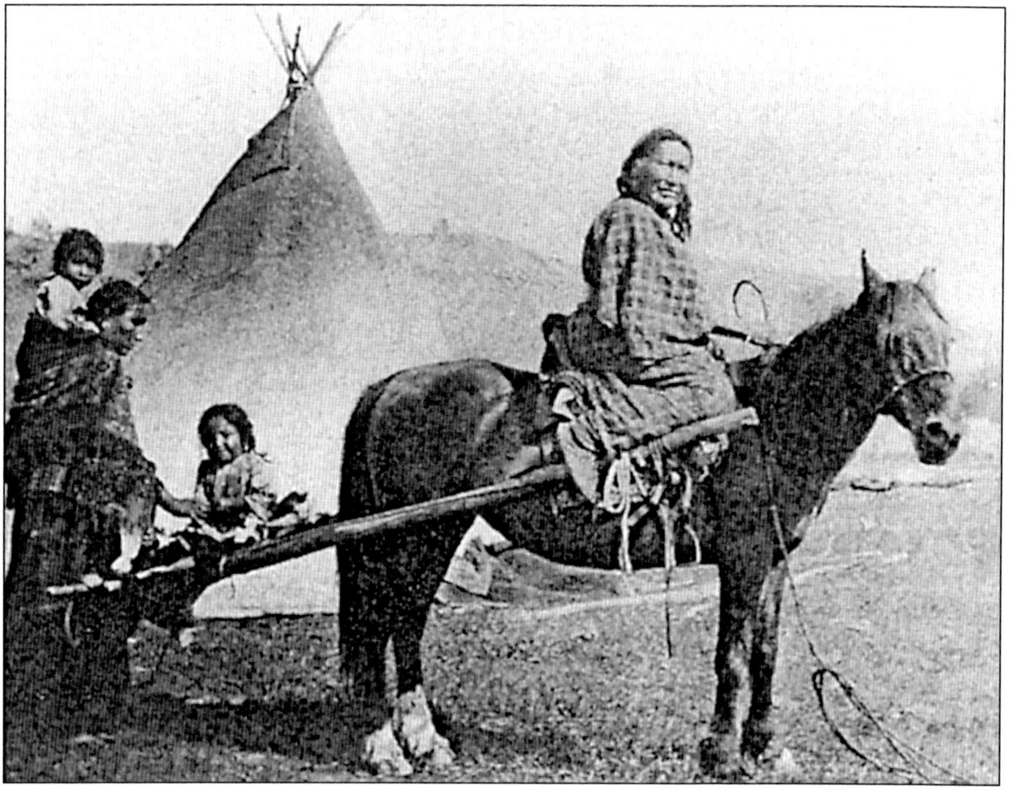

SICANGU FAMILY WITH HORSE AND TRAVOIS. This photograph is undated. (Photograph courtesy of Donovin Sprague.)

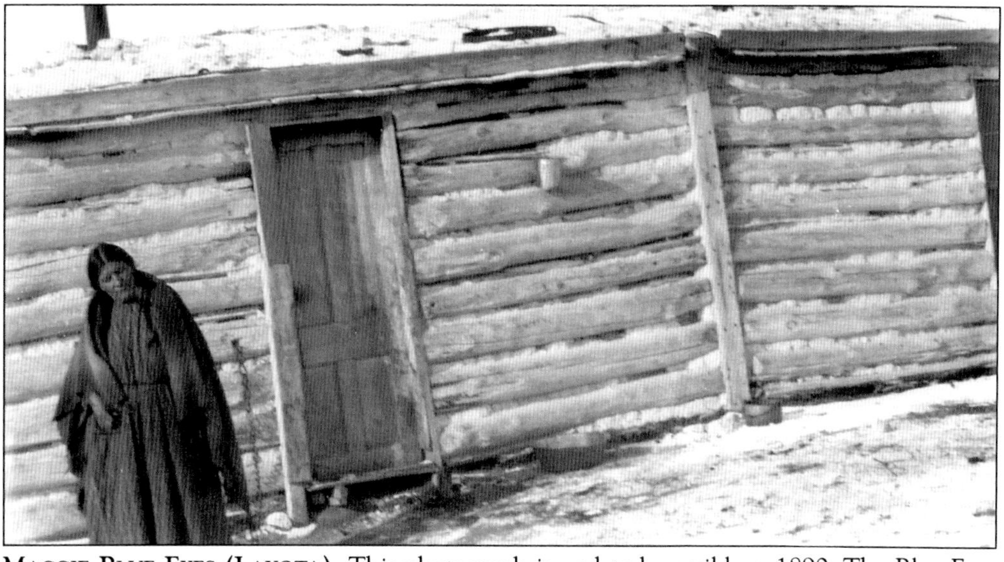

MAGGIE BLUE EYES (LAKOTA). This photograph is undated, possibly c. 1890. The Blue Eyes name came from the fact that her mother's eyes changed color from brown to gray. Maggie is pictured here at Spring Creek. The Blue Eyes family came from the northern Lakota. (Photograph courtesy of Rose Two Strike Stenstrom.)

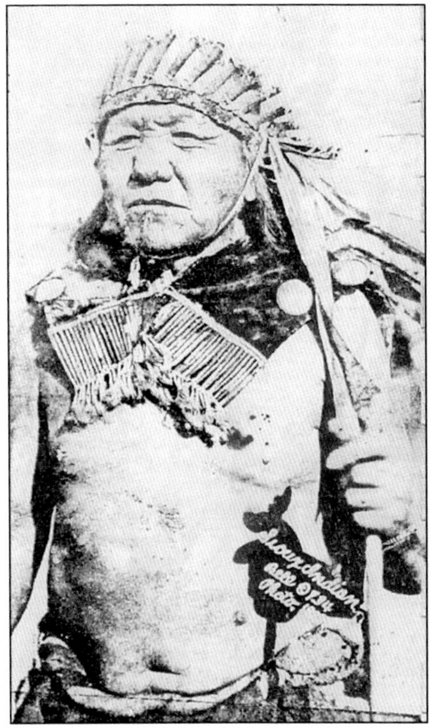

FOLLOWS THE WOMAN AT ROSEBUD FAIR (LAKOTA). This photograph was taken by Bell in 1928. This photograph was among several taken at the 1928 Indian Fair which was held in the fall at Rosebud Agency. It was reported at this time that the Sun Dance was permitted. The Sun Dance religion was banned during the early reservation era but went underground. Bell Photograph took several pictures at the Fair and of the Sun Dance, which was probably modified for the photographer. (Postcard courtesy of Donovin Sprague.)

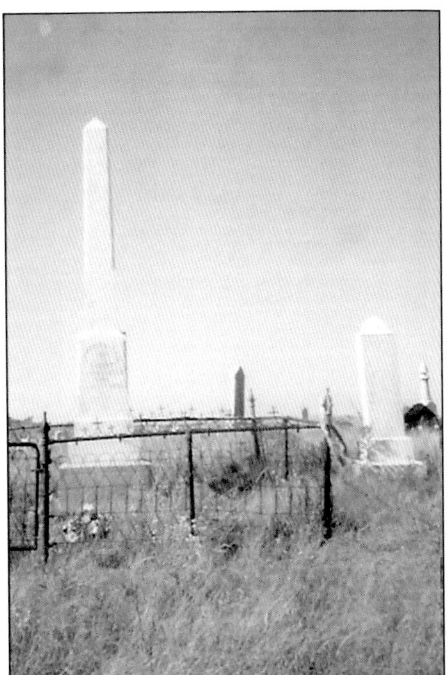

CHIEF SPOTTED TAIL AND JULIA BLACK LODGE (SICANGU). This photograph was taken at Rosebud, South Dakota, in 2004. This is the resting place and marker for Chief Spotted Tail, showing he was born in 1823 and died on August 5, 1881, when he was killed by Crow Dog. The shorter marker next to him is his wife Julia Black Lodge, who died at Rosebud on May 27, 1913, at the age of 75. The cemetery overlooks much of the community of Rosebud. It is often erroneously stated that Spotted Tail's sister was the mother of Crazy Horse. This comes from the idea that Waglula (Worm), father of Crazy Horse, married two sisters of Spotted Tail following the death of his first wife. If Waglula did marry the sisters, they would be step-mothers of Crazy Horse. The biological mother of Crazy Horse was Rattling Blanket Woman, the Minnicoujou first wife of Waglula (Worm). Rattling Blanket Woman died when Crazy Horse was a young boy. The descendants that disagree on the marriage of Waglula to the sisters of Spotted Tail say Waglula (Worm) first married Rattling Blanket Woman and Crazy Horse was born of that union, and the later wives were Iron Between Horns, Kills Enemy, and Red Leggings. Corn is the father of those three sisters. (Photograph courtesy of Donovin Sprague.)

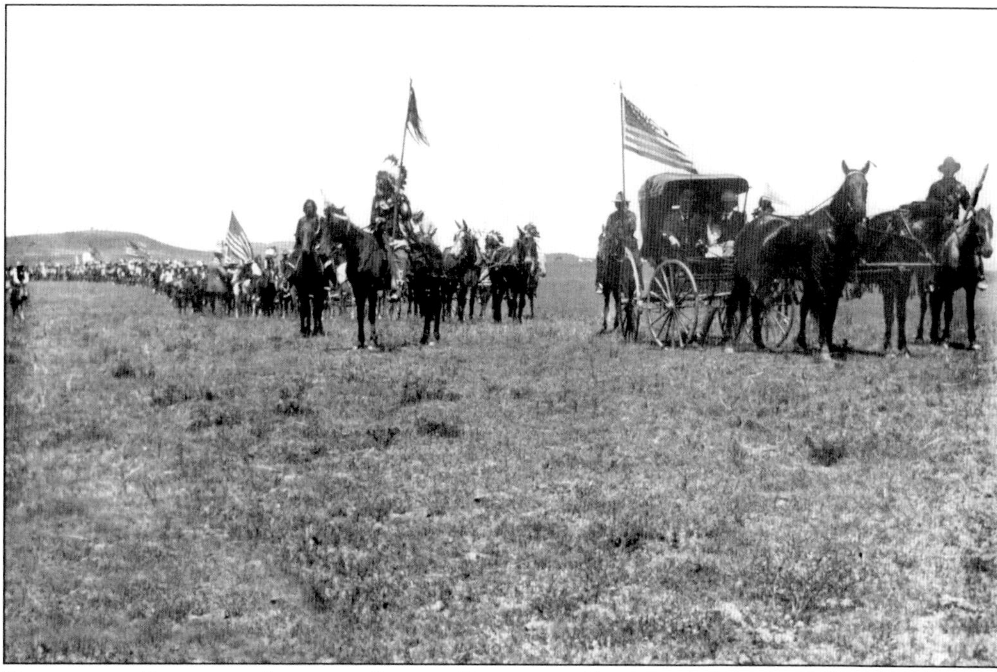

PARADE AT ROSEBUD AGENCY, SOUTH DAKOTA, (SICANGU). Photograph taken July 4, 1897. A long parade line has assembled for this July 4 celebration. (Photograph courtesy of Oglala Lakota College Archives.)

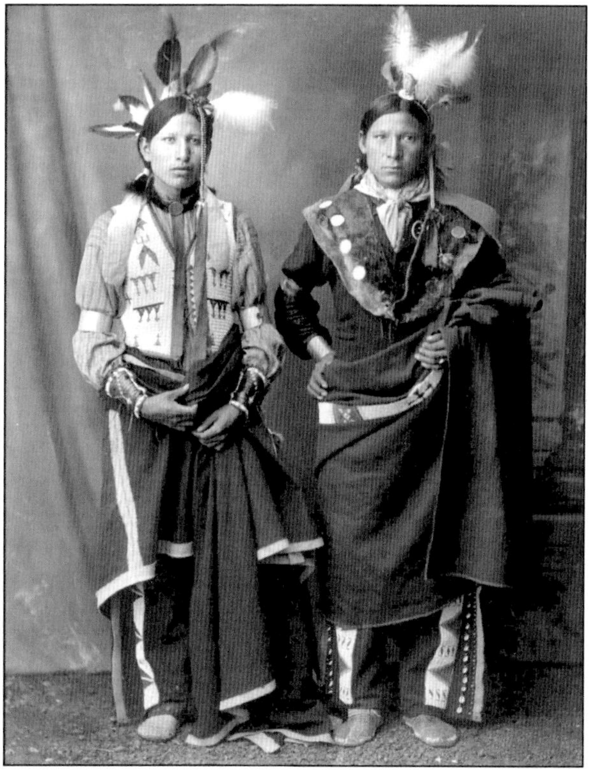

JOHN MILK AND AMOS CONQUERING BEAR (SICANGU). (Photograph courtesy of Oglala Lakota College Archives.)

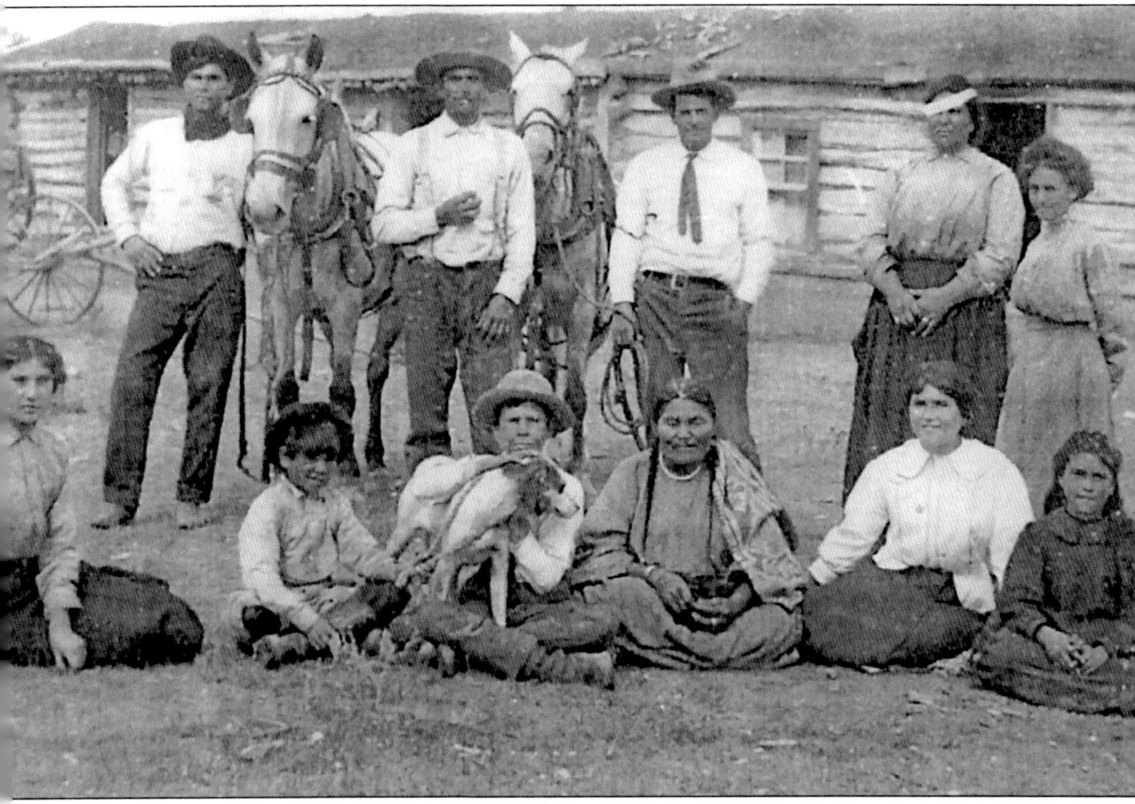

The Rousseau Family. Pictured, from left to right, are: (front row) Mary Rousseau, Abel Rousseau, Lawrence Rousseau, Red Woman/Weasel Bear, Louise Rousseau, and Keva Rousseau-Jewett; (back row) Francis Rousseau, Paul Rousseau, Oscar Rousseau, Julia Boucher Rousseau, and Mrs. Soper (Lakota). This photograph is undated. This group has ties to all the Lakota bands. Julia Boucher Rousseau is the mother and most of the people pictured are brothers and sisters, except for Red Woman and Oscar Rousseau. Red Woman was also known as Weasel Bear and arrived alone to live with the family. The family never knew where she came from and it was recalled that one day she decided to leave and vanished as mysteriously as she had arrived. Julia lost one eye and always wore a scarf as shown. Mary Rousseau is 13 years old in this photograph and married Chester Fuhrman Sr. Their son is Chester Fuhrman Jr., who provided photographs and information. His uncle is Francis Rousseau. Chester's wife was Josephine Braine Fuhrman and Josephine's grandmother was Josephine Waggoner (Hunkpapa), author of several books including *Rekindling The Campfires* and she co-wrote with Susan Bordeaux Bettelyoun (Sicangu) the book *With My Own Eyes*. Louise Rousseau married Harry Webb from Rosebud and later she was known as Louise Webb. Most of the Rousseaus settled at Cheyenne River Reservation and the photograph is believed to be taken at their home place on Goose Creek near the Moreau (Owl) River. (Photograph courtesy of Chester Fuhrman Jr.)

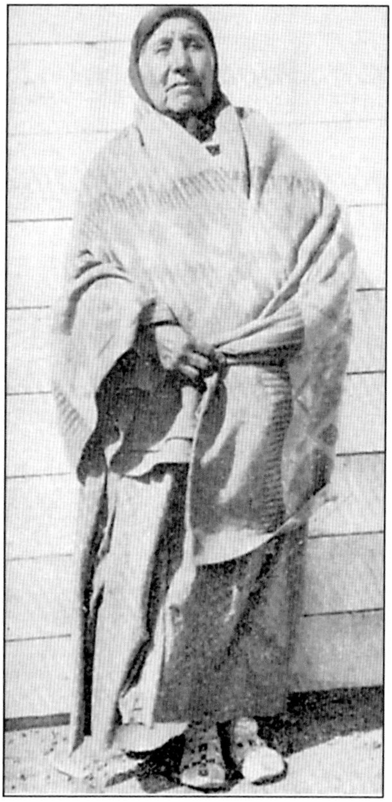

WHITE BUFFALO WOMAN (SICANGU). This photograph is undated. White Buffalo Woman married John Blue Thunder, who was captain of the Lakota Police. They had four daughters and nine sons. Three of the sisters were Harriet Bad Hand, Mary Blue Thunder, and Etta "Eagle Hail" Blue Thunder-Bad Hand. Four of the brothers were Leo, Harry, Louie, and David Blue Thunder. David "Dave" was interviewed and stated he was born in 1891 at Ring Thunder Camp. He married a daughter of Louie Roubideaux in 1915, whose land allotment name was Alice Big Face. They had five children: Mabel, Rose, Francis, Vernie, and a daughter who died in 1919. His wife Alice died in 1929. (Photograph courtesy of Donovin Sprague.)

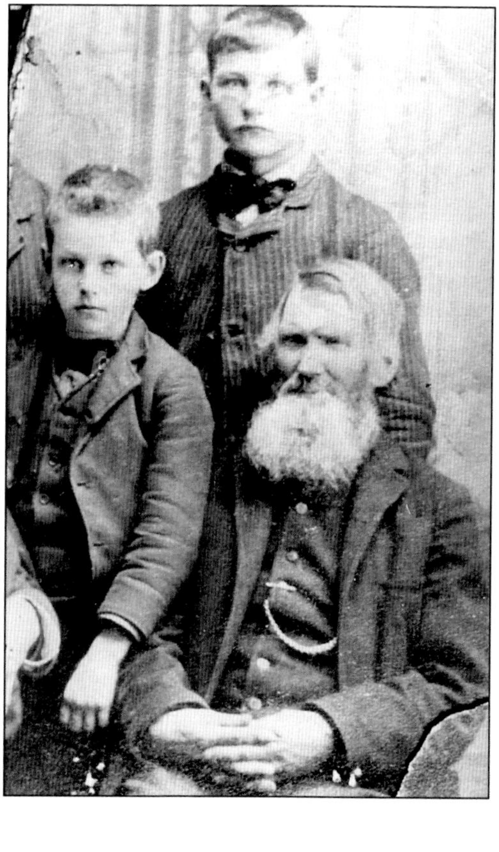

SAMUEL WILCOX WITH HIS GRANDSONS. Vernie Wilcox is on the left and William Washington's son is on the right . This photograph is undated. Samuel is pictured with the beard, and was born in 1819 in Rhode Island and died in 1905 at Ponca, Nebraska. Samuel's wife, Mary Ann McDowell, was born in 1829 in Scotland and died in 1882 in Ponca. The couple had six sons and a daughter. The children listed were William Washington, Graham (b. 1853 and died at Norris, S.D.), Alvin "Alvey" Curtis (b. 1860 and died at Long Valley, S.D.), Frank, Henry, and Albert. Samuel Wilcox was the grandfather of Fred Wilcox. (Photograph courtesy of Walter Tiedeman.)

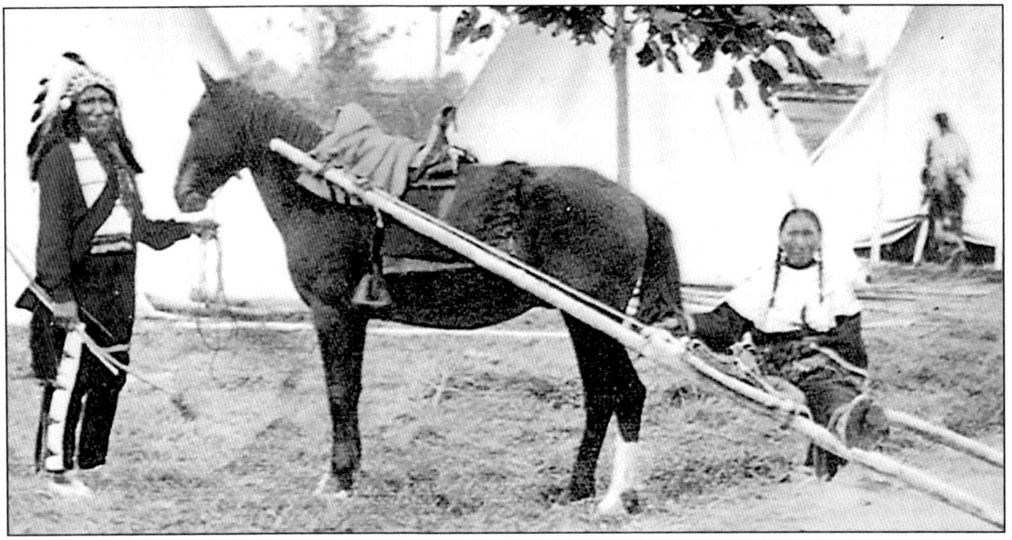

LAKOTA FAMILY WITH TRAVOIS. This photograph is undated. This couple is posing in a camp of tipis with a travois hooked up to the horse. (Postcard courtesy of Donovin Sprague.)

CRAZY IN THE LODGE (SICANGU). Photograph taken by Stanley J. Morrow. It is often claimed that this is a photograph of Chief Crazy Horse. However, the original photograph has always been clearly identified as "Crazy In The Lodge, head warrior under Spotted Tail." There is no proven photograph that exists of Crazy Horse. In 1996, a sketch of this same photograph was published in the newspaper *Indian Country Today* as the only sketch of Crazy Horse. Below the sketch contained the information that French artist Frank Taurillo sketched it in 1872. The sketch was donated to Tim Giago, editor of *Indian Country Today*, by Ed Putnam of Gilroy, California. Giago claimed to have the only sketch of Crazy Horse but the artist made an obvious sketch of this identified photograph and added the name of Crazy Horse to it. The sketch is clearly of this photograph complete with the same scarf he wears. This photograph (not the fake sketch) also appeared on the cover of a 24 page yellow booklet entitled *Crazy Horse* by H.P. Howard in 1975. The cover states: "This may be a picture of Crazy Horse. It has been so identified by some historians. There is no way of authenticating it." This photograph also appeared on the cover of *The Montana Pioneer*, published from Livingston, Montana, in August 1999. The article was entitled "Is This Man Really Crazy Horse?" and the writer chose to ignore information provided by this author which proves it is not Crazy Horse. The photograph made an earlier debut in the book *Fighting Indians of the West* by Schmitt and Dee Brown. In 1956, Hurt and Lass published a book on photographer Stanley J. Morrow and found the true label on the back of the photograph labeled "Crazy In The Lodge, head warrior under Spotted Tail." There is a growing number of fake photographs related to Crazy Horse, and readers should beware of the many inaccurate web sites about this Lakota leader. (Photograph courtesy of Bureau of Ethnology.)

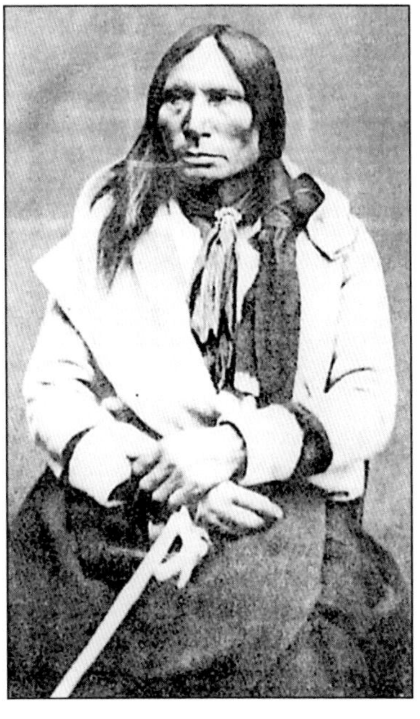

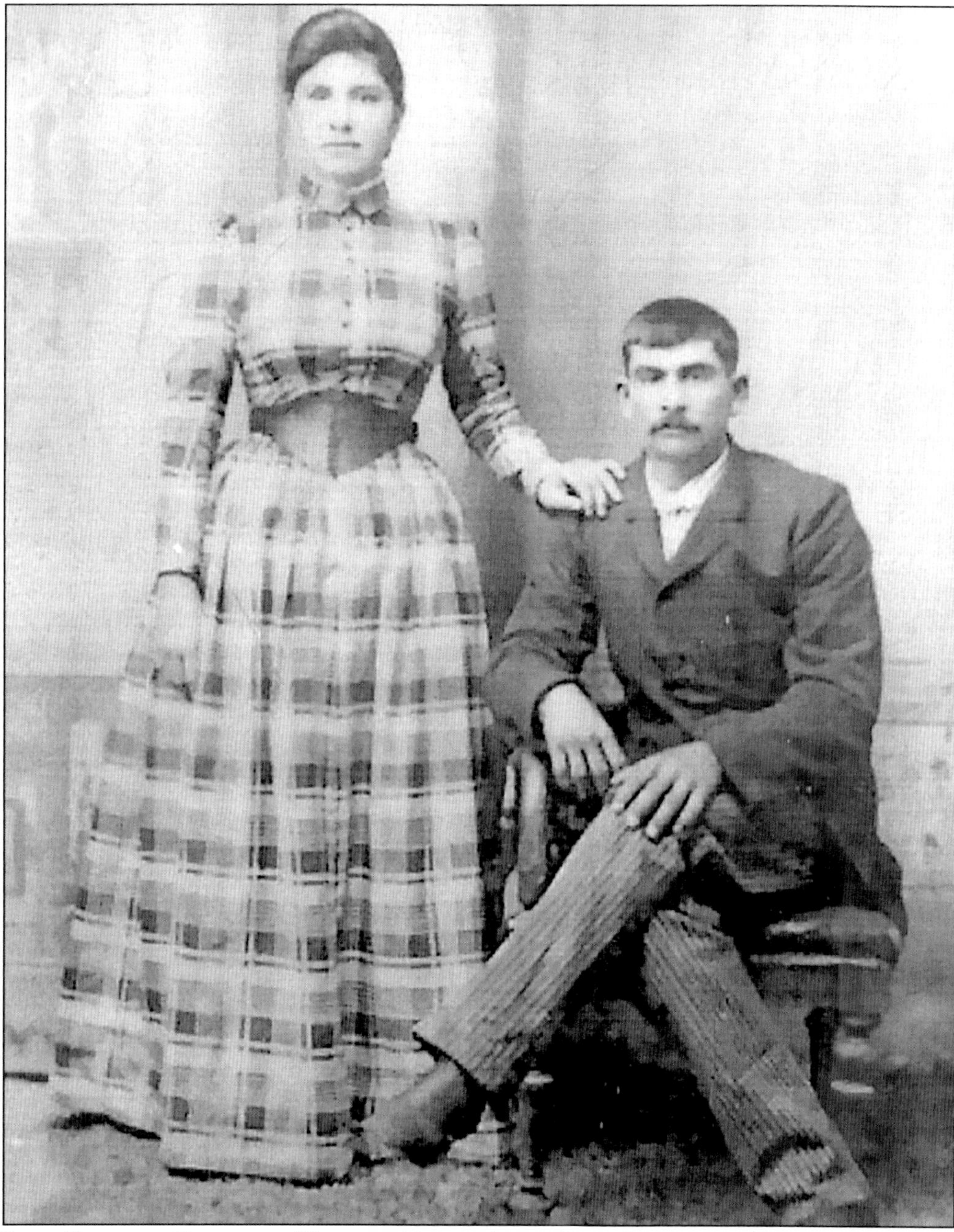

JULIA BOUCHER-ROUSSEAU (SICANGU/FRENCH) AND PAUL ROUSSEAU (CHEYENNE RIVER). The photograph, taken by R. L. Kelly, is undated. These are the grandparents of Chester Fuhrman Jr. and this is likely a photograph taken on their wedding day. It is thought that Julia Boucher/Bouche was born at Lower Brule and her father was Francio Bouche who was an interpreter at Red Cloud Agency. Julia's mother was from the family of Chief Spotted Tail. Julia enrolled at Cheyenne River when they moved to that area. Julia's husband Paul Rousseau was paralyzed from a car accident when they were on a duck hunting trip, and then died. Their daughter Louise Margaret Rousseau Red Fish married Harry Webb. (Photograph courtesy of Chester Fuhrman, Jr.)

Two

MNI TO OKICIZE (BLUE WATER FIGHT)
SICANGU VS. PALANI (BURNT THIGHS VS. PAWNEE)
OPAWINGE WICAKTEPI OKICIZE (BATTLE OF ONE HUNDRED/FETTERMAN FIGHT)
PEJI SLA OKICIZE (GREASY GRASS/BATTLE OF THE LITTLE BIGHORN)

The Sicangu Nation are a proud people whose ancestors participated in the major events in Lakota history. Early contact with non-Indians and major participation by the Sicangu occurred at these events: 1804 Lewis and Clark Expedition; 1854 Grattan Incident; 1855 Blue Water Fight; 1851 and 1868 Fort Laramie Treaties; 1866 Fetterman Fight; Bozeman Trail Wars; 1873 Sicangu vs. Pawnee (known as Massacre Canyon); 1876 Greasy Grass-Battle of Little Bighorn; 1881 Killing of Chief Spotted Tail; and 1890 Ghost Dance Movement. The southern Lakota (Sicangu and Oglala) and the Pawnee and Ponca Indians raided each other often in the southern part of Lakota territory. Spotted Tails Folk by George Hyde is a reference book for that era, though Hyde is a proponent of the Pawnee.

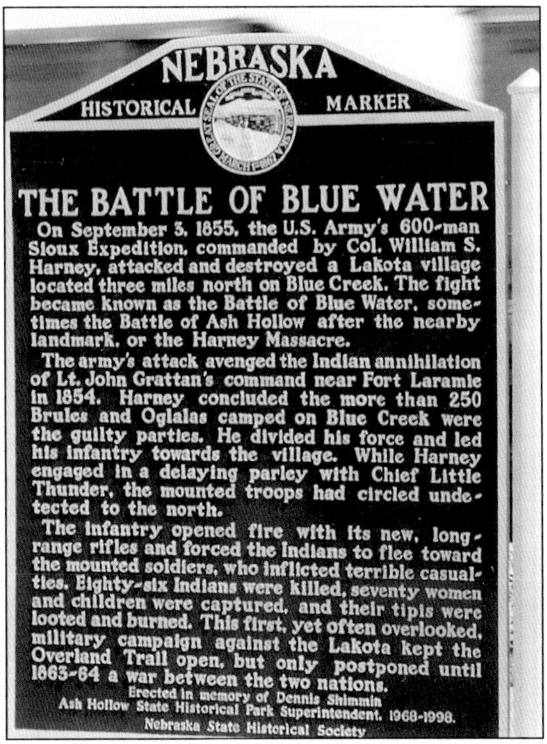

SITE OF LITTLE THUNDER'S CAMP MASSACRE (SICANGU AND OGLALA). Photographed in October 2002, this placard marks the site, near the Platte River, where Little Thunder's band of Sicangu and others were attacked by Harney on September 3, 1855, at their camp site three miles north of the Blue Water in present-day Nebraska, near the town of Lewellen. The attack was provoked by the Grattan Incident of 1854, when Lt. John Grattan and his command were defeated and killed by the Lakota. While Harney delayed a parley with Chief Little Thunder, his troops circled the village. The soldiers massacred fleeing Lakota, inflicting terrible casualties—86 Lakota men, women, and children were killed, 70 women and children were captured, and the tipis were looted and burned. (Photograph courtesy of Donovin Sprague.)

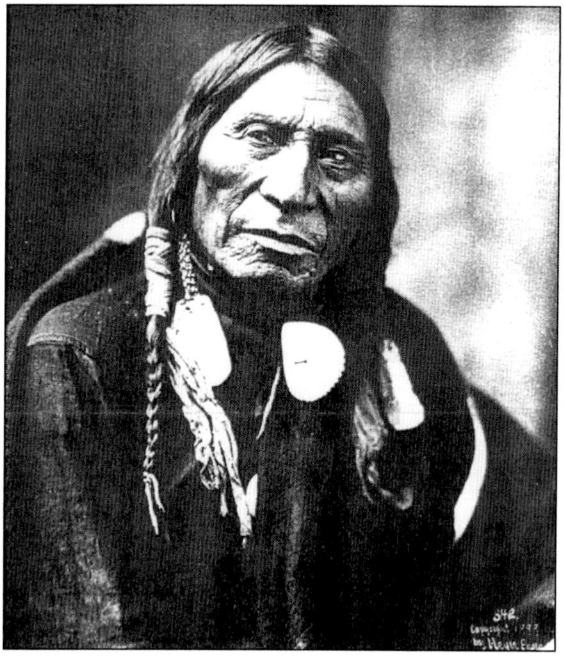

CONQUERING BEAR "MATO WAYUHI" (SICANGU). This photograph was taken by Heyn and Matzen in 1899. This is the son of the elder Chief Conquering Bear who died in 1854 in the Grattan Incident. The Conquering Bear family has ties to Rosebud and Pine Ridge. This is probably the Conquering Bear who was born in 1872 and married Susan Conquering Bear (b. 1879). The picture was taken at the Indian Congress Exposition in Omaha, Nebraska. (Photograph courtesy of Bureau of Ethnology.)

BLACK HORN "HE SAPA" (LAKOTA). Photograph taken *c.* 1899 by F.A. Rinehart. This picture was taken at the Omaha Indian Exposition. The Black Horn family of a husband, wife, and child are listed on the Rosebud Census of 1875. In 1869 Indian Agent Captain Poole recorded that he met with chiefs from the Powder River country in the north (present day Wyoming) when they arrived at the trading stores at the agency of John W. Smith and the Bordeaux family. These chiefs included Black Horn, who was described as a lieutenant of Red Leaf, old Grand Partison, and the "wild" Minnicoujou chief Roman Nose. Grand Partison signed the Fort Laramie Treaty of 1851 and may have been known as Big Eagle. Grand Partison is a translation recognizing him as a grand leader. Grand Partison was also listed as a leader of the Orphan Band after 1845 but also with the Corn Band, as the latter band evolves. Roman Nose was a son of Chief One Horn (Lone Horn). Poole noted the striking difference in appearance of the agency Indians and these non-agency Lakota. (Postcard courtesy of Donovin Sprague.)

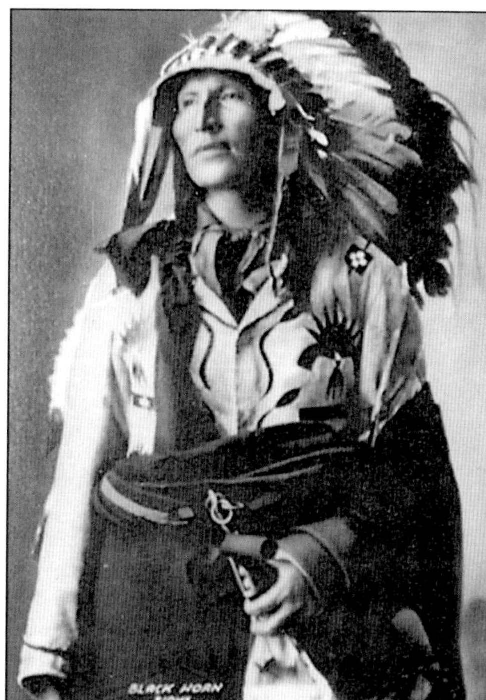

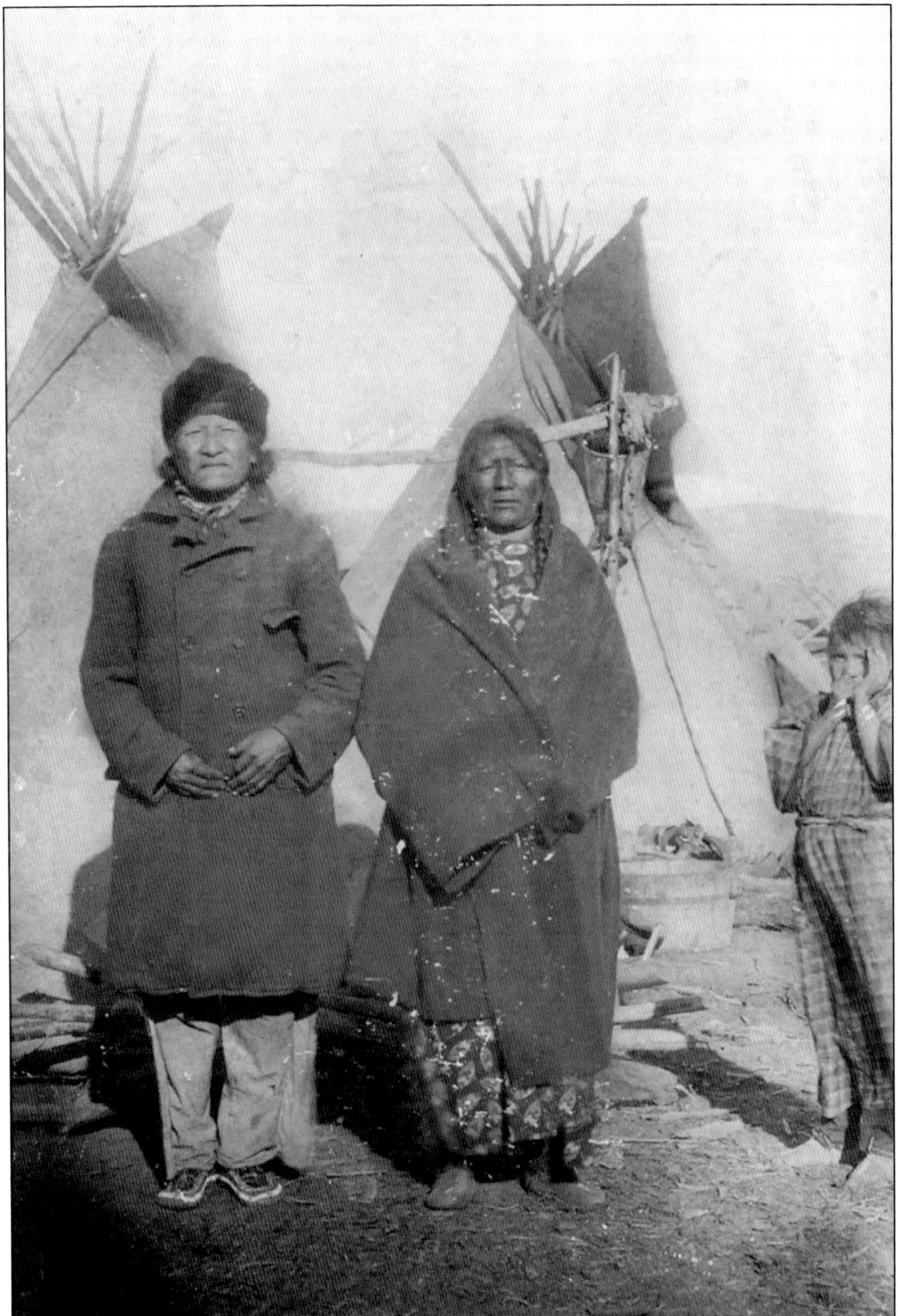

Chief Crow Dog and Mrs. Crow Dog (Sicangu). This photograph was taken January 18, 1891, just days after the Wounded Knee Massacre of December 29, 1890. Crow Dog and his wife are at Pine Ridge Agency. Earlier, Crow Dog shot and killed Chief Spotted Tail in a feud on August 5, 1881. (Photograph courtesy of Oglala Lakota College Archives.)

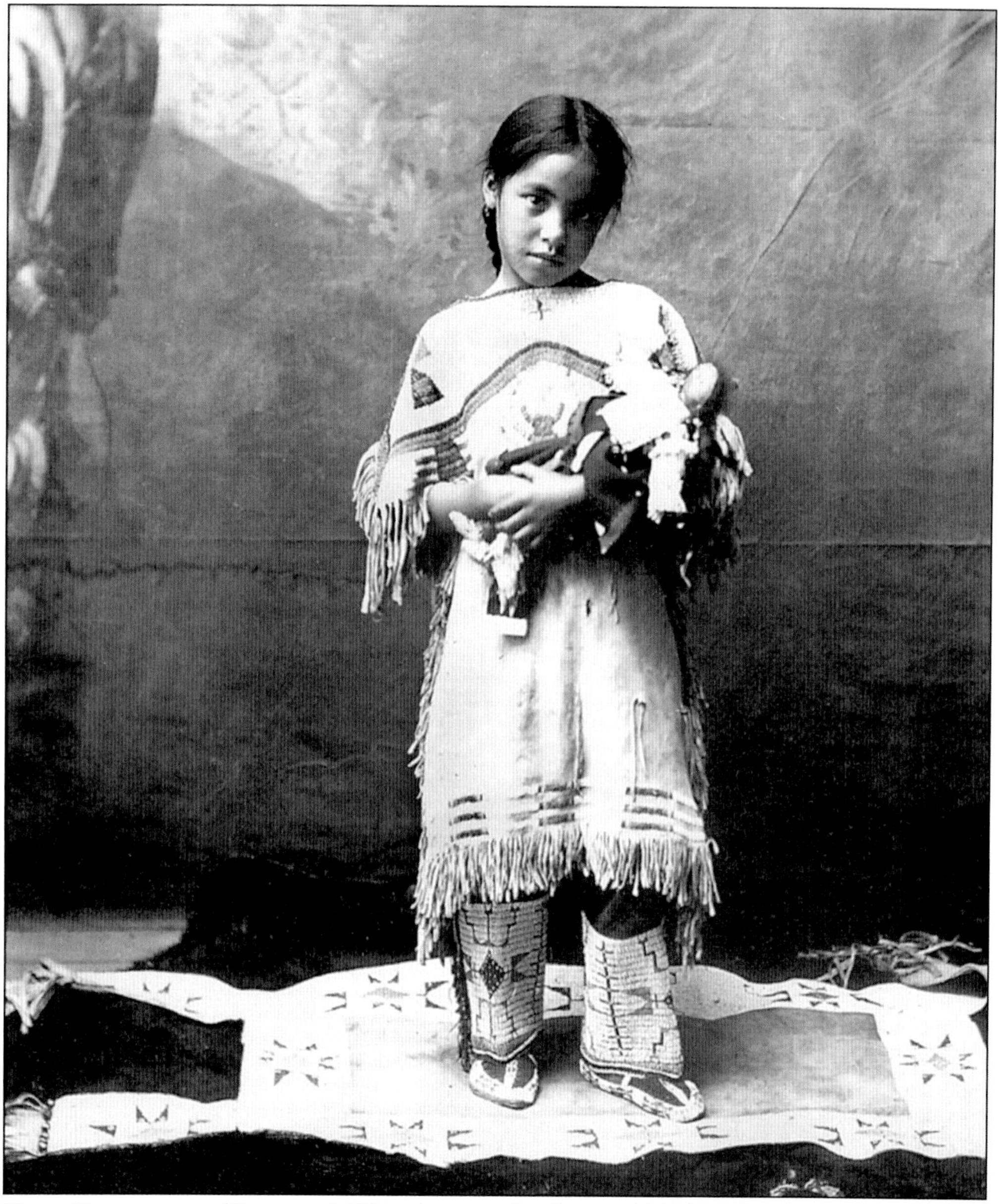

KATIE ROUBIDEAUX (SICANGU). This photograph taken in 1898 by John A. Anderson. Katie Roubideaux Blue Thunder was eight years old at this time. She was born in 1890 and was the daughter of Louis Roubideaux, official U. S. interpreter at Rosebud in the late 1880s. Louis also served as captain of the Indian Police. Adelia Roubideaux was Katie's mother. In 1909, Katie married Henry Knocks Off Two, and later married David Blue Thunder. Katie Roubideaux Blue Thunder lived to the age of 101. (Postcard courtesy of Donovin Sprague.)

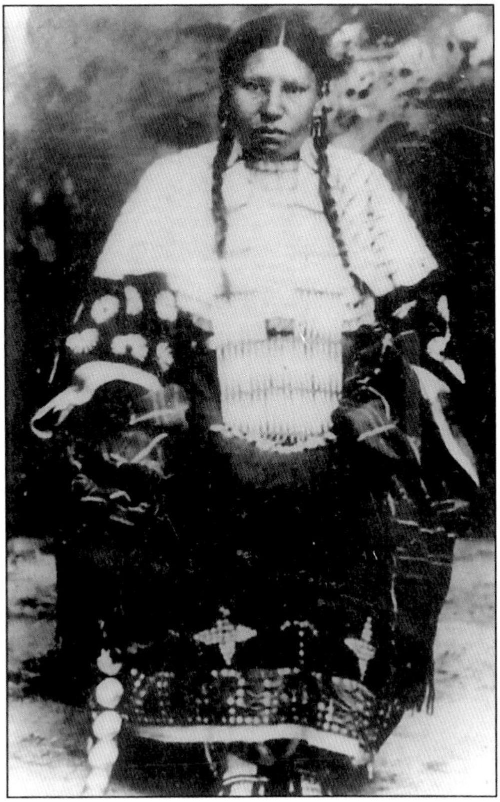

AGNES BULL WALKS BEHIND-QUIVER (OGLALA). This photograph is undated. Agnes Bull Walks Behind was born in 1895 and married Harry Quiver Sr. "Wanju" in 1895 at Pass Creek on Pine Ridge Reservation. Agnes and her parents were from Hisle, South Dakota, and Martin, South Dakota. Harry was born in 1870 and the family was close to the people and boundaries of the Rosebud Reservation. (Photograph courtesy of Walter Tiedeman.)

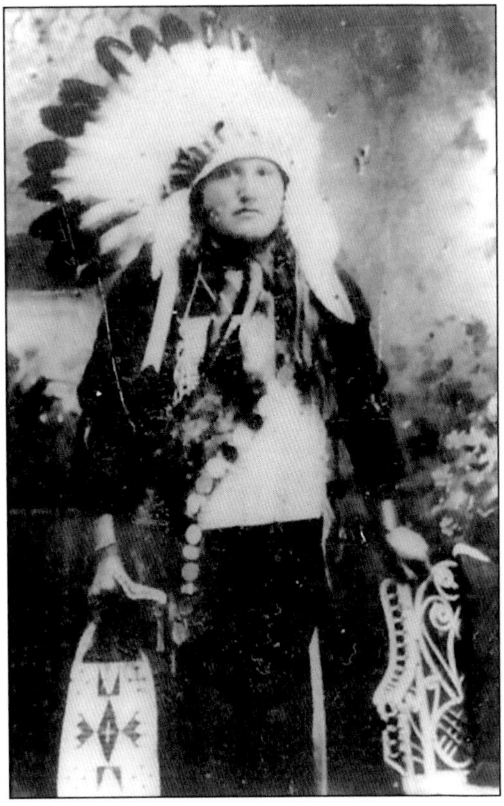

HARRY QUIVER SR. "WANJU" (OGLALA). This photograph is undated. Harry Quiver "Wanju" was born in 1870 at Pass Creek and married Agnes Bull Walks Behind in 1895. Agnes was born in 1875. A son named Harry Quiver Jr. was born in 1914. The father of Harry Quiver Sr. was Robert Quiver "Wanju." A brother of Harry Quiver Sr. was Tom Quiver. Tom married Esther Standing Bear and a son of theirs was Bert Quiver who married Lavina "Reshaw" Richards. The author works with Boots Quiver, who is the son of Bert and Lavina. Harry Quiver Sr. would be a great uncle of Boots Quiver. A daughter of Harry and Agnes was Anna Quiver, who married Fred Wilcox. The children of Anna Quiver and Fred Wilcox were Leo, Geneva Gonzales, William, Ollie, Zona Brown, Irma Kukuk, Florence Dillon, and Albert. (Photograph courtesy of Walter Tiedeman.)

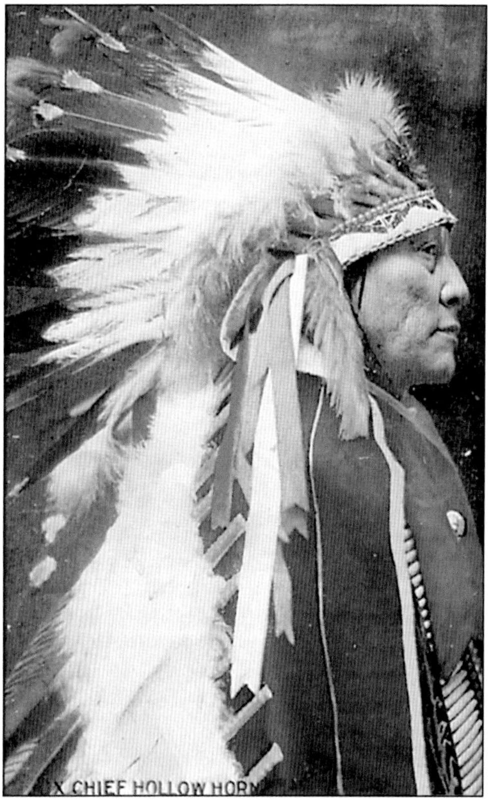

CHIEF HOLLOW HORN BEAR (SICANGU). This photograph is undated. The National Archives contain a telegram referring to the fact that Agent Pollock presented silver Presidential peace medals to Hollow Horn Bear, Spotted Tail, and others at the Missouri River agency location on August 28, 1879. "Young" Hollow Horn Bear was listed as a son of Iron Shell, chief of the Sicangu Orphan Band. (Postcard courtesy of Donovin Sprague.)

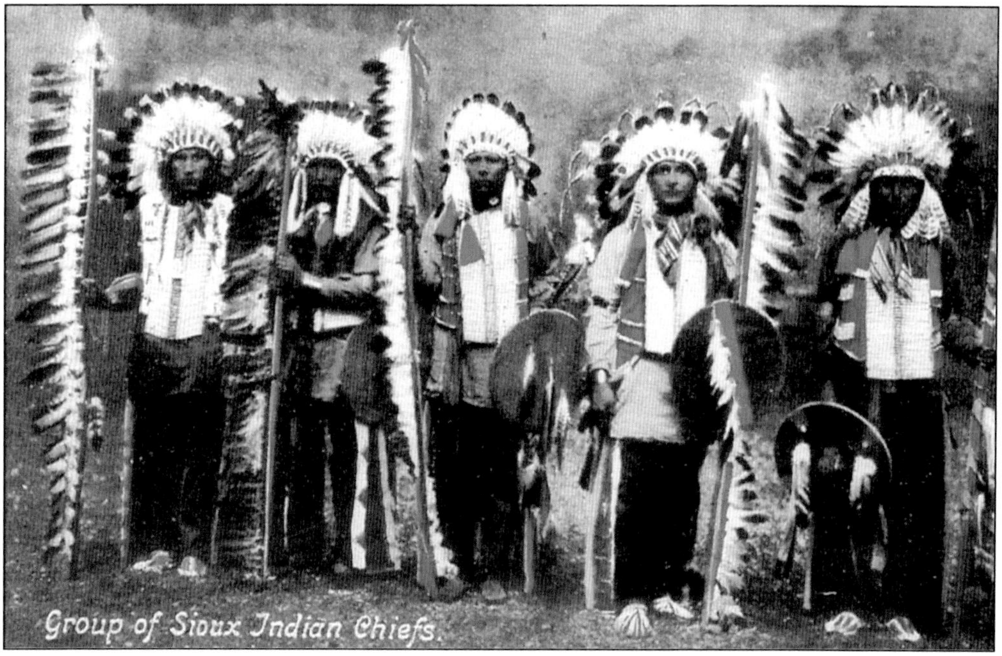

LAKOTA LEADERS IN TRADITIONAL REGALIA. This photograph is undated. These Lakota leaders are not identified and the photographer is not listed in this postcard. (Postcard courtesy of Donovin Sprague.)

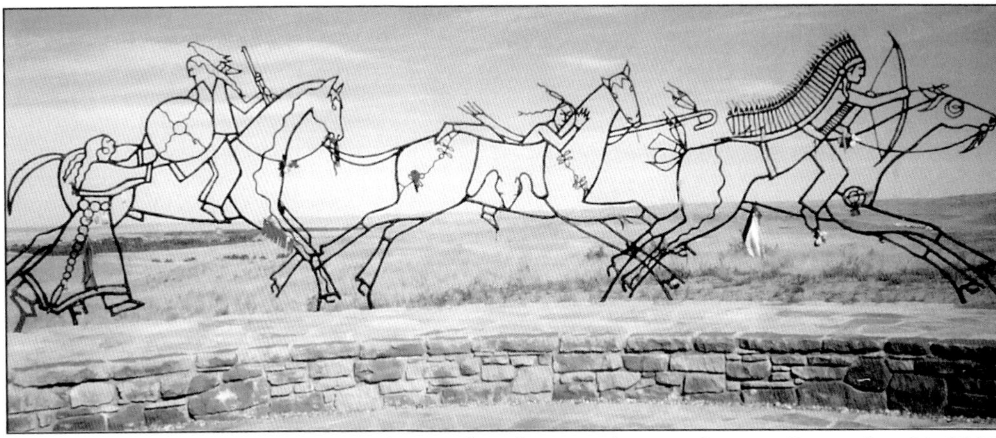

Battle of the Little Bighorn Site. This photograph was taken on September 14, 2003. This is a new design to commemorate the newly dedicated memorial to the American Indians who participated in the Battle of the Little Bighorn against Lt. Col. Custer and his soldiers. This site is next to the area where Custer and his men died atop "Last Stand Hill." The Sicangu along with their other Lakota allies, the Cheyenne, and a few Arapaho fought to defend their people and land from this attack on June 25, 1876. This battle happened in southeastern Montana where the Crow Reservation is now located. The Crow Indians were allied with the soldiers. (Photograph courtesy of Donovin Sprague.)

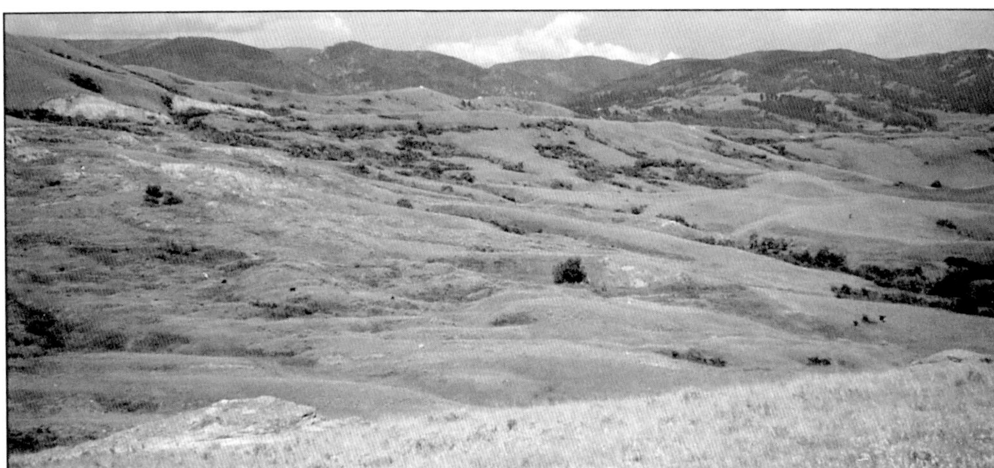

Site of the Fetterman Fight. This photograph was taken on June 25, 2004. This is the view atop the hill where Captain William Fetterman and his soldiers died fighting the Lakota and the Cheyenne on December 21, 1866. The site is just north of where Fort Phil Kearny was located and was Fetterman's location when he disobeyed his commanders orders and pursued Lakota and Cheyenne decoys over Lodge Ridge Trail, losing his entire command unit. This location is between present day Buffalo and Sheridan, Wyoming. Story, Wyoming, is just to the west of this site at the foot of the visible Big Horn Mountains. The majority of the soldiers were killed atop this hill in a running fight on horseback. Most of the soldiers' horses were lost by the end of the fighting. In this view the nearby Big Horns are to the northwest and some soldiers also died in this valley below the hill top. Fort Phil Kearny is located to the south of this hilltop. The following summer, on August 2, 1867, the Wagon Box Fight happened next to present Story, Wyoming, which is just out of view. The Sicangu Lakota were well represented in the Fetterman Fight. (Photograph courtesy of Donovin Sprague.)

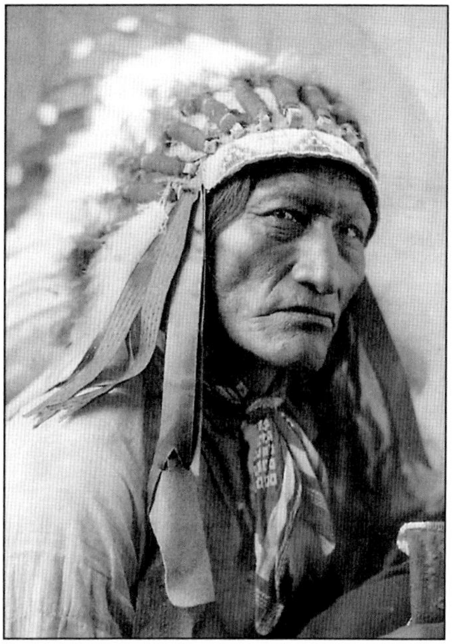

YELLOW HORSE (SICANGU). This photograph is undated. (Photograph courtesy of Rose Two Strike Stenstrom.)

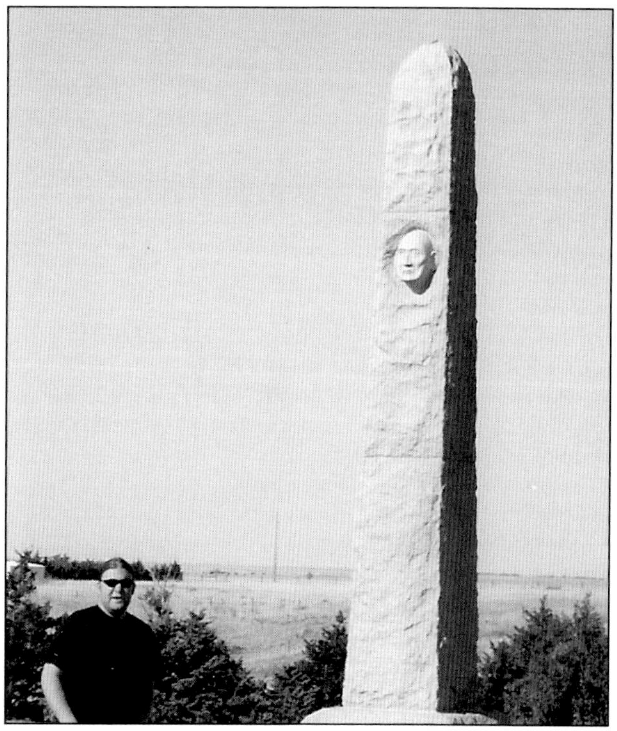

LAKOTA AND PAWNEE CANYON BATTLEFIELD MONUMENT. This photograph was taken in June 2002. This monument at "Massacre Canyon Battlefield Memorial" east of Trenton, Nebraska, was erected by authority of the U. S. Congress, "as a memorial to the frontier and Indian Wars forever ended." The face of John Grass "a noted Sioux Indian" faces west. The other image carved here facing the east is Ruling Hisson, a Pawnee chief who was in the battle. His wife and two children died in the fighting. The monument was originally on a hill overlooking the Republican River Valley but was moved to this site in 1961 to be next to the highway. It was originally dedicated on September 26, 1930, and was the first historical monument erected in Nebraska by Federal grant. Minnesota pink granite was used in the construction of the monument shaft which stands 35 feet high and weighs 91 tons. The original plan was to create a monument with "a Brule (Sicangu) Sioux named Two-Spear in combat on a horse fighting Sky Chief of the Pawnee" and to have Gutzon Borglum, head sculptor of Mt. Rushmore Memorial, do the carving. R. P. Colling of Indianola, Nebraska, erected the shaft. Brandon Sprague (Minnicoujou) is at left, facing east. (Photograph courtesy of Donovin Sprague.)

HE DOG (SICANGU). Another He Dog, Oglala, was born at Bear Butte, South Dakota, in 1840. His father was Black Rock and his mother was Blue Day Woman. He was appointed as a prestigious shirt wearer among the Oglala but had close ties to the Sicangu, and his reservation era camp was Rosebud. He Dog and his younger brother Little Shield were close friends and allies of Chief Crazy Horse. He Dog was asked to examine the body of Crazy Horse at Camp Robinson. He testified that there were two stab wounds to the back of Crazy Horse. The *Chicago Tribune* report of September 11, 1877, verified the story. Although He Dog said he was the same age as Crazy Horse and that they were lifelong friends, none of his family ever claimed any family relationship to Crazy Horse and none can be verified. He Dog's son Eagle Hawk graduated from Carlisle Indian School and was later known as Reverend Joseph Eagle Hawk. Both He Dog and his son served as judges of the Court of Indian Offenses at Pine Ridge, and He Dog lived until 1936. The following is a family unit of the He Dog family listed as living at He Dog's Camp at Rosebud: He Dog (b. 1854), his wife Holy (b. 1861), and children Yellow (b. 1877), Elk (b. 1874), White Robe (b. 1885), Looks At Things (b. 1880), and Search The Enemy (b. 1881). He Dog's Camp Day School on Rosebud Reservation opened in 1893 and closed in 1935 when a newer school was built near Parmalee, South Dakota, seven miles east of the original school. Cut Meat Day School had been located 400 yards south of the new school which still carries He Dog's name. (Photograph courtesy of Rose Two Strike Stenstrom.)

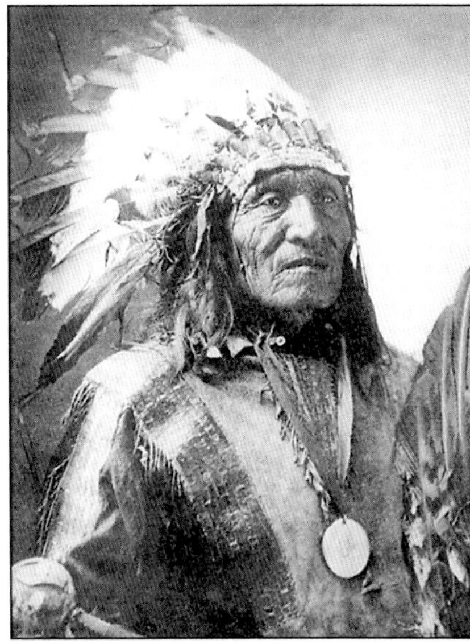

TWO STRIKE "NUMPKAHPA" (SICANGU). Photograph taken by Alexander Gardner, c. 1875. Two Strike received his name from counting coup by knocking two enemy Utes off their horses with his war club. Several other phenomena in his life occurred in pairs. He was a Ghost Dance leader in his band and was in the Stronghold area of Pine Ridge Reservation when the Wounded Knee Massacre happened on December 29, 1890. Two Strike had three wives: Bear Heart (Oglala), Standing/Her Good Horse (Oglala), and Brown Eyes. Brown Eyes may have been a Black Crow and was related to that family. The children of Chief Two Strike were Takes Pity On Them (b. 1848), Brown Woman (b. 1851), Good Whirlwind (b. 1848), Noisy/Black Spotted Horse/Noisy Black Spotted Horse (b. 1872), Plenty Pipe (b. 1858), Little Hawk (b. 1855), Arthur Two Strike (b. 1865), and Two Charger (b.1862). His daughter Brown Woman's family consisted of her sons William Brown (b. 1874), Andrew Sees Red (b. 1863), Leo Spotted Calf (b. 1881), Neck, and a daughter, Wounded (b. 1884). Two Strike's son Little Hawk became known as Joseph Little Hawk and family may include Samuel Little Hawk (b. 1904) and sons Joseph Little Hawk Jr. (b. 1932) and William Poor Bear. Two Strike's grandchildren from daughter Takes Pity On Them include her son Little Commander and daughters Mabel Plenty Bear, Julia Grass, Mary Yellow Wolf, and Martha Black Bear. Chief Two Strike died in 1913 at the age of 98. (Postcard courtesy of Donovin Sprague.)

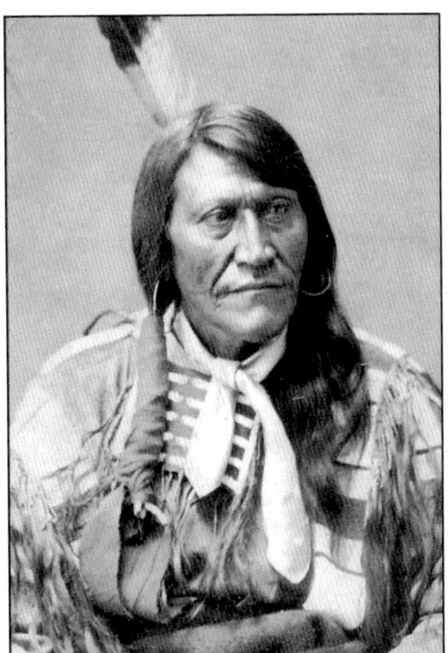

LAKOTA AND PAWNEE CANYON BATTLEFIELD SITE. This event is known in Nebraska history as "Massacre Canyon Battlefield Memorial" and the site is located just north of the Republican River in present southern Nebraska near the Kansas state line. It is three miles east of Trenton, Nebraska. This battle happened between the Lakota and Pawnee Indians on the morning of August 5, 1873. Most of the Lakota participants were the Sicangu Lakota and some of their primary itancan (leaders) in this fight were Spotted Tail, Two Strike, and Little Wound (Oglala). The principal leaders of the Pawnee were Sky Chief, Sun Chief, and Fighting Bear. In this war the Lakota inflicted terrible casualties in a surprise attack among a hunting party of about 700 Pawnee, and was the last major fight among these two long time enemies. The Pawnee retreated into and along a canyon area behind this monument clear to the Republican River. A cavalry unit arrived and the Lakota finally retreated. Captain Meinhold of the U.S. 3rd Cavalry and Assistant Surgeon D.F. Powell were the first visitors to the site following the fighting in 1873 and the *Omaha Herald* recorded the conflict which included mutilations. It was recorded that about 1,000 Lakota participated and between 70-100 Pawnee were killed or wounded compared to six killed among the Lakota. Following this, most of the Pawnee would soon cede their Nebraska land to the U.S. in exchange for land in Oklahoma and their present headquarters is at Pawnee, Oklahoma. The monument depicts a Lakota and Pawnee at opposite sides near the top. (Photograph courtesy of Donovin Sprague.)

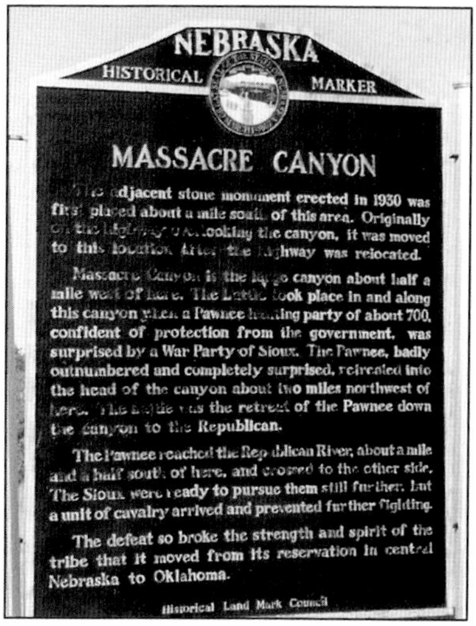

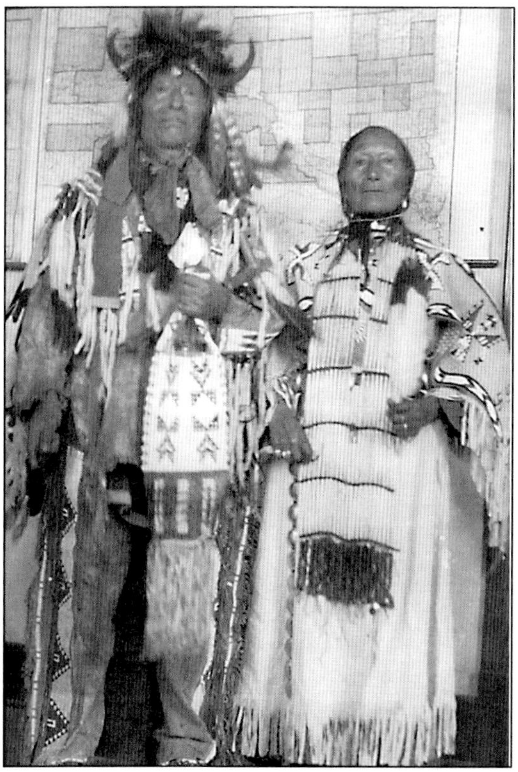

CHIEF HIGH HAWK AND NATION HAWK AKA NATION (SICANGU). High Hawk was a historian of the Sicangu Lakota. His father, Brown Hat, was born in 1821 or 1822 and was later known as Battiste Good. His father was the keeper of a Lakota winter count, which depicted important historical events of a particular year drawn on a hide. This winter count began in the year 1700 and was carried on by Brown Hat until 1880. By talking to the oldest Sicangu elders he gained factual information. It is possible that Brown Hat created the drawings as late as 1863. Then the winter count was handed down to High Hawk and he carried on the historical record. In a trip to Washington, D.C., High Hawk was given a silver topped walking cane. High Hawk had three wives and at least 12 children. His oldest son was also named High Hawk. There were other High Hawk families throughout Lakota country, including several who were killed or wounded at the Wounded Knee Massacre in 1890. (Photograph courtesy of Rose Two Strike Stenstrom.)

UNIDENTIFIED LAKOTA. This photograph is undated. This is a picture of a Lakota man and the photographer and identity was not recorded. (Photograph courtesy of Oglala Lakota College Archives and Musee de l'Homme, Paris, France, and Bureau of Ethnology.)

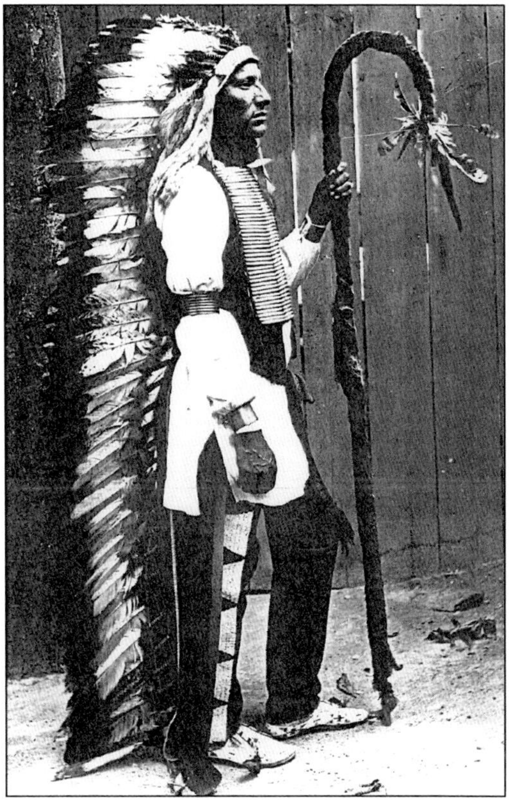

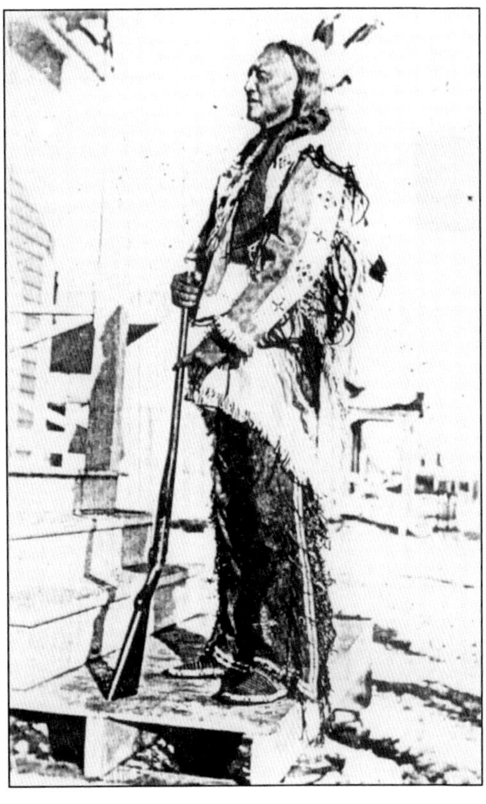

CHIEF HOLLOW HORN BEAR "MATO HE OKLOGECA" (SICANGU). This photograph is undated. Hollow Horn Bear was a recognized headman, and the son of Chief Iron Shell. He participated in many Lakota Plains Wars in the 1860s including the Fetterman Fight near Fort Phil Kearny south of present day Sheridan, Wyoming. He was born in 1850 and later became known as Daniel Hollow Horn Bear. He also had sons named Daniel, John, and Luther. He was a great orator, and was a guest at President Theodore Roosevelt's inauguration. He was also present at President Wilson's inauguration and while in Washington, D.C., Hollow Horn Bear contracted pneumonia and died. His body was shipped back to Rosebud in 1913 when he was about the age of 63. (Postcard courtesy of Donovin Sprague.)

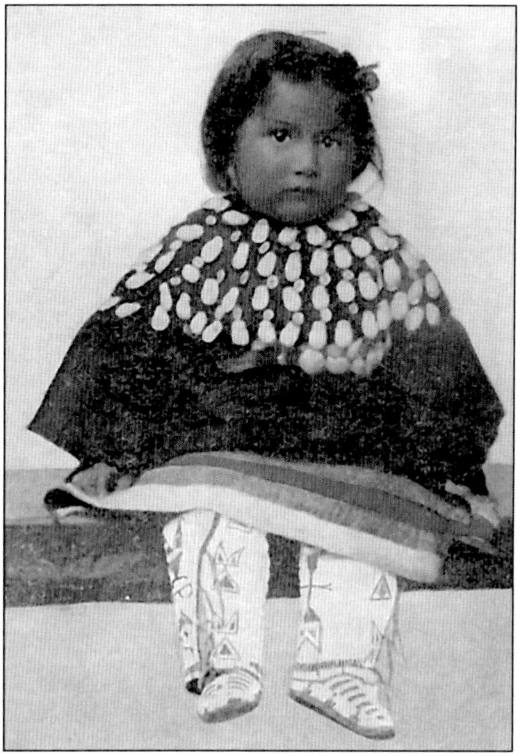

LOST BIRD (LAKOTA). This photograph was taken in 1905 by F.A. Rinehart. Rinehart and his assistant Adolph Muhr were also hired to document in photographs the 1898 World's Fair, also known as the Trans-Mississippi and International Exposition in Omaha, Nebraska. Most of the photographs were taken in 1898, but some were taken later. (Postcard courtesy of Donovin Sprague.)

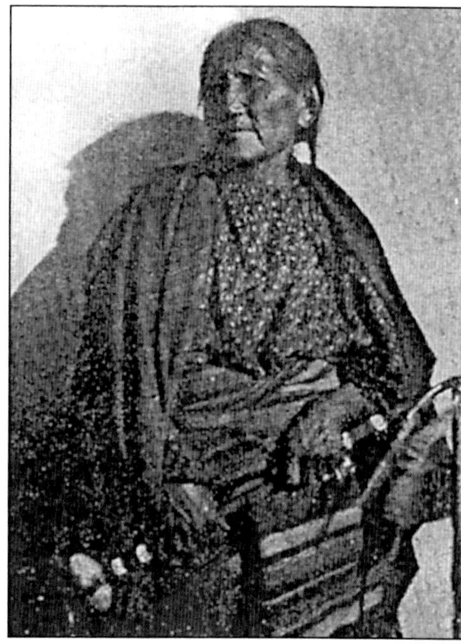

WHITE BUFFALO WOMAN (SICANGU). This photograph is undated. (Photograph courtesy of Donovin Sprague.)

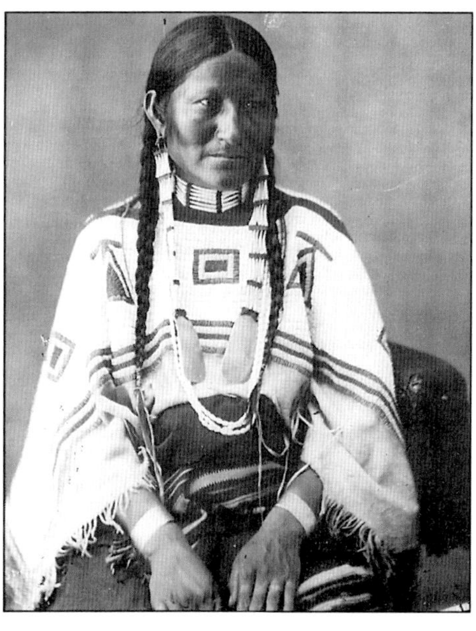

MRS. SPOTTED TAIL (SICANGU). Photograph taken by Alexander Gardner, Washington, DC, 1872. This is one of the wives of Chief Spotted Tail. Spotted Tail had a house built for him by the U.S. at the old Spotted Tail Agency in Nebraska and another one when he settled just north of Rosebud Agency. The latter home was considered a mansion and cost $5,000, a huge sum in those days. The Rosebud agent was not happy because the home was much larger than his, however the family of Spotted Tail preferred living in their nearby tipi. (Photograph courtesy of Bureau of Ethnology.)

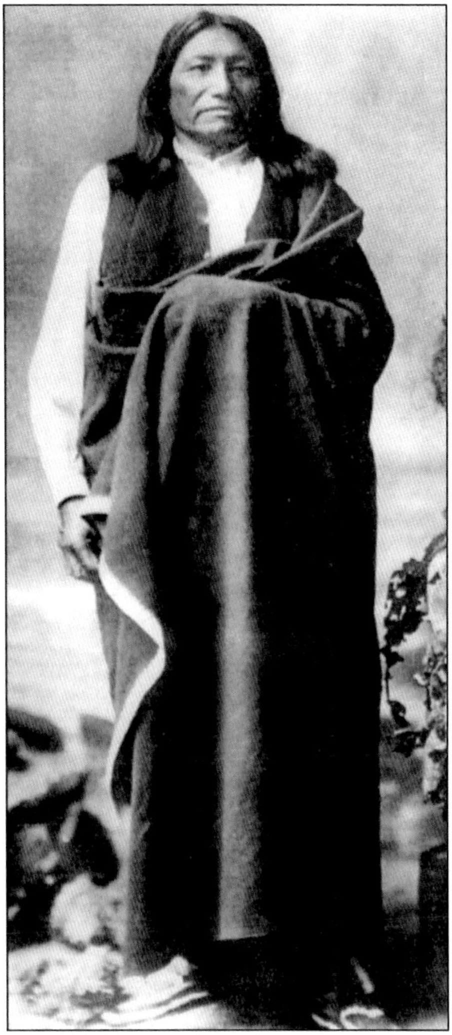

CHIEF SPOTTED TAIL "SINTE GLESKA" (SICANGU). Chief Spotted Tail was the most famous Sicangu leader since non-Indian contact with the Lakota. He was born in 1823 on the White River west of the Missouri River in South Dakota and was previously known as Jumping Buffalo. He earned the name Spotted Tail when a white trapper gave him a raccoon tail, which he carried into battle and used in his headdress. His father was Tangle Hair and his mother was Walks With The Pipe. Tangle Hair was Sicangu but the family was related to the Saones, a French name for some of the northern Lakota bands who were at that time around the upper Missouri River area of present South Dakota. Of these bands, he was closest to the Siha Sapa. He had five wives and an estimated 34 children. According to Susan Bettelyoun, who knew the family, four of his wives were sisters and the youngest of these sisters was Minniscurrin. Some of his children from his wife Blue Haired Horse were Annie (b.1883), Charlie (b. 1880), Louis (b. 1879), and George (b. 1880). One family's genealogy shows Spotted Tail and Chief Smoke were brothers, and Lois White Thunder Woman as their sister. Spotted Tail was a great leader in war, particularly at the battle at Julesburg, Colorado, in 1865 in retaliation for the attack by Col. John Chivington on Black Kettle's Cheyenne camp. Spotted Tail did not participate in the Fetterman Fight and Wagon Box Fight near Fort Kearny. At the time of the Fetterman Fight in December of 1866, his daughter had died and he traveled to Fort Laramie where she was buried on a scaffold near the fort with full military honors. He was once captured and spent time at Fort Leavenworth and learned to read and write in English. Spotted Tail went to Washington, D.C., with Red Cloud and others in 1870 where he was a noted spokesperson for the Sicangu. Spotted Tail was a great proponent of education and sent his sons to Carlisle Indian School. In the spring of 1877, he was designated to lead a group from the agency into the Powder River country to try to induce Crazy Horse and others to surrender. In 1877, General Crook made Spotted Tail the head chief of the Sicangu and Oglala bands because they felt Red Cloud (Oglala) was uncooperative. Spotted Tail was shot off his horse by Crow Dog in a power struggle after Crow Dog lost his position as chief of police because of Spotted Tail's influence. (Photograph courtesy of Bureau of Ethnology.)

COFFEE "WAKALYAPI" (SICANGU). This photograph of Coffee was taken in early 1930s at Parmelee, South Dakota. The Coffee name goes back to Old Coffee who was born in 1831 and later generations received a non-Indian first name. Some records show Old Coffee's wife as Red Leg who was born in 1835. Their children included Hand Old Coffee born in 1884 and Kills A Little Old Coffee who was born in 1874. Sons of Old Coffee included Lawrence Coffee (b. 1864 and d. 1918), who married Agnes Fast Wolf (b. 1891) in 1909. Lawrence married Tall Woman II about 1893, and married Mary Long Woman (b. 1872) in 1890. John Coffee (b. 1897) was the son of Lawrence and Mary Coffee. Amelia Oglala Win Coffee was born in 1843 and married John Rames about 1870. Their son John Rames Jr. was born in 1875. Peter Coffee (b. 1859) married Gone In Lodge (b. 1875) in 1890 and their children included Lizzie Wounded Coffee (b. 1893), Sampson Coffee (b. 1898), and Mollie Coffee (b. 1902). The Coffee name also was referred to as "Makes Coffee" and "Coffee #2." This photograph is Lawrence or Peter Coffee, the next generation of Coffees, called Coffee #2. Coffee #2 was a deaf mute and knew Chief Crazy Horse and claimed relationship to him but the claim is unproven by blood. A rumor that has appeared in book print was that Coffee #2 was a caretaker of a possible grave of Crazy Horse which is also unproven. After the death of Crazy Horse, Coffee #2 submitted a claim to the U.S. Government for loss of some horses as an heir to Crazy Horse. The claim was denied after checking agency records, on the basis that Coffee was not a blood relative of Chief Crazy Horse. Henry Standing Bear also wrote letters denying Coffee's relationship to Crazy Horse. Henry Big Crow was an heir to the Rosebud land allotments of Coffee #2, Wounded Coffee, Mary Coffee, and Pine Ridge allotments of Iron Heart and Eagle Feather. (Photograph courtesy of Donovin Sprague.)

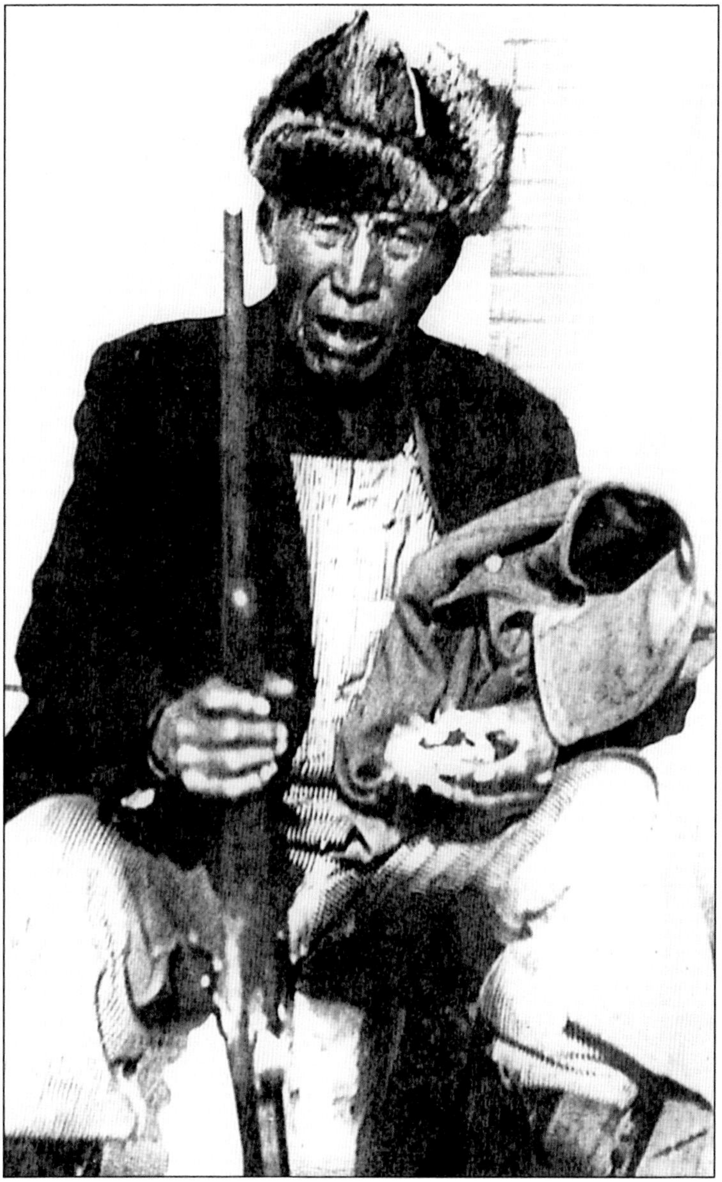

GOES TO WAR "ZUYA HIYAYA" (SICANGU). This photograph is *c.* 1899 by F.A. Rinehart. This picture was taken at the Omaha Indian Exposition where thousands of photographs were taken of American Indians who attended the event. The family of "Go To War" is listed with a total of 14 people in the Rosebud Census of 1875, including two wives. Goes To War was born in 1855, and was a brother of Hollow Horn Bear. One of his wives was Comes Amongst Them. (Postcard courtesy of Donovin Sprague.)

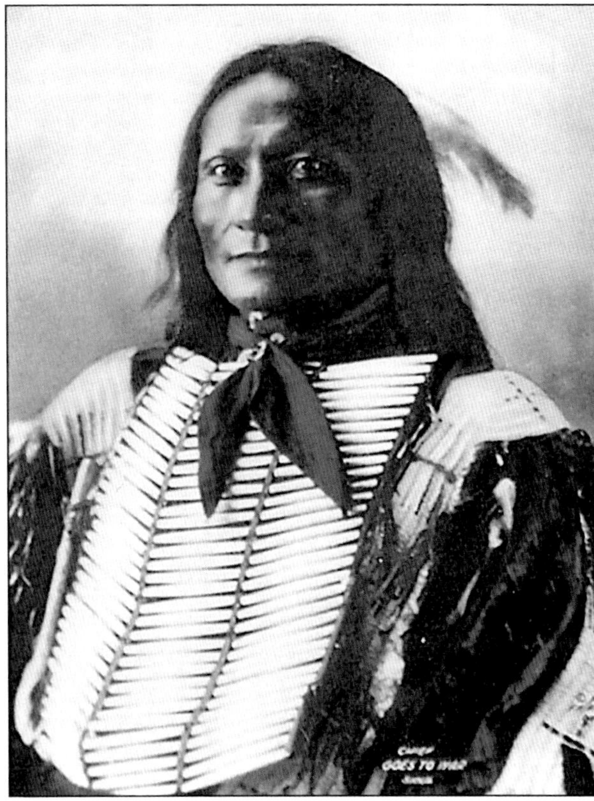

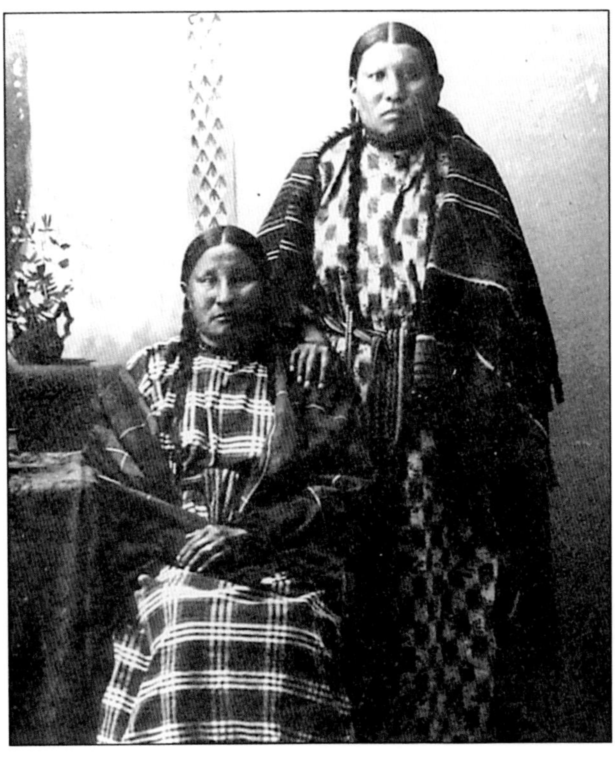

MRS. SORREL HORSE (TWO STRIKE) (SEATED) AND WEARS THE BIRD (STANDING) (SICANGU). This photograph is undated. This photograph shows the daughter and granddaughter of Chief Two Strike. Sorrel Horse was a daughter of Chief Two Strike and she had six or seven children, all of whom died. Wears The Bird was a daughter of Mrs. Sorrel Horse. When all the children had passed on, the Sorrel Horse name ended. Early records obtained by the author show a Mr. Owns Sorrel Horse who was born in 1808 at Rosebud and his wife Owns Sorrel Horse, born in 1810 at Rosebud. They married about 1830. (Photograph courtesy of State Historical Society of South Dakota.)

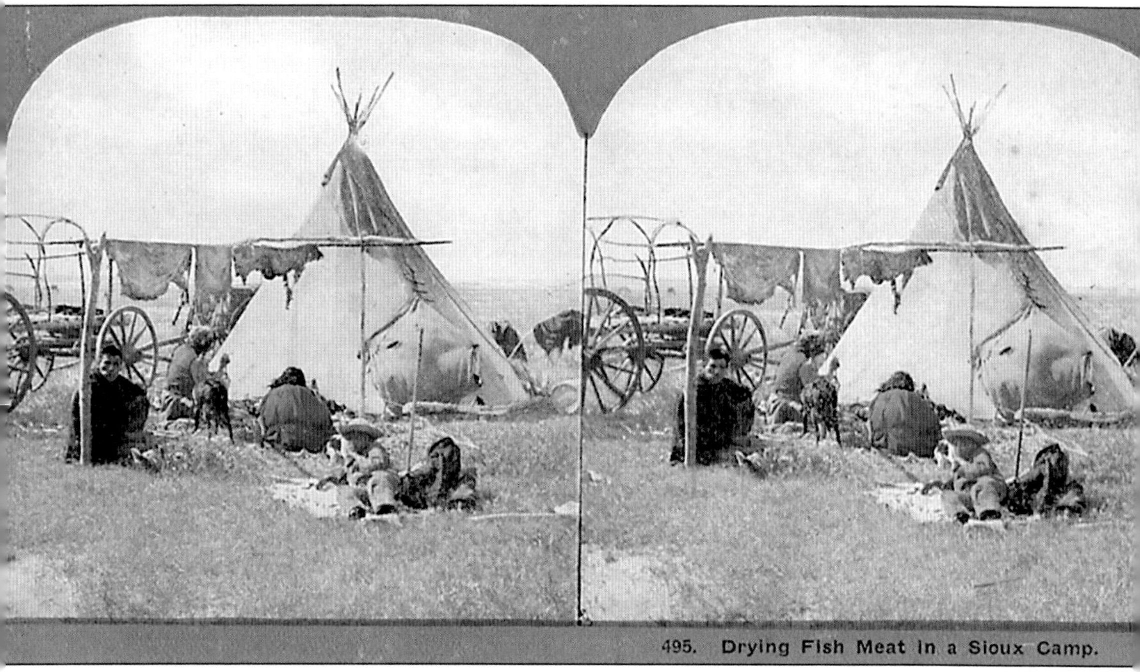

LAKOTA CAMP. This photograph was taken *c*. 1899. This is a stereoview postcard which depicts a Lakota camp at the start of the reservation era. The two women are preparing a recently obtained deer for buckskin, rawhide, meat, and probably will have some dried jerky ready. The two sunkas (dogs) are waiting for any offering which might be given to them. The boys in the foreground are posing for the camera while the young boy tries some meat. A tipi was constructed of buffalo hides. The drying rack can hold hides and jerky, which would be placed upon it to dry, out of reach of animals. A wagon sits in the background. The caption on this card incorrectly states that the Sioux are drying fish and the back of the card explains an incorrect history of the fishing process and preparation by the Sioux. Buffalo meat was a favorite among the Lakota and they were not known for their fishing ability or appetite for fish. (Stereoview postcard courtesy of Donovin Sprague.)

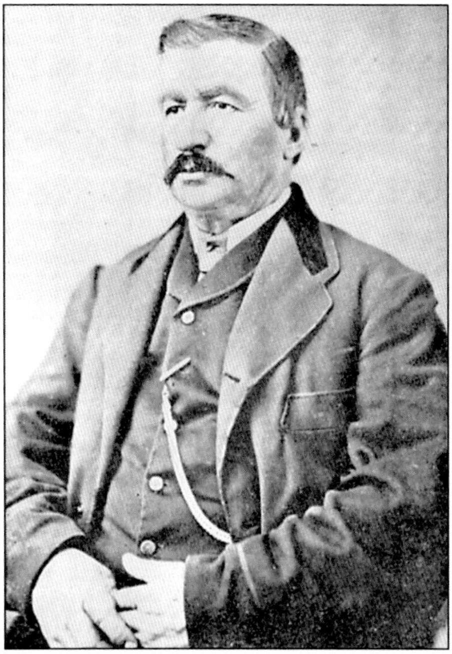

JAMES BORDEAUX (FRENCH). This photograph is undated. James Bordeaux came from France as a boy and arrived at New Orleans. The family moved north to St. Louis and then to St. Joseph, Missouri, where he married a woman from the Otoe Tribe. Following her death, James traveled west to Laramie in Dakota Territory which was in present day Wyoming. He started a trading post on the Platte River, within sight of Fort Laramie. Later by 1846, he established a sub-station on Bordeaux Creek just east of the present town of Chadron, Nebraska. During this time James married the sister of Chief Swift Bear (Sicangu). The last post he would establish was at the old Wheeler Crossing on the Missouri River in Charles Mix County, South Dakota which he operated until 1878. At this time the Sicangu had a brief home agency there but the Upper Sicangu would be moved to Gregory, Tripp, Mellette, and Todd counties, which is the present location of Rosebud Reservation. James Bordeaux lived in the area where events such as the Grattan Incident happened, 1868 Treaty of Fort Laramie, and the last years of Chief Crazy Horse when the leader was fleeing from Red Cloud Agency to Spotted Tail Agency and then back to Red Cloud Agency where he would be stabbed in the back while under surrender. Crazy Horse passed by the Chadron location of Bordeaux's post during this flight in 1877. James died the following year in 1878 at the agency. Today the Bordeaux Trading Post has been rebuilt on the east edge of Chadron, along with a Fur Trade Museum. (Photograph courtesy of Bureau of Ethnology.)

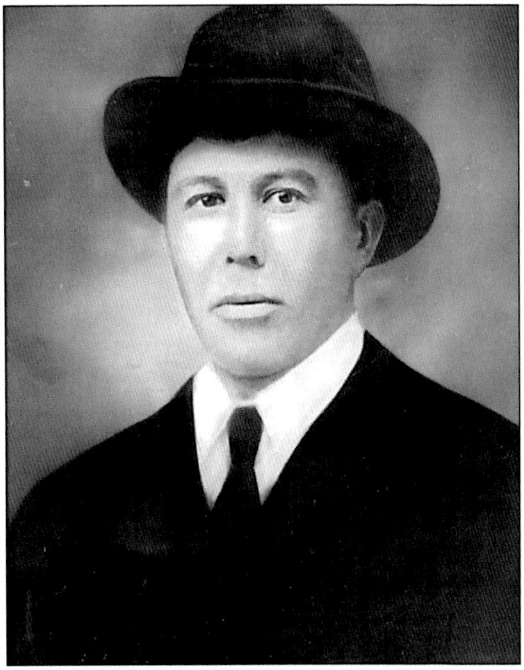

JOHN MOSES HUDSON (SICANGU). This photograph is undated. John married Rose Marie Drapeau and their children were Henry (called Hank), Donald, Paul, Fauniel, Alvina, Gloria, and Hayden. (Photograph courtesy of James and Lenora Hudson.)

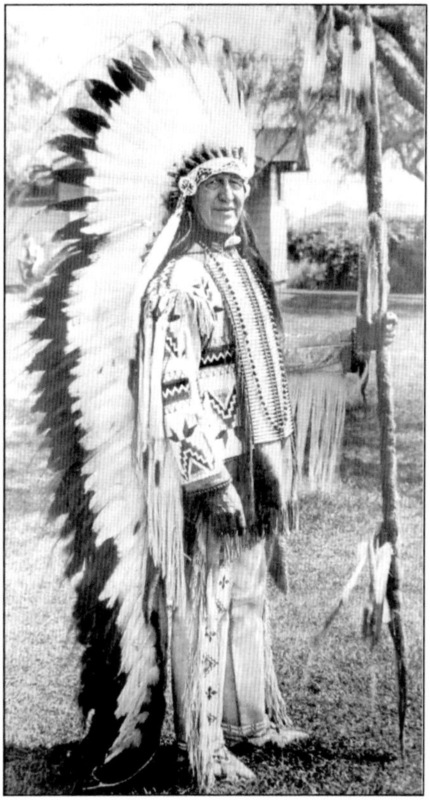

Luther Standing Bear (Sicangu). This photograph is undated. Luther's Lakota name was Ota Kte (Plenty Kill) and he was asked to choose his English first name from a list of names on a blackboard while at the Carlisle Indian School. (Courtesy of Crazy Horse Memorial Foundation and Luther Standing Bear Collection.)

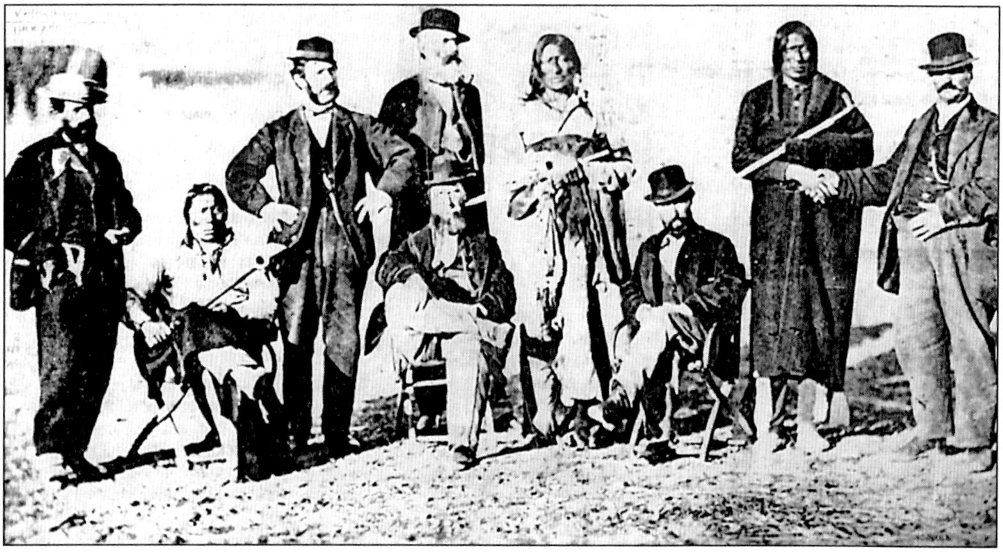

A Group of Oglala With John Bordeaux. Pictured from left to right are unidentified, Packs His Drum (Oglala), John Finn, Amos Bettelyoun, W.G. Bullock (seated), Old Man Afraid Of His Horses(Oglala), Benjamin Mills, Red Bear, and James Bordeaux. (Photograph courtesy of Bureau of Ethnology and James and Lenora Hudson.)

BIG MAN (LAKOTA). This postcard is dated 1903, and was taken by F. A. Rinehart. (Postcard courtesy of Donovin Sprague.)

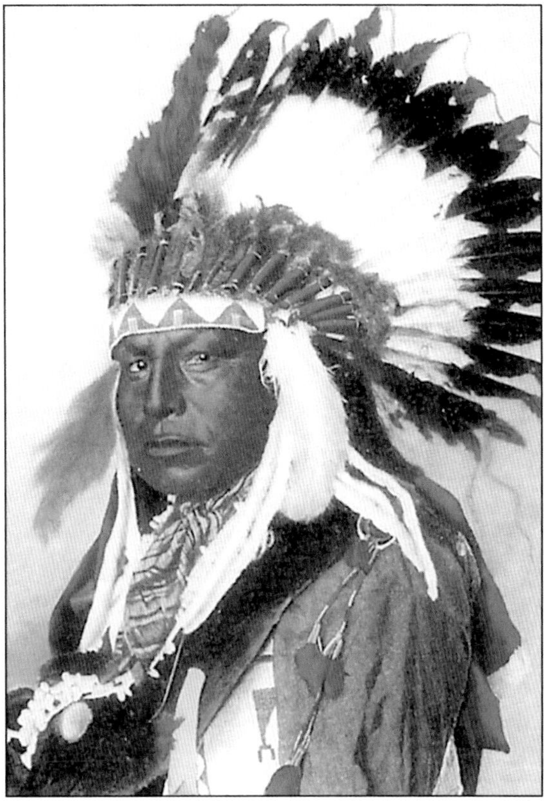

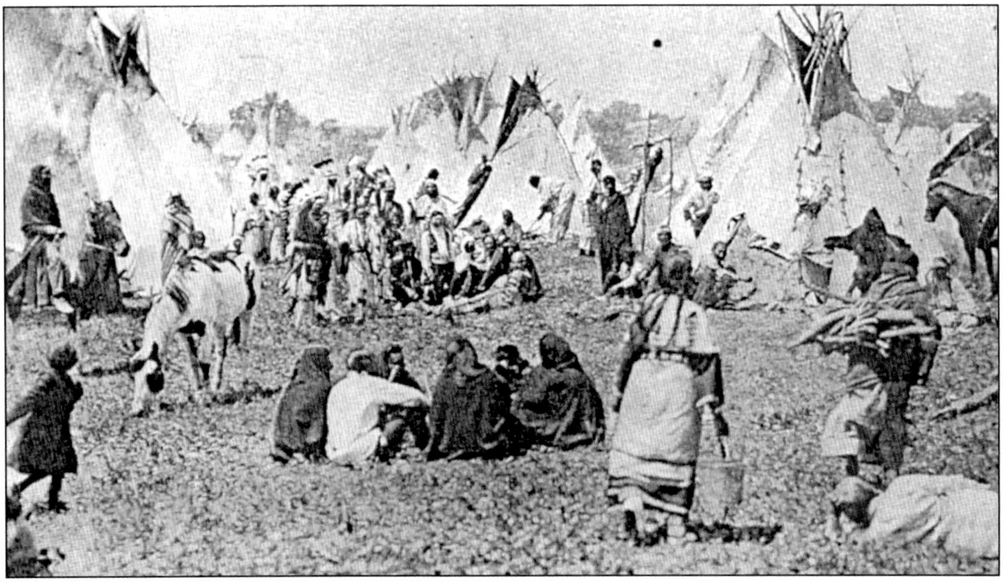

SICANGU CAMP. This photograph is undated. This is a busy camp which was located in Tripp County. (Photograph courtesy of Tripp County Historical Committee.)

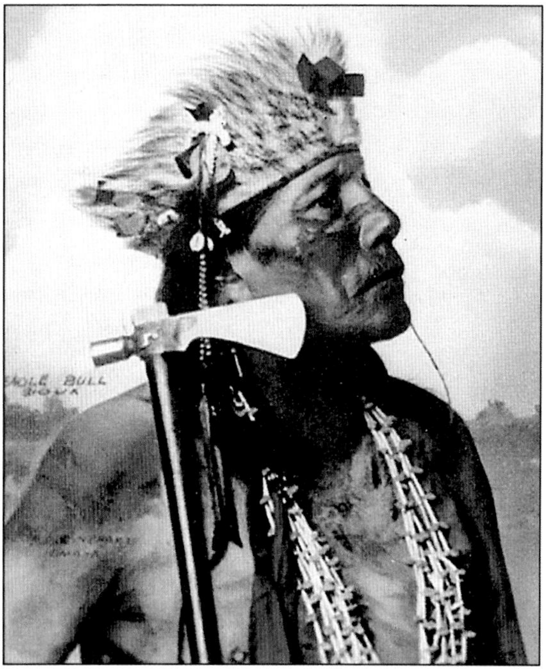

EAGLE BULL "TATANKA WANBLI" (SICANGU). This photograph, c. 1899, was taken by F. A. Rinehart at the Omaha Indian Exposition. The Eagle Bull family is listed in the Rosebud Census of 1875. (Postcard courtesy of Donovin Sprague.)

(below) **LUTHER STANDING BEAR (SICANGU).** The first son of Chief Standing Bear and Pretty Face, Luther's Lakota name was Ota Kte (Plenty Kill). Luther identified himself as Oglala but his father was Sicangu. The Standing Bear family was living at Spotted Tail Agency in June of 1876 when some of the people went north to join Lakota bands in present Montana; Luther's father participated in the Battle of the Little Bighorn. The family resided briefly at Whetstone Agency, and later Standing Bear built a store at Spotted Tail Agency. Luther attended Carlisle Indian School, and authored *My People, The Sioux*, *My Indian Boyhood*, *Land of the Spotted Eagle*, and *Stories Of The Sioux*. Luther returned to Rosebud from Carlisle; his father received a land allotment on Pine Ridge Reservation but Luther remained at Rosebud. Luther began teaching at the Allen school, opened a store at Pass Creek, and raised horses and cattle. His brother Ellis ran the store. Luther married Nellie DeCory and Laura Cloud Shield-Levering, and lived with Mrs. Jones (Sunflower). A marriage is listed to Millie Standing Bear in 1886, but it may be Nellie, as they were married that year. Luther and Nellie's children were Lily (b.1887), Luther Jr., and Alexandra Birmingham Cody Standing Bear (b. about1898), the latter named after the Queen of England when Luther was traveling with William F. Cody's "Wild West Show." The children died at young ages. Some records list a son named Arthur, born in 1888. Eugene George (b. about 1900) was the son of Luther Standing Bear and Laura Cloud Shield. Luther became active in Hollywood and lived in the Los Angeles area with May Jones Montoya/Sunflower. Luther died in 1939 at age 71, and Sunflower died in 1973 at the age of 89. (Postcard courtesy of Donovin Sprague.)

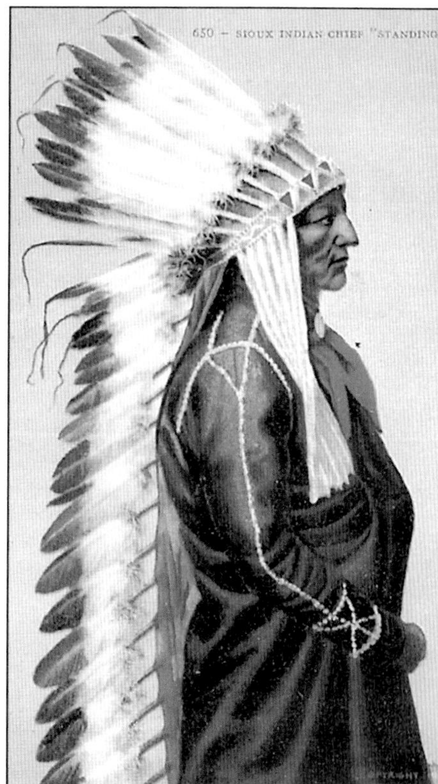

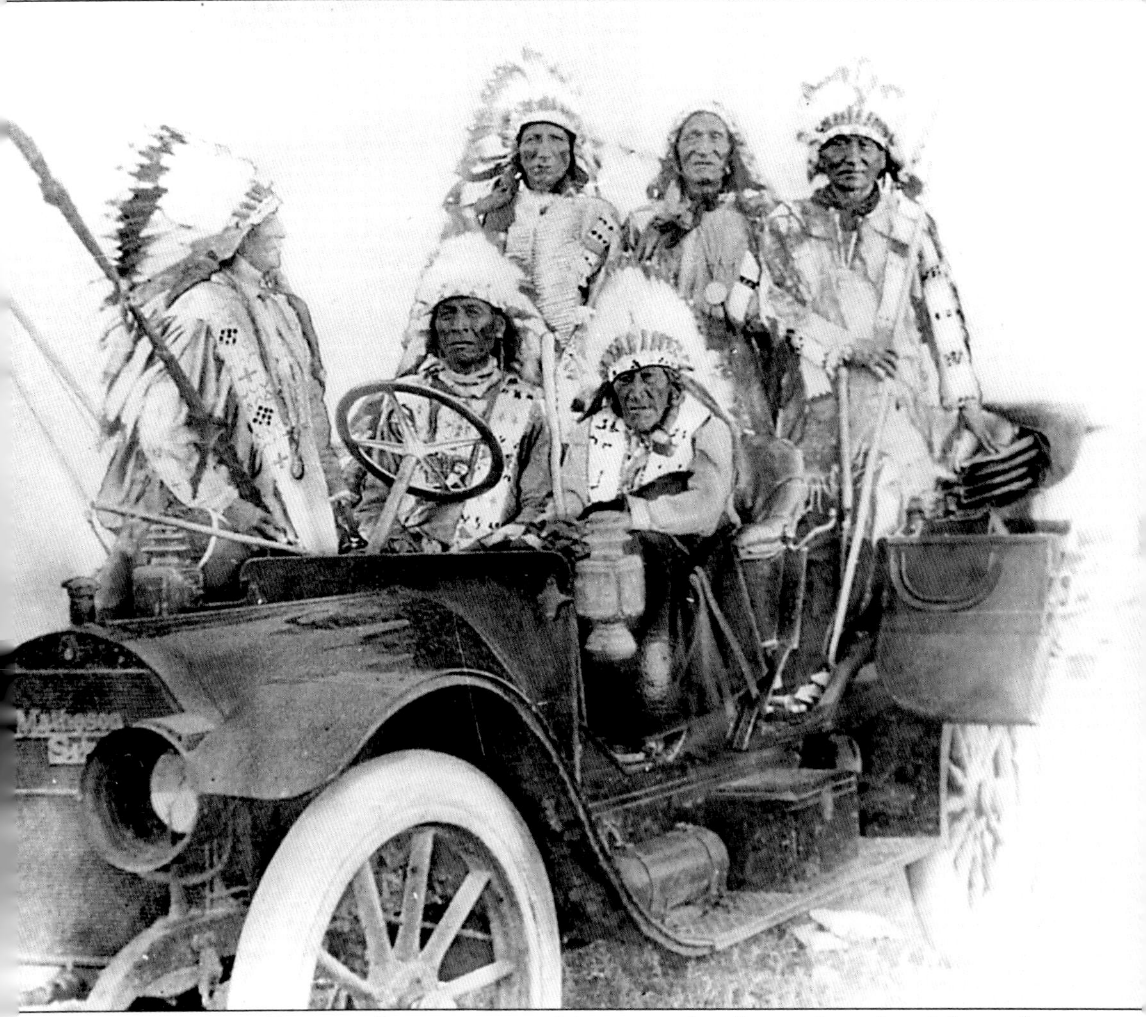

THE FIRST CAR ON ROSEBUD RESERVATION, A MATHESON SIX. Pictured are, from left to right: (front seat) Hollow Horn Bear (standing at far left), High Pipe, and Chief Two Strike; (back seat) Turning Bear, He Dog, and Eagle Pipe. This photograph was taken by John A. Anderson c. 1910. High Pipe was a Crow Indian who joined the Sicangu. Turning Bear was later run over by a train in Valentine, Nebraska, in 1910. (Photograph courtesy of State Historical Society of South Dakota.)

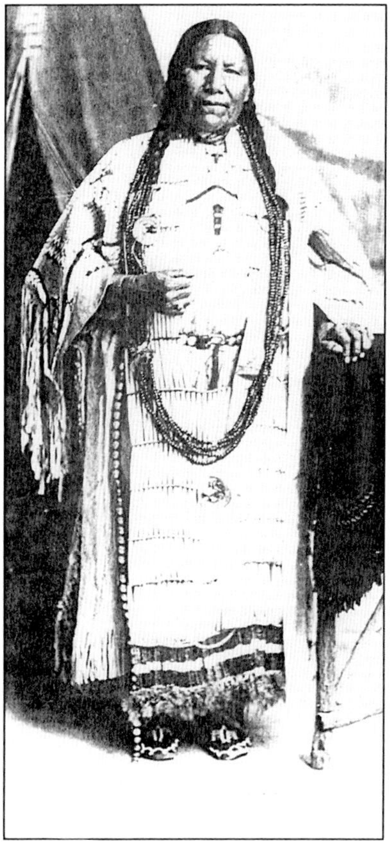

Mrs. Mary Cedar (Lakota). This photograph is undated. Mary Cedar was born in 1859 and married James Cedar in 1881. James was younger, born in 1865. Some of their records come from the Porcupine District at Pine Ridge Reservation. (Postcard courtesy of Donovin Sprague.)

Quick Bear, Spotted Tail, Swift Bear, and Yellow Hair. This photograph was of a deputation of Sicangu's under Capt. D. C. Poole who is on the right in the back row. Charles Guerue is at left in the back row. The photograph may be from 1870 but it looks later. Spotted Tail made several trips to Washington, D.C. with other leaders such as Chief Red Cloud of the Oglala. He learned early of the vast numbers and power of the white people in the East. U.S. military demonstrations of cannon firing down the Potomac River was a regular part of the presentations made to impress the Lakota delegations. Spotted Tail would become an advocate for peace. He died on August 5, 1881, when Crow Dog of the Sicangu shot and killed him in a feud. Crow Dog said Spotted Tail was making advances toward his wife but some people say it was a political plot. (Photograph courtesy of Birmingham Library, England.)

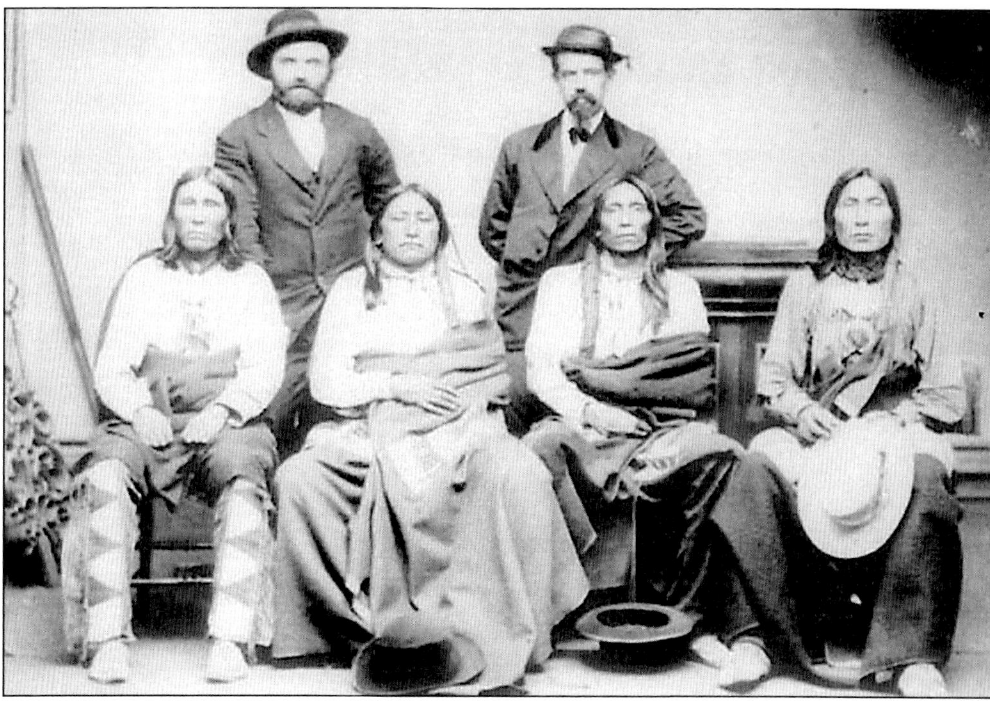

PETER IRON SHELL (SICANGU). This photograph was taken by F. A. Rinehart in 1898. Peter Iron Shell was born in 1877 and married Hannah Big Girl Eagleman who was his same age. The date of this marriage was recorded as 1907. A probable son of Peter's was also named Peter Iron Shell (b. 1900), and he married Stella Alice (b. 1884) in 1900. This picture was taken at the Trans Mississippi and International Exposition held in Omaha, Nebraska. The old Chief Iron Shell was itancan (leader) of the Orphan Band and following his death other itancan of that band were Hollow Horn Bear, Crow Dog, White Thunder, and Dog Hawk. (Photograph courtesy of Bureau of Ethnology.)

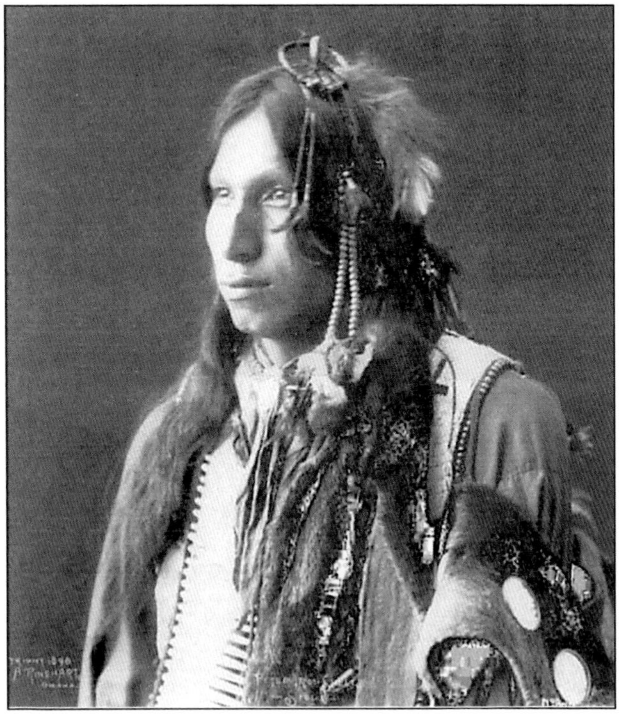

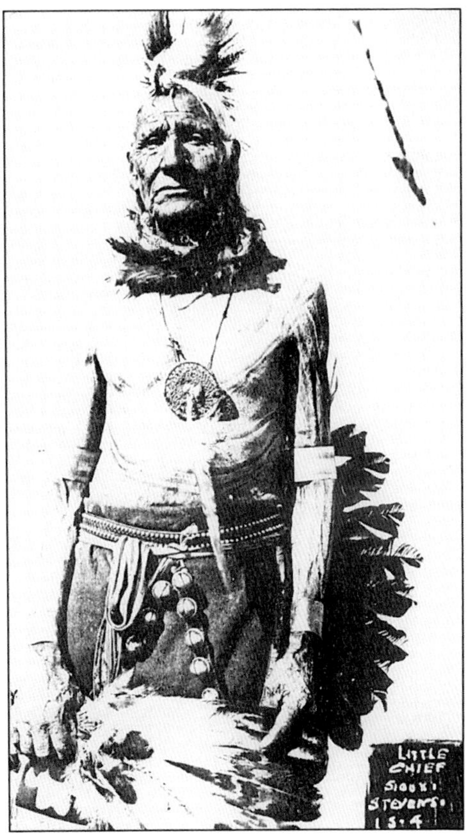

LITTLE CHIEF "ITANCAN CIKALA" (SICANGU/ OGLALA). This photograph was taken in the 1940s. This was a postcard by Stevens which had circulation in the Black Hills and western South Dakota. The Little Chief name is listed as born into the Standing Rock area long before that agency was created and the family is connected to Rosebud and Pine Ridge. (Postcard courtesy of Donovin Sprague.)

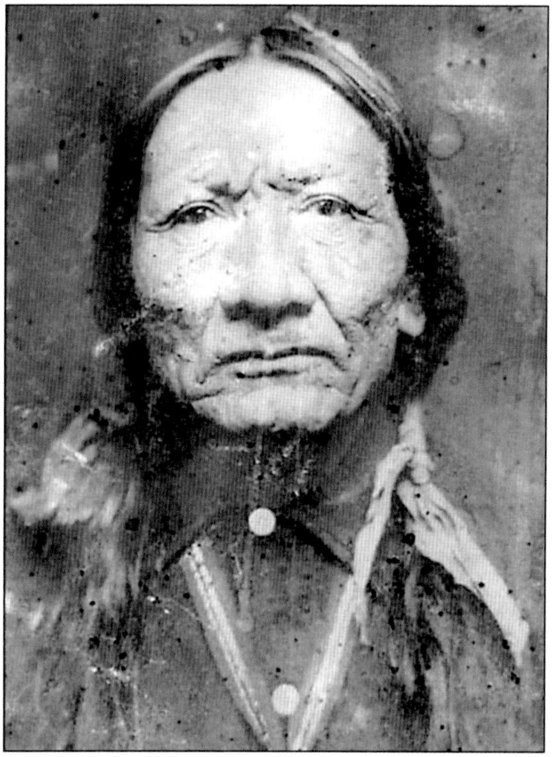

CRAZY BULL (LAKOTA). This photograph was taken between 1890-1910. Crazy Bull is listed on a Rosebud Agency census of 1875 with his wife, three sons, three daughters, and two other men (extended family/ tiospaye), for a total of 13 people. (Photograph courtesy of Bureau of Ethnology.)

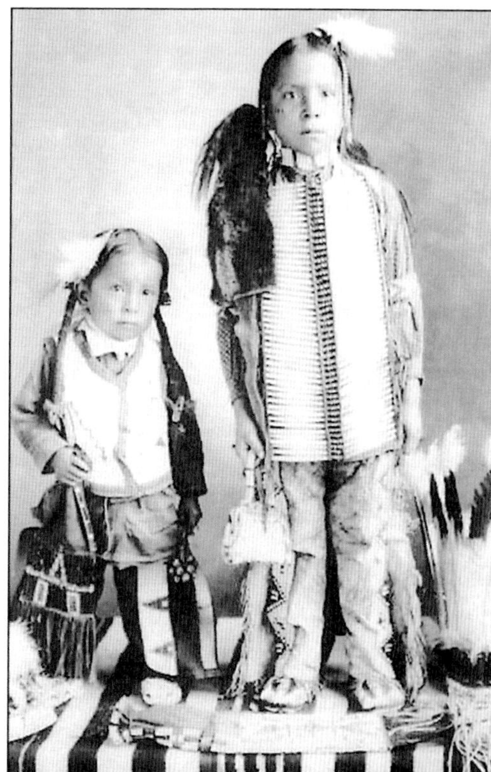

UNIDENTIFIED LAKOTA CHILDREN. This photograph is thought to have been taken sometime between 1880-1910. (Postcard courtesy of Donovin Sprague.)

Three

SINTE GLESKA OWAKPAMNI (SPOTTED TAIL AGENCY)

When the Sicangu were moved from Spotted Tail Agency to Rosebud Agency, bands were still intact and families received land allotments. Prior to agency life the Lakota were scattered throughout the Plains but were now confined to the boundaries of what would become the Rosebud Reservation. The people were now dependent upon the U.S. Government for food and ration supplies. Rosebud, South Dakota, would become the tribal headquarters for the Rosebud Sioux Reservation. Rosebud Reservation would consist of 20 districts throughout the reservation of bands which evolved into communities.

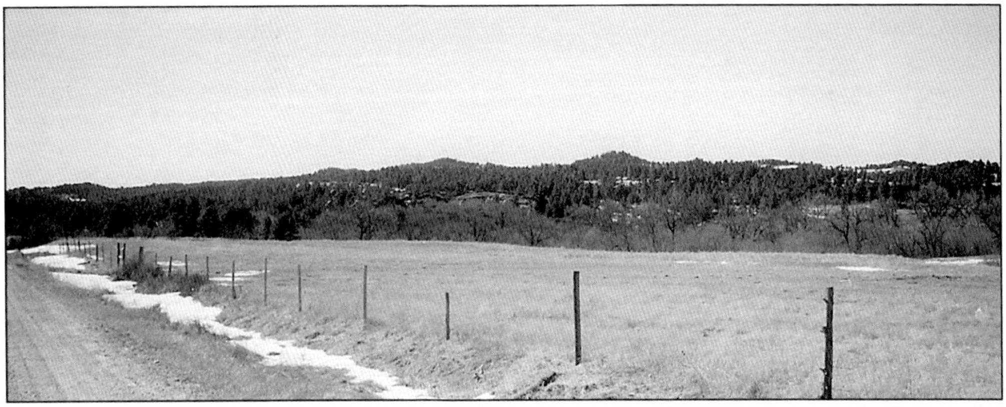

SPOTTED TAIL AGENCY LOCATION. This photograph was taken in spring 2000. This is the location of the old Spotted Tail Agency #1 in present day Nebraska, which was established as the agency for the Sicangu. Other Lakota bands and a few Cheyenne and Arapaho were also present in fewer numbers here. The site is north of Hay Springs, Nebraska, and south of Pine Ridge Reservation. The next location for Spotted Tail Agency #2 was briefly south of Fort Randall, South Dakota. The Whetstone Agency was the first government headquarters for both the Sicangu and Oglala bands. Whetstone was on the west side of the Missouri River in far southern present South Dakota. It was about 18 miles west of Fort Randall. The last shuffling of the agency locations would be to the present Rosebud Sioux Reservation in South Dakota. (Photograph courtesy of Donovin Sprague.)

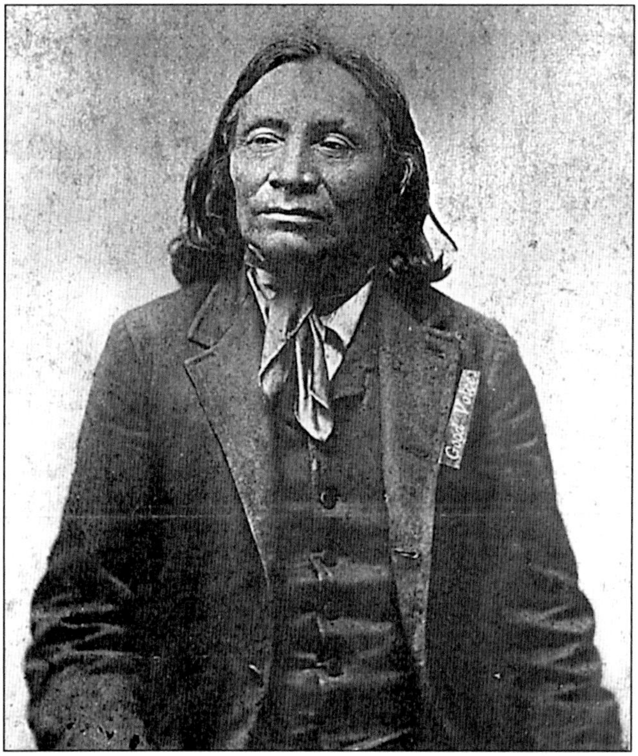

Good Voice "Ho Waste" (Sicangu). This photograph was taken by J.N. Choate and is undated. Good Voice lived at Two Strike community. This photograph was taken at Carlisle Indian School when Good Voice visited the school. The school listed these names in 1879 as children and relatives of Good Voice: Bull Man, Kills, Looking Woman, and White Woman. (Postcard courtesy of Donovin Sprague.)

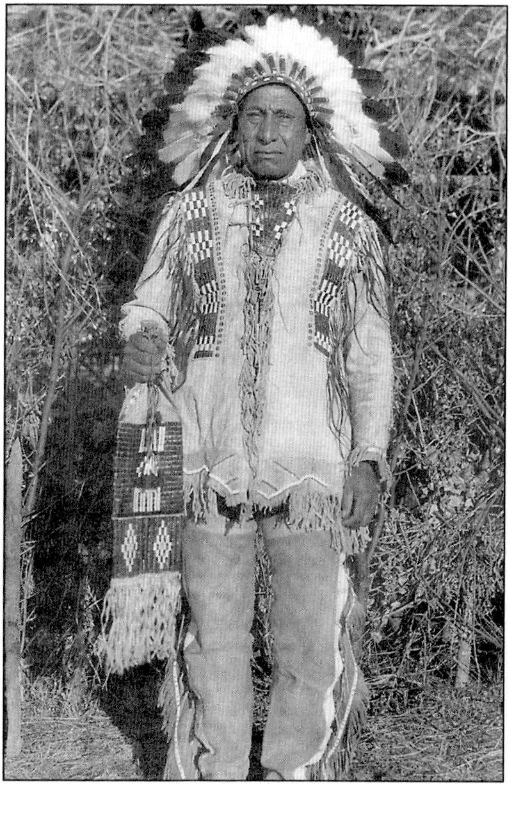

Whirlwind Soldier (Sicangu). This photograph is undated. In 1879, the Carlisle Indian School listed these names as children and relatives of Whirlwind Soldier who were attending the school: Frog, Kills Without Wounding, Running Horse, and Big Boy Earth. A son of Whirlwind Soldier was also listed as Hugh Whirlwind Soldier in a print photograph. Upon returning from Carlisle, many of the children's Lakota names were never used again and were substituted for English names. (Photograph courtesy of Rose Two Strike Stenstrom.)

HARRY QUIVER SR. "WANJU" (OGLALA). This photograph is undated. Harry Quiver Sr. "Wanju" married Agnes Bull Walks Behind and they were from Wanblee, South Dakota, but had ties to Rosebud Reservation, with later generations related to the Standing Bears, Witts, and Wooden Knifes from Corn Creek. A son was named Harry Quiver Jr. and was born in 1914. One of his daughters, Anna Quiver, married Fred Wilcox. A brother of Harry Quiver Sr. was Tom Quiver who married Esther Standing Bear (Sicangu) of Corn Creek. The father of Harry Quiver Sr. and Tom Quiver was Robert Quiver. (Photograph courtesy of Walter Tiedeman.)

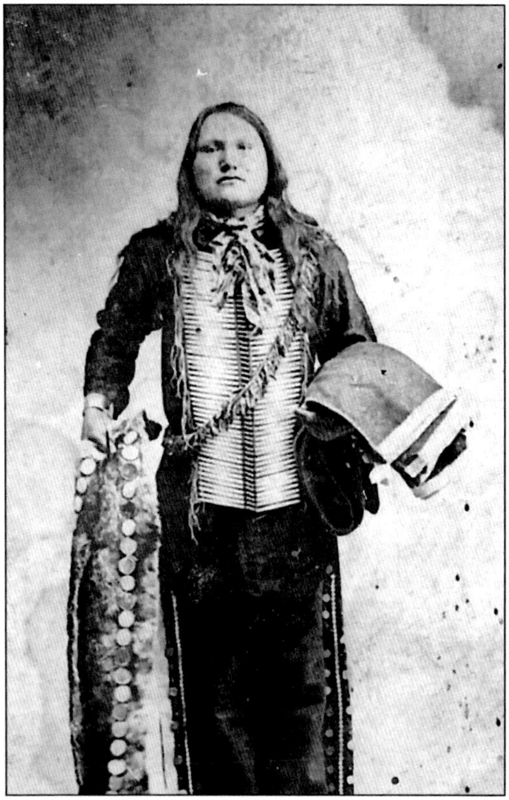

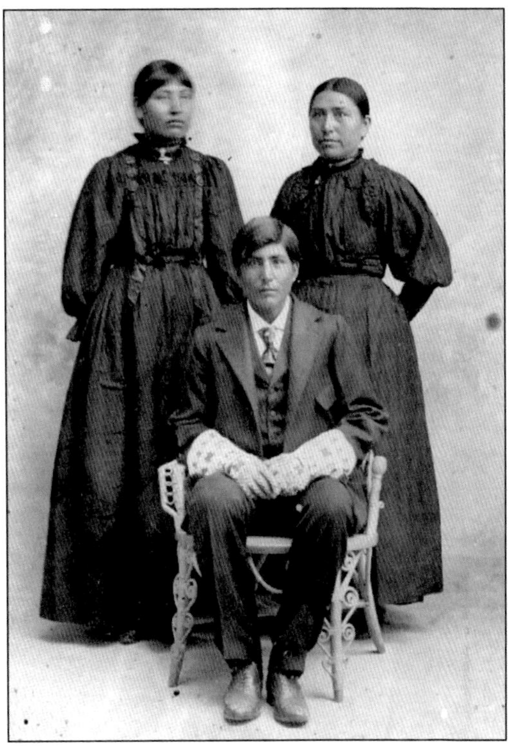

THE STANDING BEAR FAMILY. Pictured are Anna Standing Bear-Dillon, Emily Standing Bear-Dillon, and (seated) Alfred Standing Bear (Sicangu/Oglala). This photograph is undated. Anna, Emily, and Alfred were the children of George Standing Bear and his wife Lena One Horse-Standing Bear. Other daughters were Victoria Standing Bear-Conroy and Lucy Standing Bear-Hunter. The children from this family would be half-sisters and half brother of Luther Standing Bear. Anna Standing Bear married Peter Dillon but died young in 1902 at the age of 23. Emily Standing Bear then also married Peter Dillon and lived a long life with many descendants. Alfred Standing Bear died in 1914 at the age of 33. According to the Standing Bear family Lena (also Hawk) One Horse was a first cousin to Crazy Horse. Ben Sherman supplied the photograph and information and his great grandmother is Lucy Standing Bear-Hunter. (Photograph courtesy of Ben Sherman.)

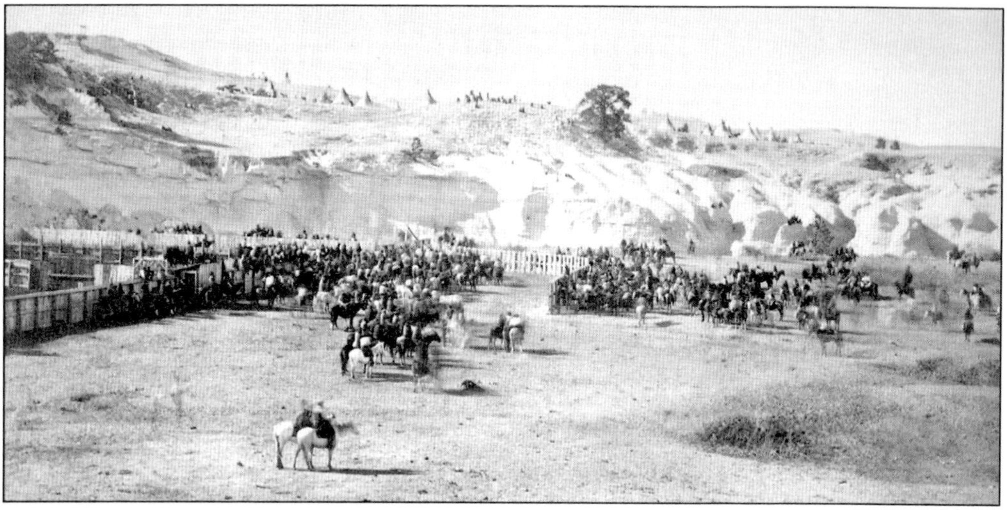

SPOTTED TAIL AGENCY. This photograph by Howard is undated. This is the monthly beef issue day at Spotted Tail Agency in Nebraska. The fences hold the cattle and on the horizon in back Sicangu tipis are visible. This agency would later be moved to become Rosebud Reservation in present South Dakota. (Photograph courtesy of Princeton Collections of Western Americana.)

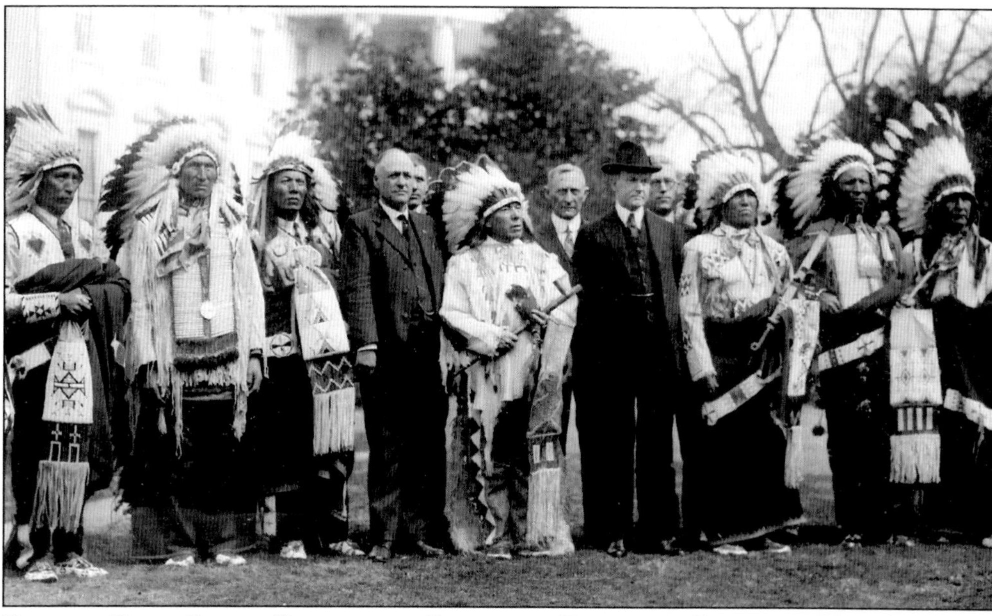

ROSEBUD SIOUX INDIAN REPUBLICAN CLUB WITH PRESIDENT COOLIDGE. This photograph was taken in Washington, D.C., in 1925. This group from Rosebud Reservation met with President Calvin Coolidge on the White House lawn. President Coolidge is at right center with the hat. White man clothes are visible under the regalia of the Lakota. American Indians had just received the right to vote under the Indian Citizenship Act of 1924, four years after women in the U.S. received voting rights. Some American Indians had received citizenship prior to this because of their service with Teddy Roosevelt's Rough Riders and service in World War I. Today, American Indians still have the highest rate of participation in the U.S. military of any ethnic group in America. Statistics vary but as high as 50 percent of all American Indians are veterans. (Photograph courtesy of Donovin Sprague.)

IRON SHELL "TUKIHA MAZA" (SICANGU). The elder Chief Iron Shell was the father of Chief Hollow Horn Bear. He participated in the fighting on the Blue Water in 1855 against the surprise attack by General Harney near present day Lewellen, Nebraska. Iron Shell escaped but two of his wives were taken captive. Until this incident, the Sicangu had never had such a large camp taken by the military with heavy losses of life and property. He also led several attacks on the Pawnee and Omaha Indians. In 1867, the U.S. was implementing a Peace Commission and the *New York Herald* reported on September 4 that Iron Shell came in to North Platte with 180 Sicangu of the Orphan Band from Powder River country in the north. Chief Iron Shell was the son of Shot In The Heel (d. 1816) and had a brother named Holy Circle. Children and relatives of Chief Iron Shell attending Carlisle Indian School in 1879 were recorded and included these names: Thunder, Short Leg, Runs After The Moon, Her Pipe, and Looking Woman. Iron Shell lived in the Upper Cut Meat District and is buried near St. Francis. This photograph was taken by Alexander Gardner, Washington, D.C., 1872. (Photograph courtesy of Bureau of Ethnology.)

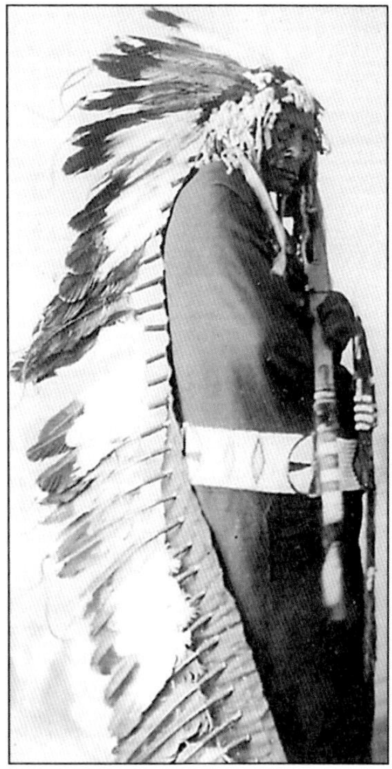

CHIEF SWIFT BEAR "MATO LUZAHAN" (SICANGU). There is a winter count of Sicangu and Lakota history compiled by the Swift Bear family. After 1865, Swift Bear was listed as the second chief of rank of the Sicangu (if such a title existed), and his grandfather was listed as Red War Bonnet, a Sisseton Wahpeton from Minnesota. As contact with white traders increased, Swift Bear's people became more settled and did less traveling than other Sicangu. As the French word Brule became more common than Sicangu, it was the Lower Brule group who traveled less and traded along the Missouri River and did some farming. Generally, the Upper Brule traveled more, hunted, and made excursions for warfare against Nebraska tribes during this era. This movement was called Kheyatawichasha, "People away from the Missouri River," later known as Highland or Upper Brules. Dakota tribes from Minnesota were also arriving. After 1845, Swift Bear was the main leader of the Corn Band, which would have had a different name in earlier years. The Swift Bear winter count shows that a white man taught this band how to plant corn on White River in 1823–24. The band was then named Wagmezayuha (They Have Corn). The Corn Band also became divided between those who wanted some hunting and traveling, and those like Swift Bear who favored farming. He would later lose many of his relatives to smallpox. Swift Bear was a brother-in-law of fur trader James Bordeaux. Next to Spotted Tail, Swift Bear received the best house from the government, and then other leaders received houses. (Postcard courtesy of Donovin Sprague.)

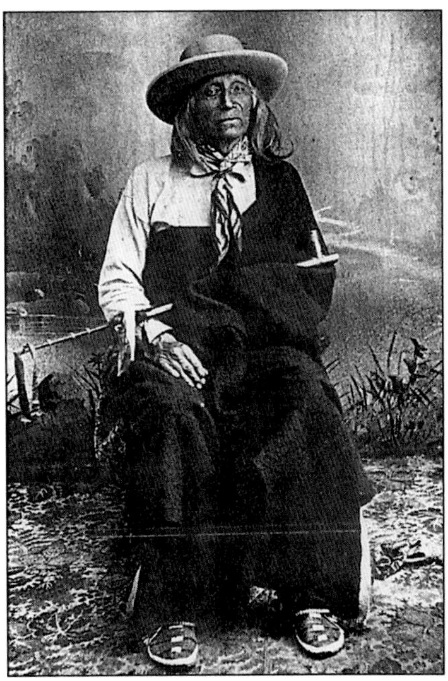

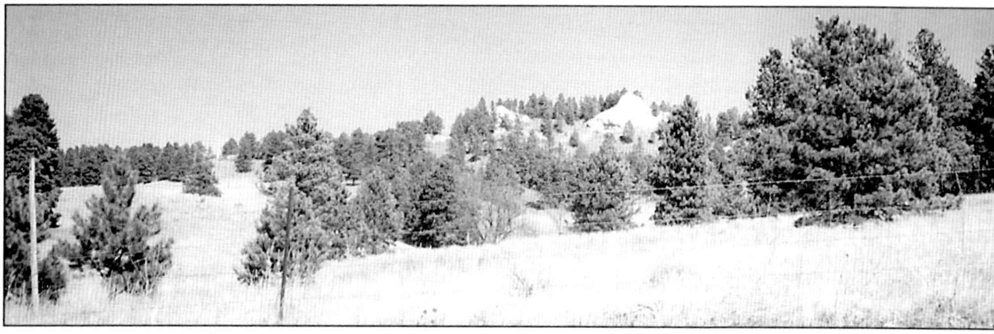

Beaver Valley. This photograph was taken in the spring of 2000. Beaver Valley is located in present day Nebraska, and is just south of the old Spotted Tail Agency #1, north of Hay Springs, Nebraska, and south of Pine Ridge Reservation. This view is looking to the east to where two of three prominent butte tops are visible. The area is a good camp site and location of ceremonies. About 100 yards west of where the picture was taken is Beaver Creek, a known favorite camp site of people including the Crazy Horse family. It was to this camp on Beaver Creek that Crazy Horse fled to when he left the Red Cloud Agency while soldiers were attempting to arrest him. His father Waglula (Worm), his step-mothers, and his first cousin Touch The Cloud were camped here and Crazy Horse arrived in September 1877. His cousin Touch The Cloud suggested they report in to Spotted Tail Agency just to the north, to commanding officer Agent Jesse Lee. Lee supposedly did not know an arrest party was en route from Red Cloud Agency. Crazy Horse vented his frustration to Jesse Lee about problems he was experiencing with the "politics" at Red Cloud Agency. Lee would suggest they return to Red Cloud Agency and problems could be worked out. It was upon the arrival of Crazy Horse onto the parade grounds at Fort Robinson when the events would unfold which led to his being stabbed in the back by a soldier while under arrest. Fort Robinson was right next to the Red Cloud Agency, the home agency for the Oglala. The Minnicoujou Touch The Cloud would remain at his cousins side until death came. Touch The Cloud also insisted that the mortally wounded Crazy Horse be placed in the Adjutants Office instead of being placed in the guardhouse to die. (Photograph courtesy of Donovin Sprague.)

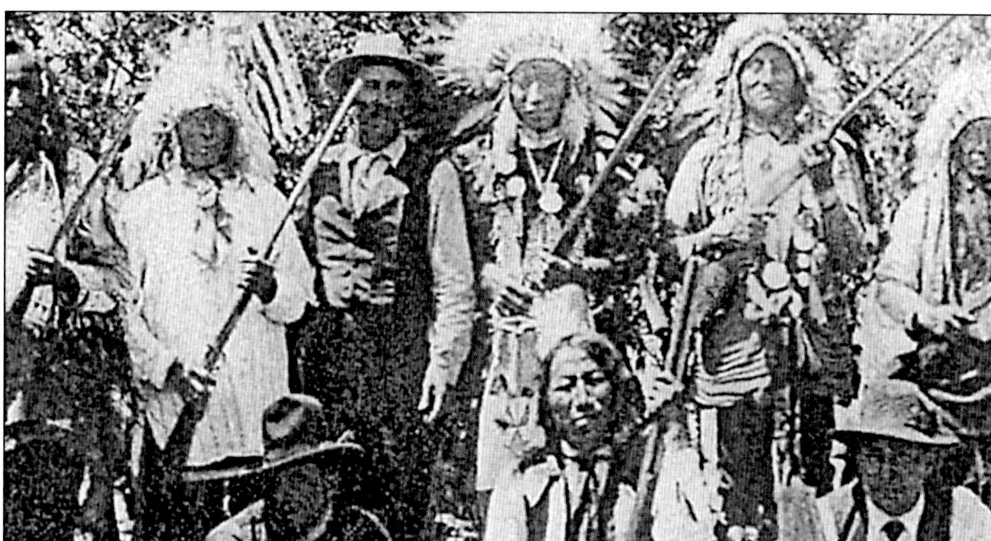

Men at Mellette County. This photograph is undated. This picture was taken at a July 4th celebration in Mellette County. (Photograph courtesy of Mellette County Historical Committee.)

Four

Wanagi Wacipi (Ghost Dance)

Leaders of the Ghost Dance at Rosebud in the era of the Wounded Knee Massacre were Chief Two Strike (Sicangu), Kicking Bear (Minnicoujou/Oglala), and Chief Short Bull (Sicangu). Each had large followings in which some aspects of the religion were learned from the Paiute Ghost Dance leader Wovoka. Main prophecies recorded were that the white man would disappear and that deceased relatives, along with the buffalo, would return.

The Ghost Dance movement and the December 15, 1890, killing of Chief Sitting Bull at Standing Rock set the stage for later events, including the December 29, 1890, Wounded Knee Massacre of Si Tanka (Big Foot) and his band of Minnicoujou Lakota. After the killing of Sitting Bull, Hunkpapa Lakota Ghost Dance followers at Standing Rock traveled to the Minnicoujou Ghost Dance camps of Chief Hump and Chief Si Tanka (Big Foot) near Cherry Creek at Cheyenne River. By this time soldiers pursued the group, and General Nelson Miles sent a representative to the camp of Chief Hump, asking him to report to Fort Bennett. Chief Hump led a large Minnicoujou band into the fort, joined by some of the Hunkpapas. Si Tanka and his band fled south to the Badlands, and to the site at Wounded Knee where about 300 Lakota would be killed. Most of these Lakotas were Minnicoujou, with some Siha Sapa, Hunkpapa, Itazipco, and Oohenumpa. Much of the history of the Sicangu surrounding this event would be in Ghost Dancing, and in warfare against soldiers and home guard units. All of the Lakota were greatly affected by the Wounded Knee Massacre, which marked the end of an era and of America's Indian "wars," 114 years ago.

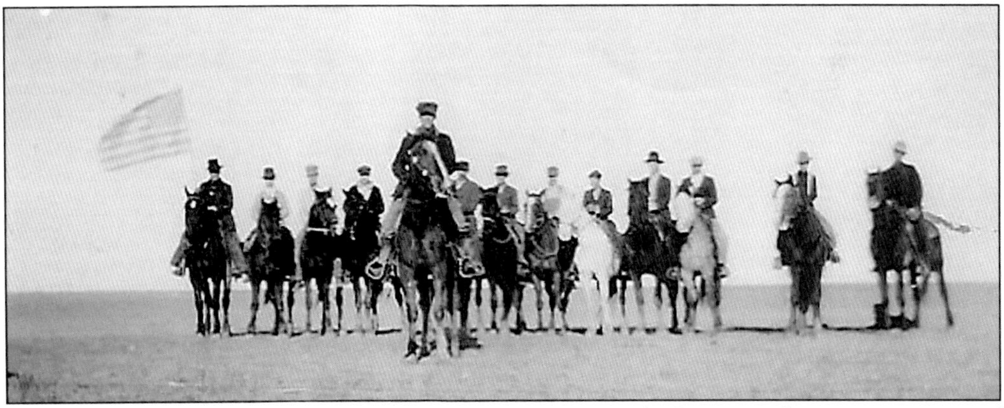

Hereford, South Dakota Home Guard, 1918. Hereford is a rural community east of Sturgis. Home guards were farmers, ranchers, or businessmen who worked to quell the Lakota population, authorized by territorial governors such as Arthur C. Mellette. Home guards often administered their own law and killed Lakota without judge or jury—Lakota too often raided a settler's farm or ranch for cattle and horses. An undocumented war existed between the home guards and the Lakota prior to and following the 1890 Wounded Knee Massacre, including fighting in the southwestern part of Rosebud Reservation. Other conflict occurred in the Stronghold, Holy Rosary Mission, and Red Shirt Table areas of Pine Ridge Reservation, and in off-reservation areas. (Photograph courtesy of Donovin Sprague.)

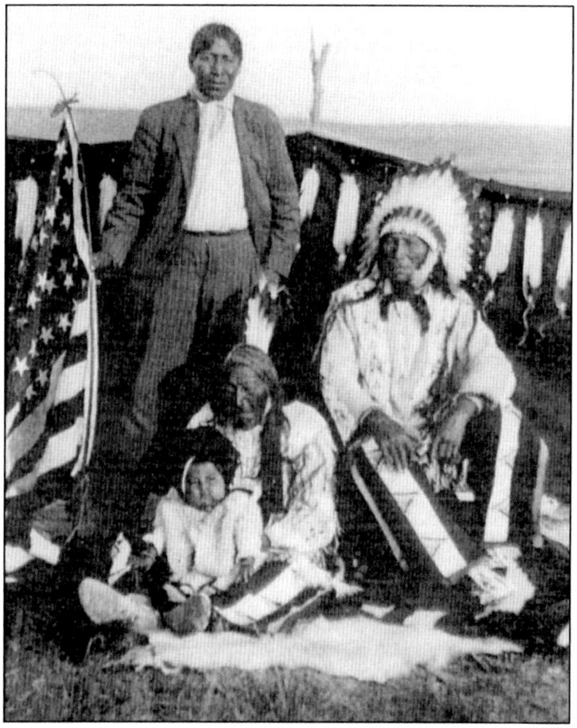

CHIEF TWO STRIKE HOLDING BABY ROSE TWO STRIKE, WITH POOR BEAR AND LITTLE HAWK (SICANGU). This photograph was taken about 1906. Four generations are represented in this picture. Poor Bear, standing at left, was nicknamed Jumping "Psica" and his father is Little Hawk, also called Joseph Little Hawk. Little Hawk, wearing a headdress, also had a daughter. Then Little Hawk died and this family bloodline soon ended. Rose Two Strike was the daughter of Poor Bear, and she married Steve Spotted Tail. They never had children. Four daughters of Chief Two Strike were Brown Woman, Good Whirlwind, Takes Pity On Them, and Noisy. Takes Pity On Them married John Grass (Hunkpapa). Noisy was later known as Black Spotted Horse and then Noisy Black Spotted Horse. It is believed that the mother of Chief Two Strike was connected with Sitting Bull's Hunkpapa band. (Photograph courtesy of Rose Two Strike Stenstrom.)

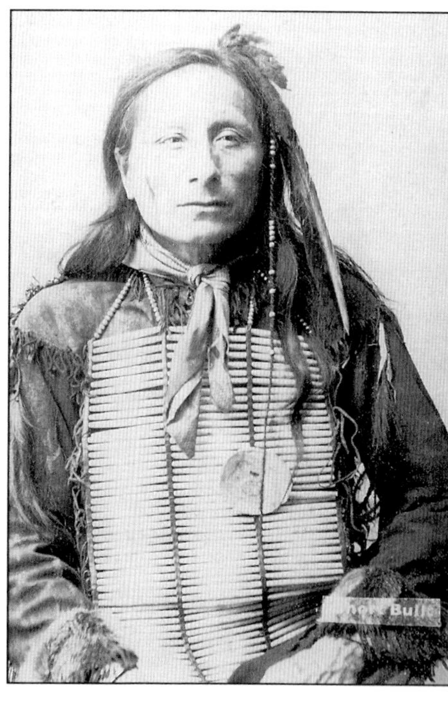

SHORT BULL "TATANKA PTECELA" (SICANGU). This photograph is undated. Short Bull was a Ghost Dance leader and was allied with both the Sicangu and Oglala. When the Rosebud and Pine Ridge Reservations were established, he lived in close proximity to both reservations. (Postcard courtesy of Donovin Sprague.)

Lakota Woman with Travois. This photograph is undated. This woman is traveling with her sunka (dog), pulling a travois loaded with her luggage. This was the method of travel for the Lakota before the arrival of the horse. The Spanish brought the present "domesticated" horse to South America, which arrived on the northern Plains of the Lakota in the early 1700s. Lakota society and travel was greatly transformed and enhanced as a result. The Lakota name for horse is "sunka wakan," which means God/ Great Spirit dog. It was a sacred being and the biggest "dog" anyone had ever seen! (Photograph courtesy of Mellette County Historical Society.)

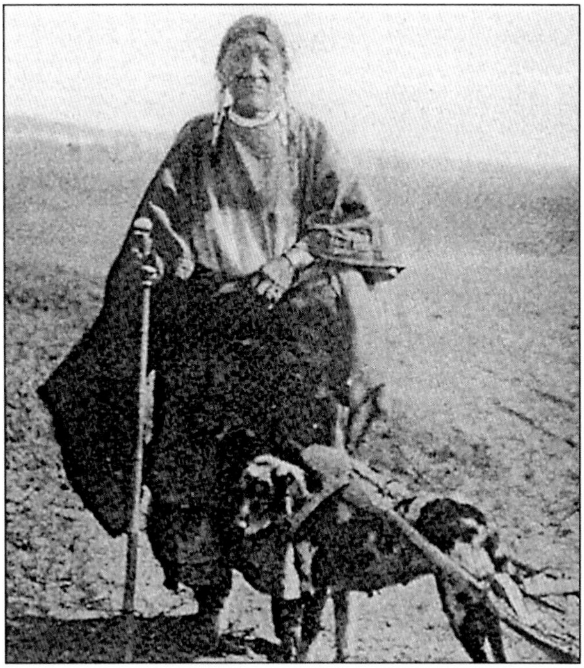

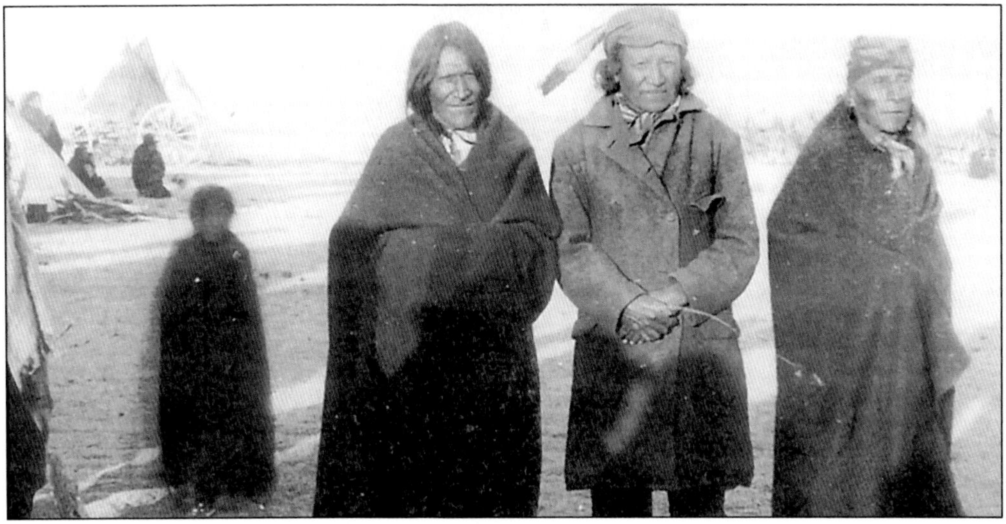

Chief Two Strike (Sicangu), Chief Crow Dog (Sicangu), and Chief High Hawk (Lakota). This photograph was taken by George Trager in 1891, shortly after the Wounded Knee Massacre. The picture is at Pine Ridge Agency. George Trager was an area photographer from Chadron, Nebraska, who took many photos of the Wounded Knee Massacre, many of which show slain Lakota bodies on the ground or burial details. Chief High Hawk lived at Rosebud but the High Hawk family includes people from Rosebud, Pine Ridge, and Cheyenne River. Two Strike was at the Stronghold area with his Ghost Dancers at the time of the massacre and led them through the uncertain days which followed the massacre. Crow Dog was a leader of the Orphan Band of the Sicangu and was a nephew of Brave Bear, who was killed in the Grattan Fight in 1854. Crow Dog would gain notoriety when he killed Chief Spotted Tail in a dispute. Crow Dog was also present during the killing of Crazy Horse. (Photograph courtesy of Bureau of Ethnology.)

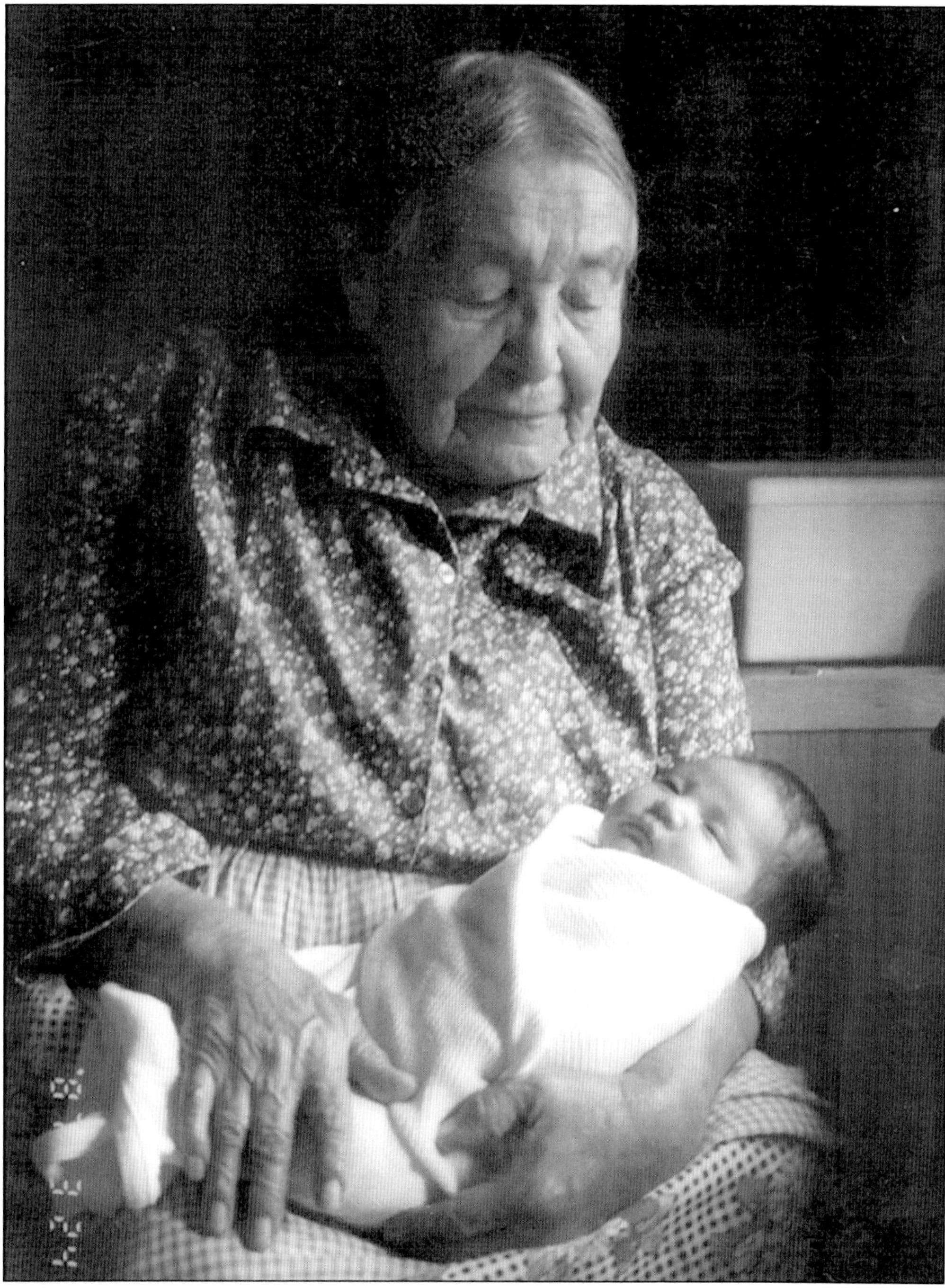

Edna Little Elk-Leighton and Jemma MacKichan-Moccasin (Sicangu). Edna was born in 1916 and was raised by Susie Moccasin Face. Edna is a descendant of Baptiste Good/Brown Hat and is now 90 years old and living at Grass Mountain. Jemma is the great-great-granddaughter of Edna. Margaret MacKichan painted a portrait of this photograph. (Photograph courtesy of Margaret MacKichan and Virginia Broncho Bill.)

Five

Sicangu Lakota Owakpamni (Rosebud Sioux Reservation) 1900–1950

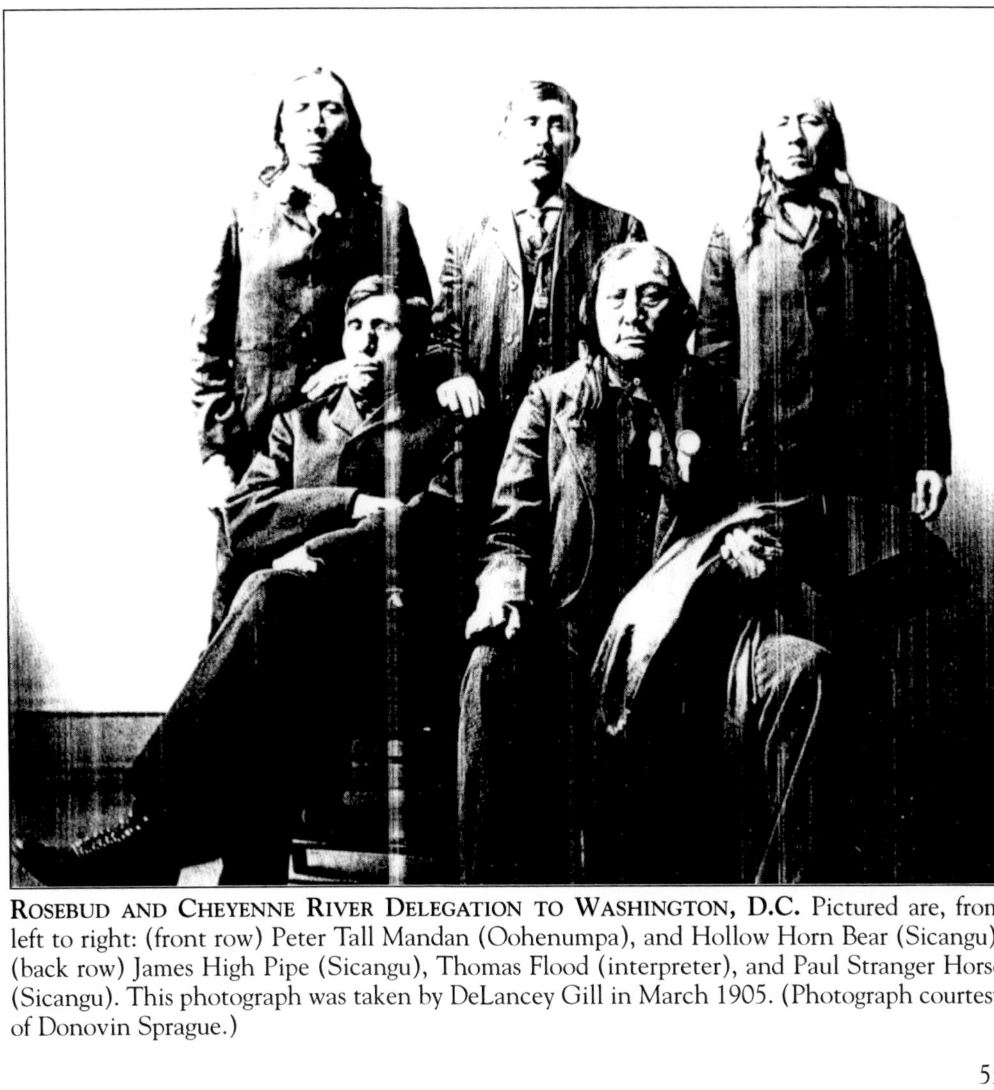

Rosebud and Cheyenne River Delegation to Washington, D.C. Pictured are, from left to right: (front row) Peter Tall Mandan (Oohenumpa), and Hollow Horn Bear (Sicangu); (back row) James High Pipe (Sicangu), Thomas Flood (interpreter), and Paul Stranger Horse (Sicangu). This photograph was taken by DeLancey Gill in March 1905. (Photograph courtesy of Donovin Sprague.)

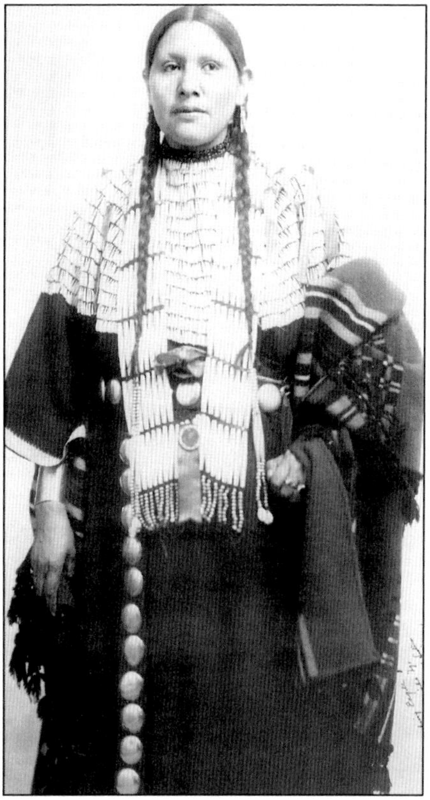

NELLIE JUMPING EAGLE (LAKOTA). This photograph of Nellie Jumping Eagle was taken by the Gerhard Sisters in 1904 at the Louisiana Purchase Exposition held in St. Louis, Missouri. The Gerhard Sisters had a photo booth there and took pictures. Nellie has an elaborate yoke decorated with dentalium shell and hair pipe of deer bone or shell around her neck. Her silver concho belt is wrapped around a trade-cloth dress and her blanket is a trade-cloth item as well. (Photograph courtesy of Donovin Sprague.)

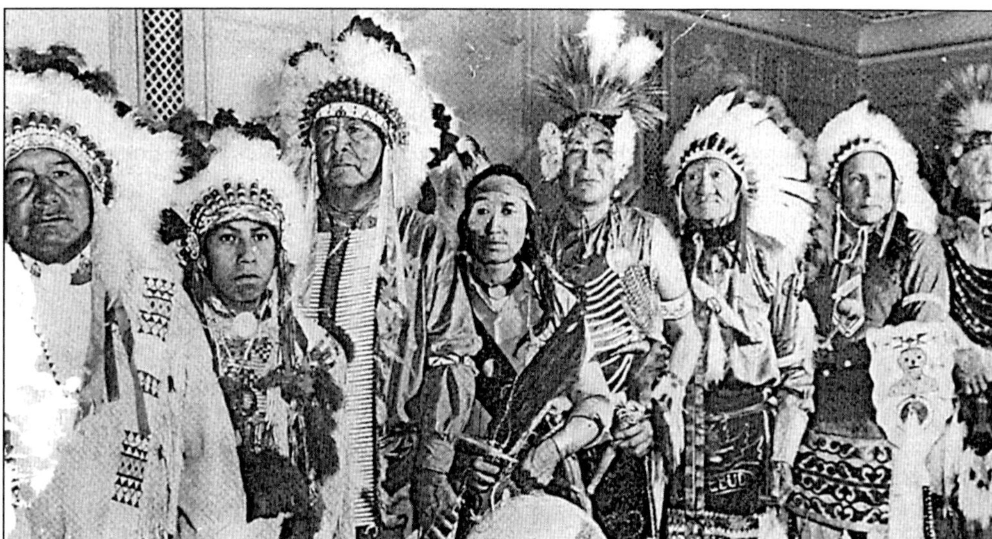

WILD WEST SHOW AND PETE THOMPSON. This photograph is undated. This picture was taken of a group that traveled to Europe for a show. Pete Thompson is the man fourth from the right and the others are unidentified. (Photograph courtesy of Jackson Washabaugh County History Book Committee.)

LUTHER STANDING BEAR (SICANGU). This photograph is undated. (Photograph courtesy of Donovin Sprague.)

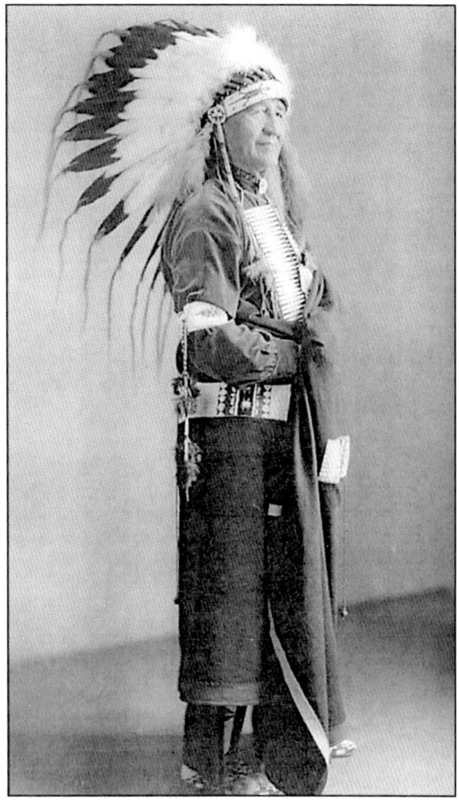

WOOD, SOUTH DAKOTA TRAVELERS. This photograph was taken before 1922. This picture was taken at the community of Wood and the travelers are unidentified. The picture is labeled "Bert Humphrey Stage Line." Bert carried mail between White River and Carter in a stripped down Ford. The Ford had the fenders and any unnecessary parts removed to make traveling through the muddy gumbo easier. (Photograph courtesy of Mellette County Historical Society.)

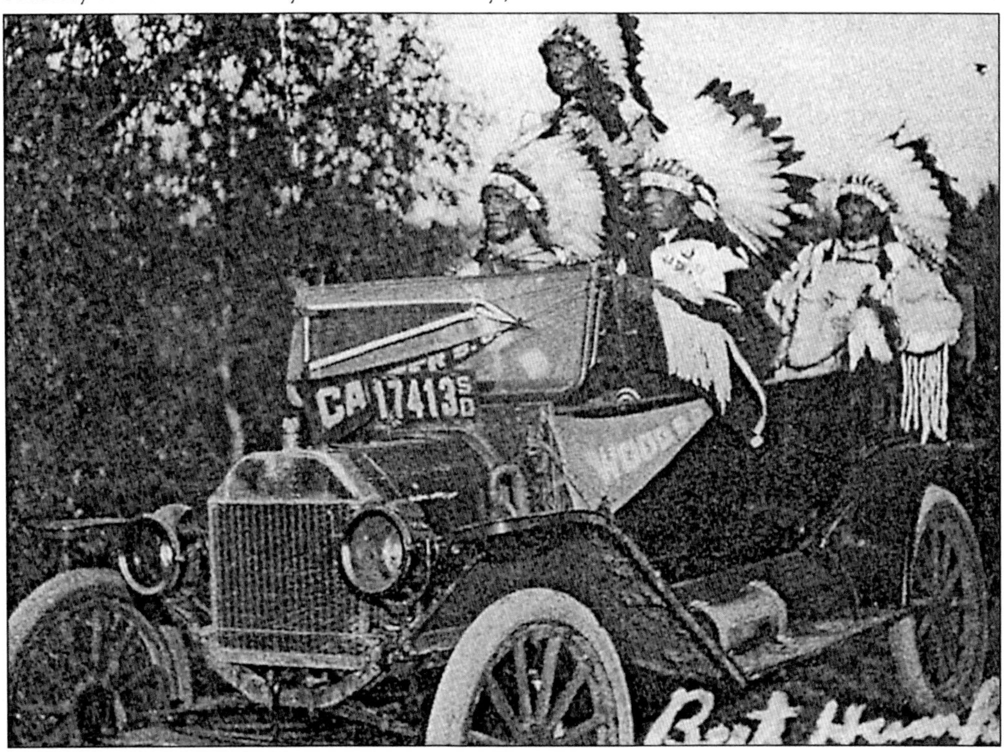

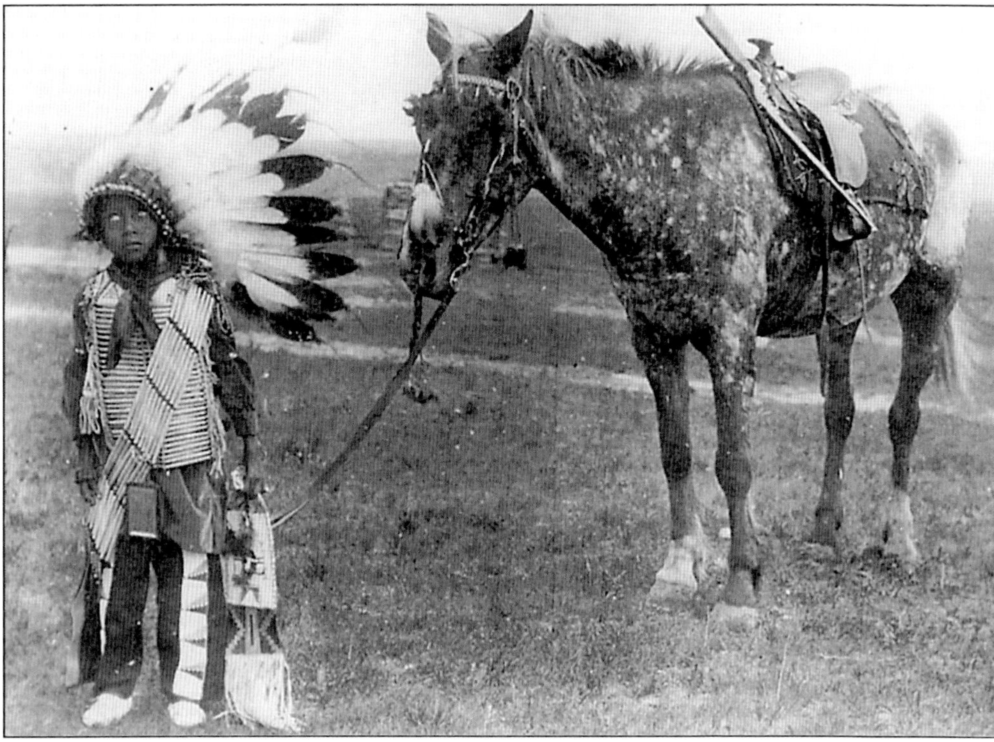

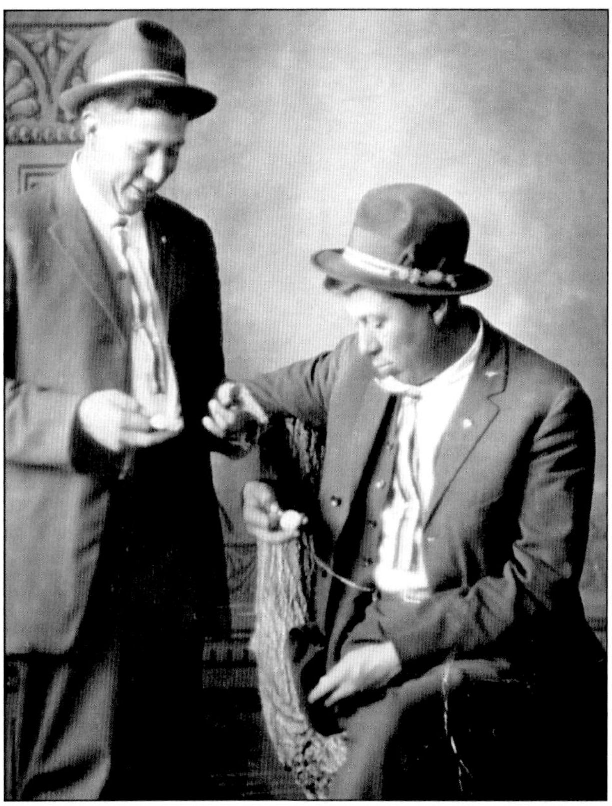

HENRY WITH HORNS (SICANGU). This photograph was taken by Jesse Hastings Bratley between 1895-1899. Henry is dressed up and ready to hunt on his sunka wakan (horse). (Photograph courtesy of Donovin Sprague.)

JOHN MOSES HUDSON (SICANGU). This is a double exposure photo. John Hudson's son, Donald, assisted the author. Donald is now 87 years old. Hudson family members James and Lenora also assisted in the project. John Hudson's daughter, Gloria Hudson Traversive, is a long-time neighbor of the author. (Photograph courtesy of James and Lenora Hudson.)

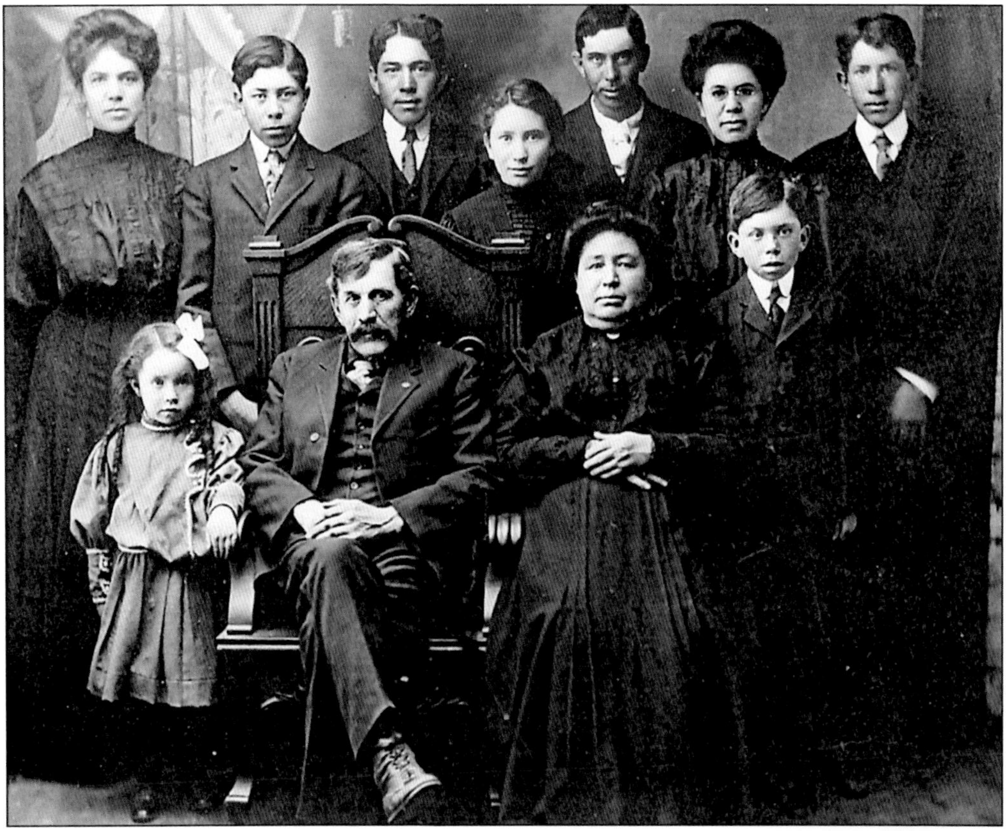

EDWARD LAMOYNE WHITING SR. FAMILY (SICANGU). Pictured in April of 1908 are, from left to right: (front) Louise Evelynia, Edward Lamoyne Sr., Mary Herman Whiting, and William Lawrence; (back) Nellie Sophie, Jacob Herman, David Blaine, Mary Ellen, Edward Lamoyne Jr., Harriet Elizabeth, and Thomas Francis. Edward L. Lamoyne Sr. was born in 1885 and married Mary Herman. David Blaine Whiting is the father of Harriet Minnie Whiting, who married Donald Francis Hudson. Donald and Harriet are the parents of James Vincent Hudson, who provided this photograph. (Photograph courtesy of James and Lenora Hudson.)

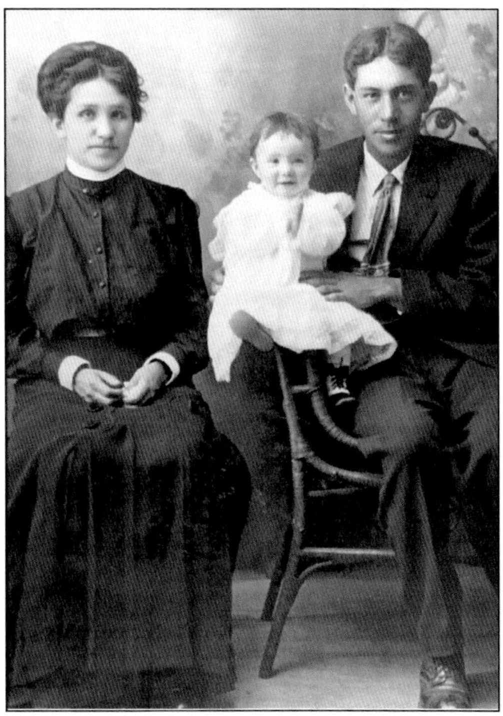

THE WHITING FAMILY (SICANGU). Pictured, from left to right, are Phoebe Bordeaux, Nellie, and David Blaine Whiting (Sicangu), c. 1912. David was born in 1887 to Edward Whiting Sr. and Mary Herman Whiting. Phoebe was born in 1888 to William and Mary Bordeaux. (Photograph courtesy of James and Lenora Hudson.)

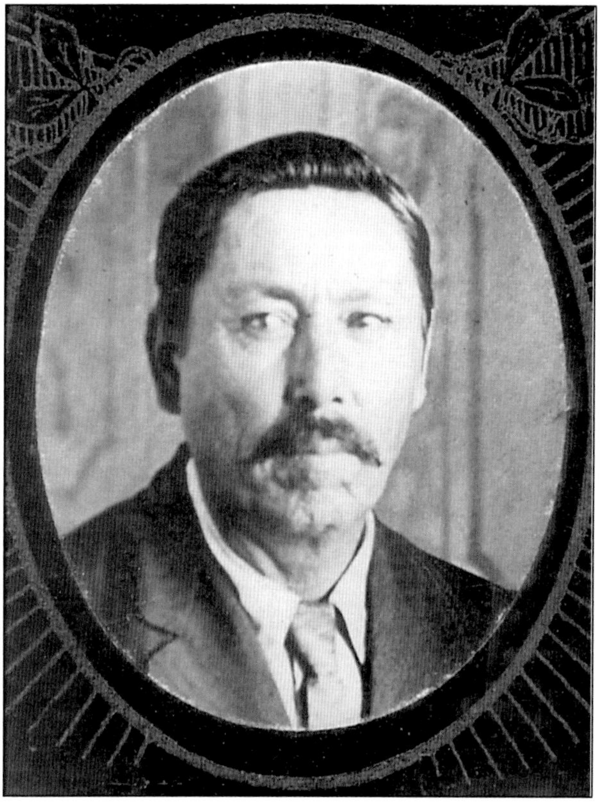

Henry Hudson (Sicangu). This photograph is undated. Henry Hudson married Julia Douville and their children were Phillip, Joe, Lawrence, Clara, Minnie, and Pauline. Henry's father was married to either the daughter or the niece of Chief Spotted Tail. (Photograph courtesy of James and Lenora Hudson.)

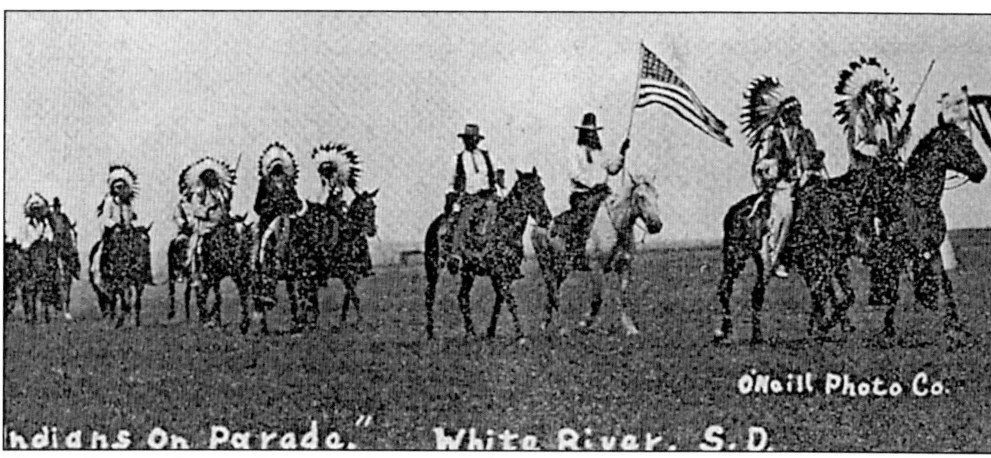

White River, South Dakota, Parade. This photograph was taken by O'Neil Photo Co. This is a parade of Sicangu Lakota at the White River Frontier Days. When people first settled at White River they noted the barking of the numerous prairie dogs at the town site. An area called Two Kettle was about eight miles northeast of White River. Mrs. Iron Road Hungry lived in a house nearest to the church there for many years. After she died, her daughter Ms. Hungry married Reuben Little Cloud and they lived there. The cemetery there is old and goes back to the 1800s. (Photograph courtesy of Jackson Washabaugh County History Book Committee.)

HENRY STANDING BEAR (SICANGU). This photograph was taken in 1943. Henry Standing Bear is pictured here visiting the home of sculptor Korczak Ziolkowski in Segwich, West Hartford, Conn. Henry wrote letters beginning in 1939 requesting the sculptor to carve a mountain in the Black Hills of South Dakota to honor Chief Crazy Horse and American Indians. The author has a copy of a letter Henry wrote to James H. Cook of Agate, Nebraska, dated August 4, 1933, in which Henry explained his plan to "get an Indian head carved some place in the Black Hills" and proposed "that the head of the Warrior Crazy Horse be the one to be carved…" Henry began his correspondence in a July 27, 1933 letter and in his September 19, 1935 letter to James Cook he relates that "I have now some members in my organization known as Crazy Horse Memorial Association." (Photograph courtesy of Crazy Horse Memorial Foundation.)

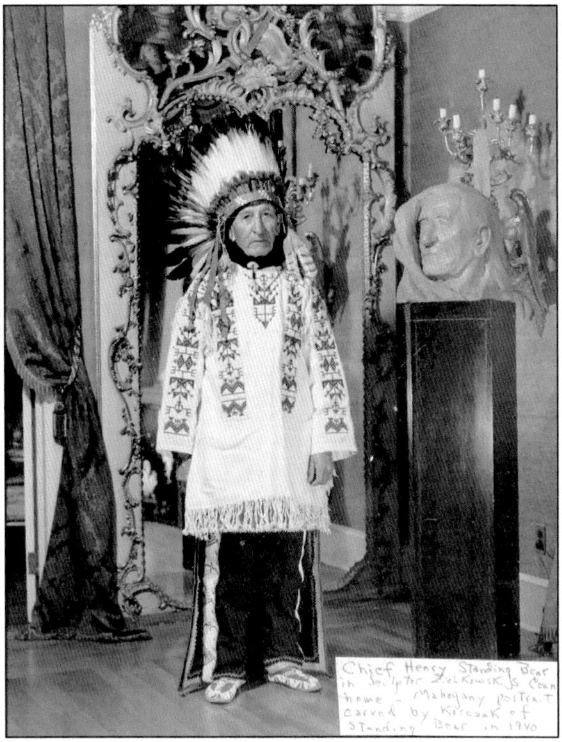

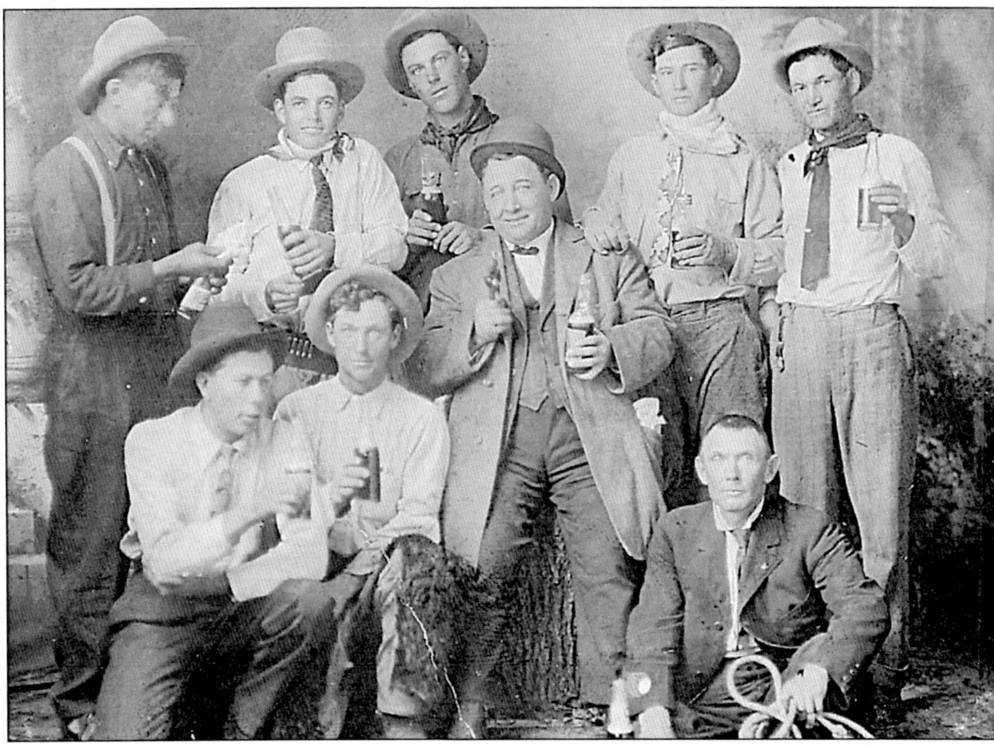

JOHN MOSES HUDSON (SICANGU) AND GROUP. John Hudson is seated in the front row on the far left in this undated photograph. (Photograph courtesy of James and Lenora Hudson.)

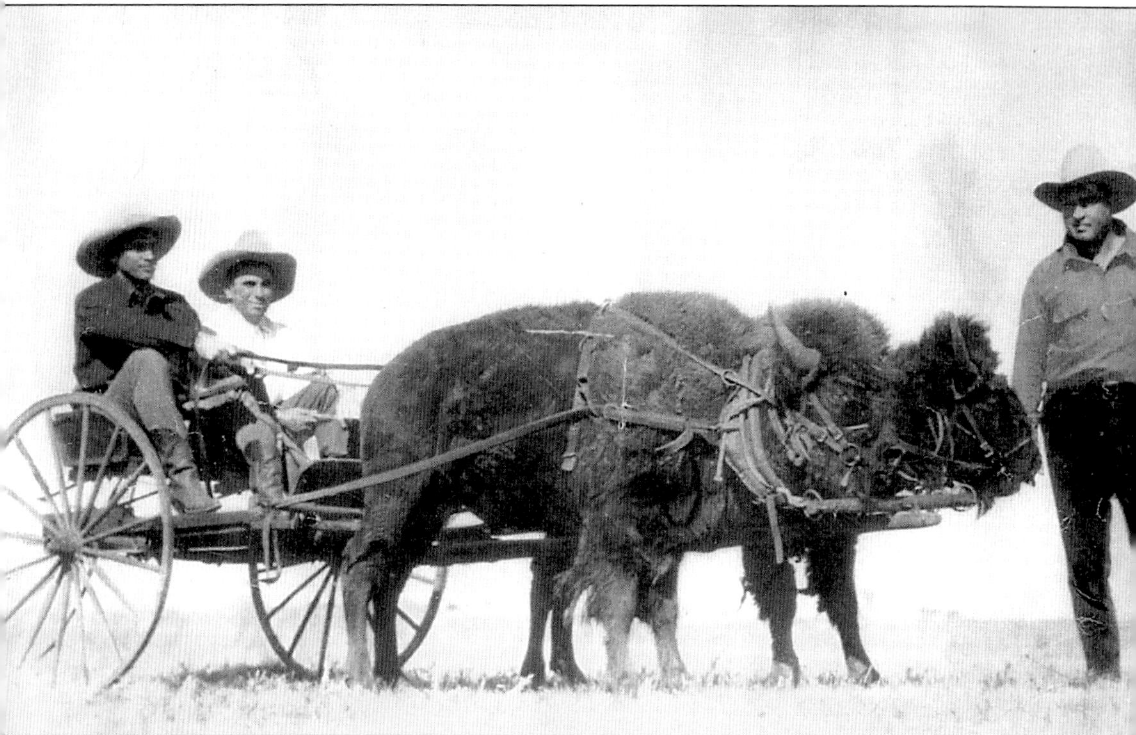

ORIGINAL FRED DUPREE BUFFALO. This photograph is undated. This buffalo team is pictured at the Scotty Philip Ranch north of Rosebud Reservation. It is not certain who the men are but they may be George and Jess Powell in the buggy and Rod Philip at right. Rod was a son of Scotty Philip. The buffalo are an essential part of the life and culture of the Lakota. These buffalo belonged to Fred Dupree from Cheyenne River, who is in the South Dakota Hall Of Fame and credited with being one of six people in the United States who saved the buffalo from extinction when the family captured calves in 1883 and raised them; they grew into a herd. After Fred died in 1898 his son settled his estate and sold the herd to Scotty Philip. By 1918, the herd numbered 500 and in 1914 the Custer State Game Preserve in South Dakota purchased 36 of the buffalo from James "Scotty" Philip. The purchased herd included 6 bulls, 18 cows, and 12 calves. By the 1960s, the Custer State Park herd had grown to 2,500, the largest in the U.S. Scotty Philip died at a young age. The cities of Dupree, South Dakota, on Cheyenne River Reservation and Philip, South Dakota, north of Rosebud Reservation are named for these men/family. Fred Dupree and his wife Mary Ann Good Elk Woman are the great-great-great-grandparents of the author, Donovin Sprague. (Photograph courtesy of Chester Fuhrman Jr.)

BIG EAGLE "WANBLI TANKA" (LAKOTA/DAKOTA/NAKOTA). This photograph, taken by Doubleday, is undated. This photo is thought to be taken in the Winner, South Dakota, area. Big Eagle has floral designs on his regalia typical of tribes to the east of the Sicangu. Many families from the Yankton "Ihantonwan" and Crow Creek "Kangi Okute" tribe tie into this eastern side of the Rosebud Reservation. Big Eagle is a common name among many tribes in this area, and the Omaha Tribe in Nebraska. (Photograph courtesy of Tripp County Historical Society.)

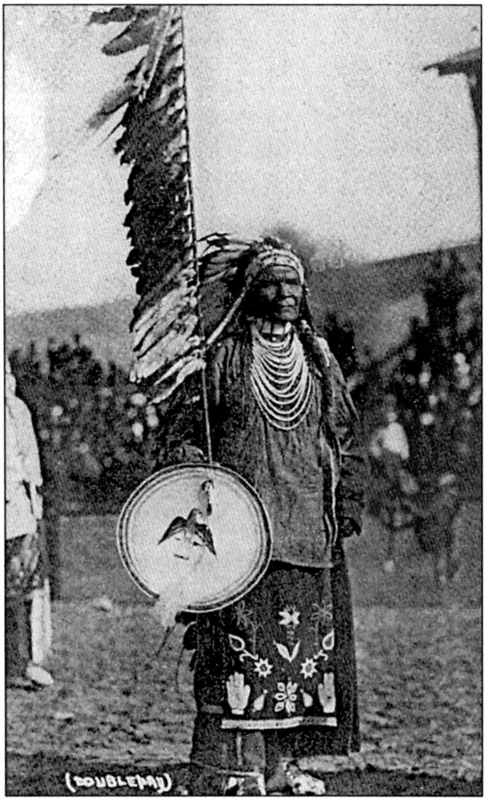

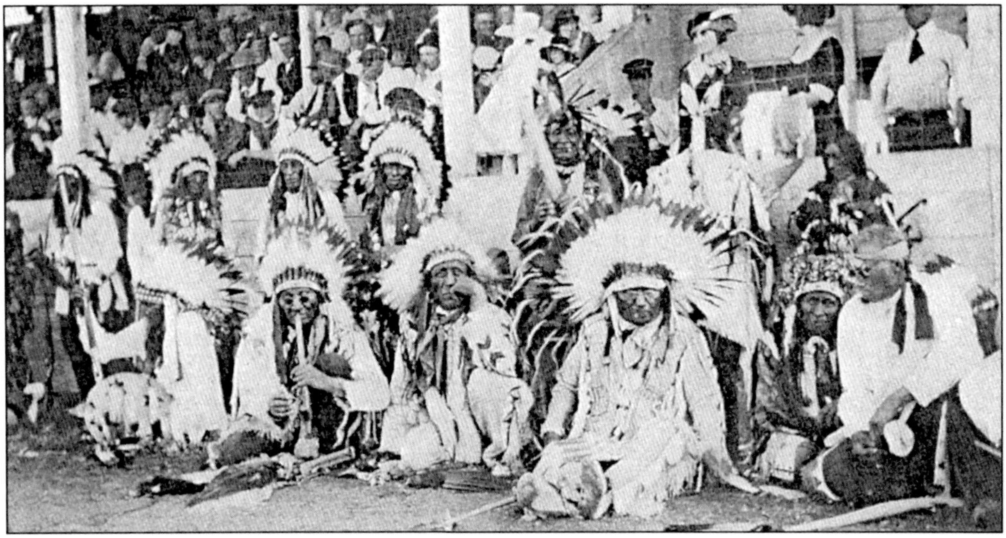

WINNER, SOUTH DAKOTA, CELEBRATION. This photograph was taken about 1928. This photo was taken at the Winner Fair *c.* 1928, where Sicangu Lakota dancers performed for the audience in the grandstand. (Photograph courtesy of Tripp County Historical Society.)

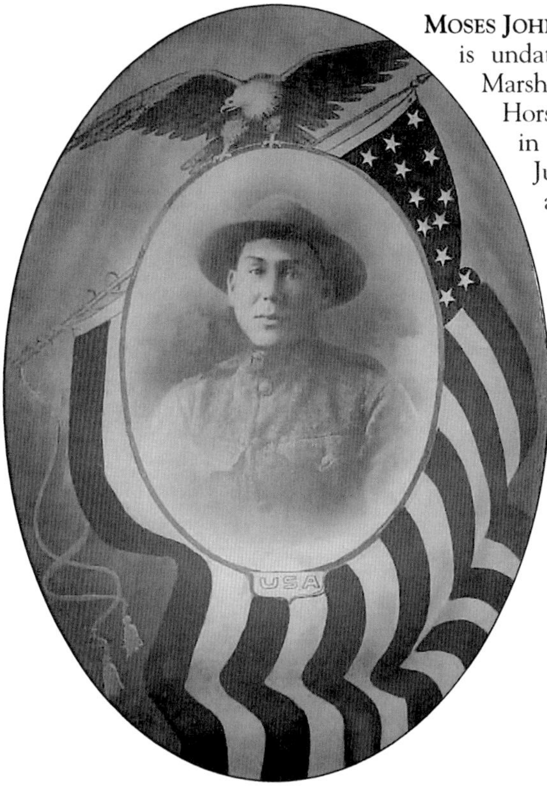

MOSES JOHN MARSHALL (SICANGU). This photograph is undated. The father and mother of Moses Marshall were Morris Janis and Josephine Black Horse. Moses was born about 1895 and lived in Mission, South Dakota. He married Anna Julia Grant, the daughter of William Grant, a half Lakota/Irish man. Moses and Anna "Julia" had 13 children. Moses was the grandfather of Karen Swan who provided the nice photo. (Photograph courtesy of Karen Swan.)

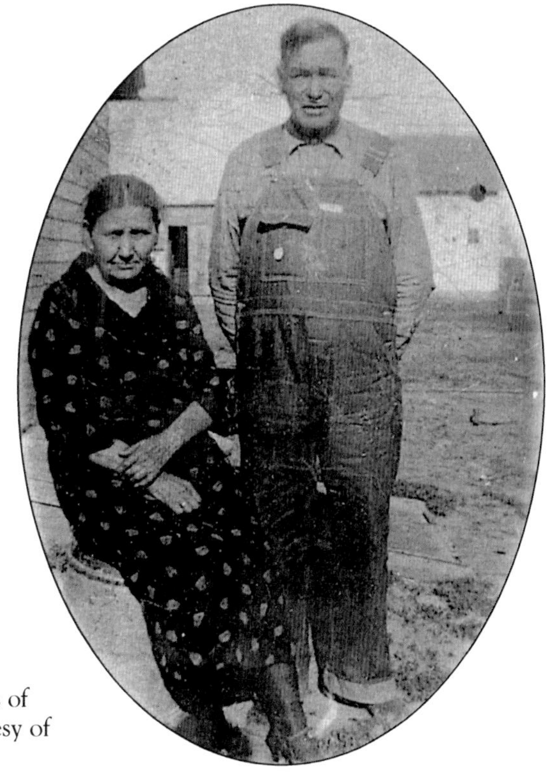

EMMA LAROUCHE DRAPEAU AND LEON DRAPEAU (SICANGU). This photograph is undated. Emma and Leon were the parents of Rose Drapeau Hudson. (Photograph courtesy of James and Lenora Hudson.)

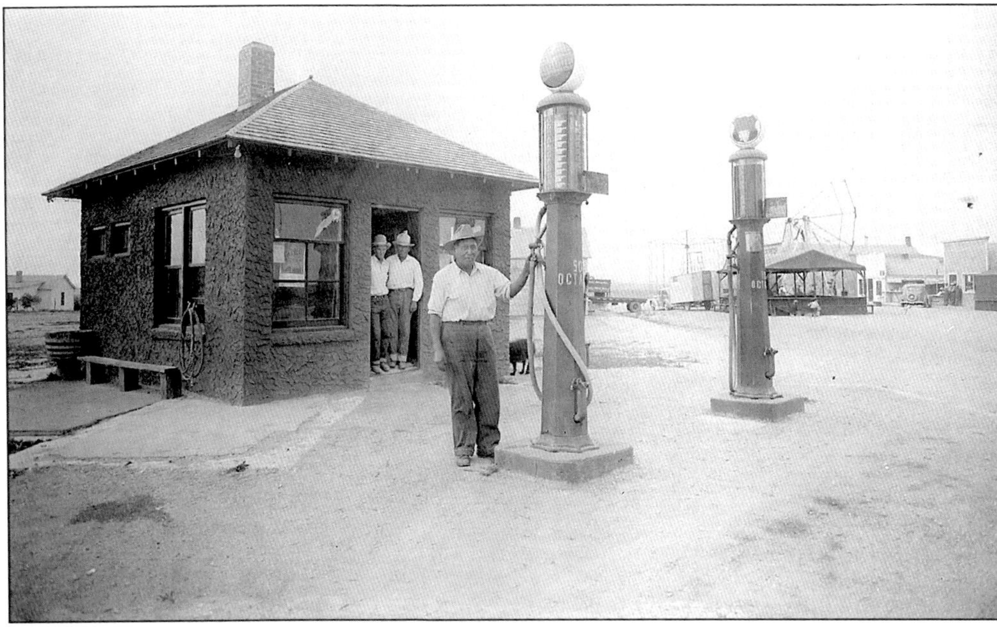

ROBERT DRIVING HAWK (SICANGU). This photograph was taken August 3, 1936. Robert Driving Hawk operated the Phillips 66 gas station in Mission, South Dakota. It also appears in the background that the carnival has set up in Mission. (Photograph courtesy of Virginia Driving Hawk Sneve.)

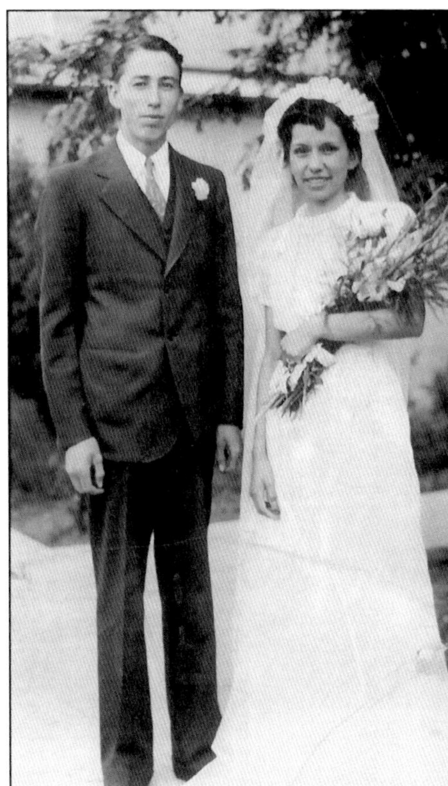

DONALD FRANCIS HUDSON AND HARRIET MINNIE WHITING (SICANGU). This photograph was taken July 16, 1938. This photo was taken on Donald and Harriet's wedding day at St. Francis, South Dakota. Their sons are James, Thomas, and Michael. William Bordeaux was one of Harriet's grandfathers. Her grandmother was Mary Little Battle Nichols, who was born in 1862. Harriet's mother, Phoebe Bordeaux, died in 1926, and her father, David Blaine Whiting, lived from 1887 to 1935. Ptesanwin was Harriet's great-great-grandmother (1779-1887). Her other great-great-grandmother was Huntkalutawin, who married James Bordeaux. (Photograph courtesy of James and Lenora Hudson.)

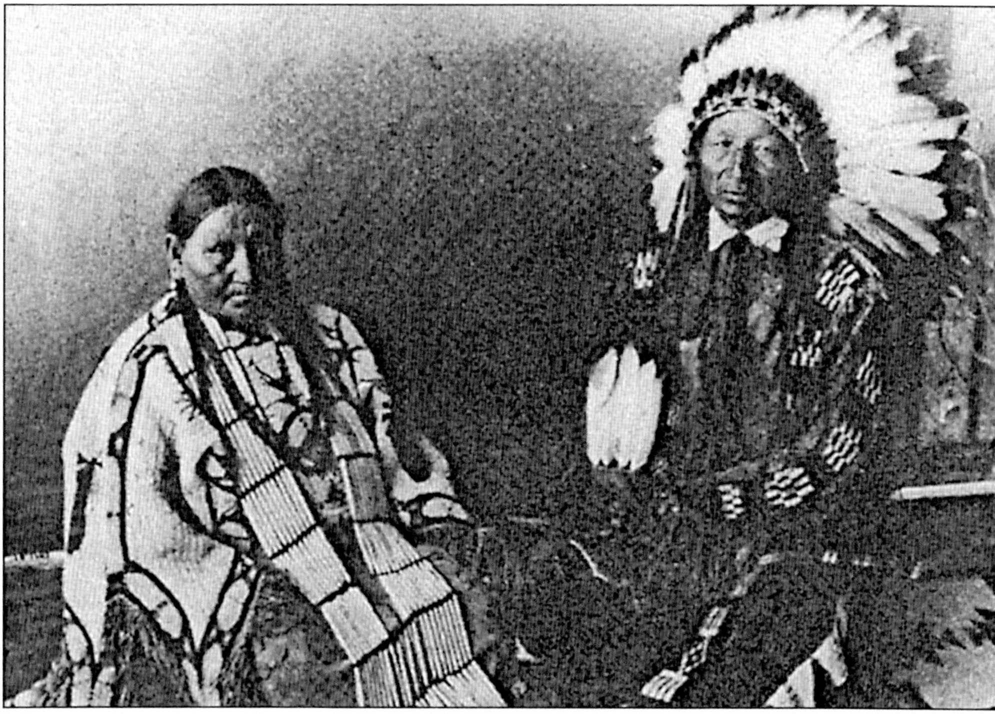

MR. AND MRS. FAST HORSE "SUNKA WAKAN LUZAHAN" (SICANGU). This photograph is undated. The Fast Horse family was from Bad Nation. The Fast Horse name is common on all Lakota reservations. The Fast Horse tiospaye (extended family) of 17 members is included on the Rosebud Census of 1875. (Photograph courtesy of Tripp County Historical Society.)

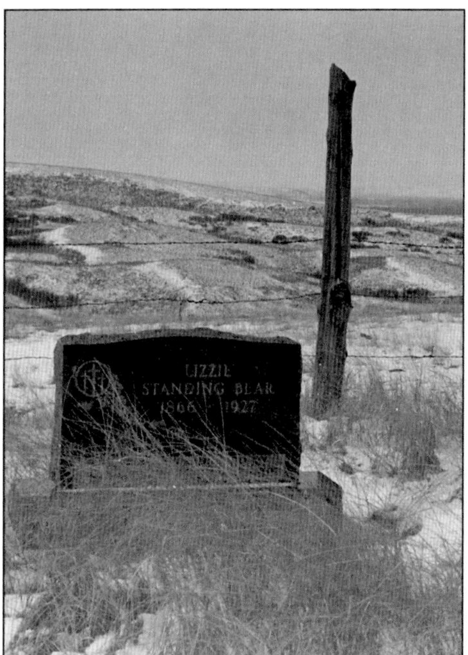

LIZZIE STANDING BEAR MARKER. This is the resting place of Lizzie Quiver Standing Bear who was born in 1866 and lived until 1927. The location overlooks the White River. Lizzie Quiver married Willard Standing Bear about 1888 in Bennett County. Willard was born in 1867 and their daughter was Esther Standing Bear who was born in 1890 at Rosebud. Esther married Tom Quiver and they lived at Corn Creek. A son of Tom and Esther's was Bert Quiver. Willard Standing Bear was the son of George Standing Bear (b. *c.* 1830) and Her Eagle Blanket (b. *c.* 1830). Willard's sisters were Ella Standing Bear and Sarah Standing Bear. Willard's brother was Cyrus Standing Bear. The land was sold by the Standing Bear family and Elizabeth Quiver Standing Bear bought the headstone which was erected in the 1960s and is on private property. (Photograph courtesy of Mildred Thoede Sleep.)

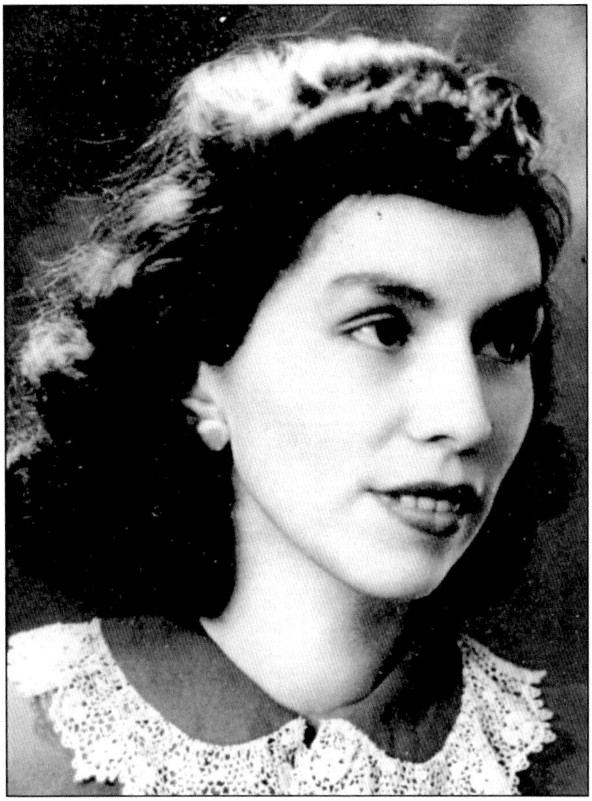

HARRIET MINNIE WHITING-HUDSON (SICANGU). This photograph is undated. Harriet Whiting was born in 1916 at Hidden Timber on Rosebud Reservation. She married Donald Hudson in 1938 and lived until 2001. Harriet's great-grandparents were James Bordeaux and Huntkalutawin, who was later known as Marie. James and Marie had seven children, one of whom was author Susan Bordeaux Bettelyoun. (Photograph courtesy of James and Lenora Hudson.)

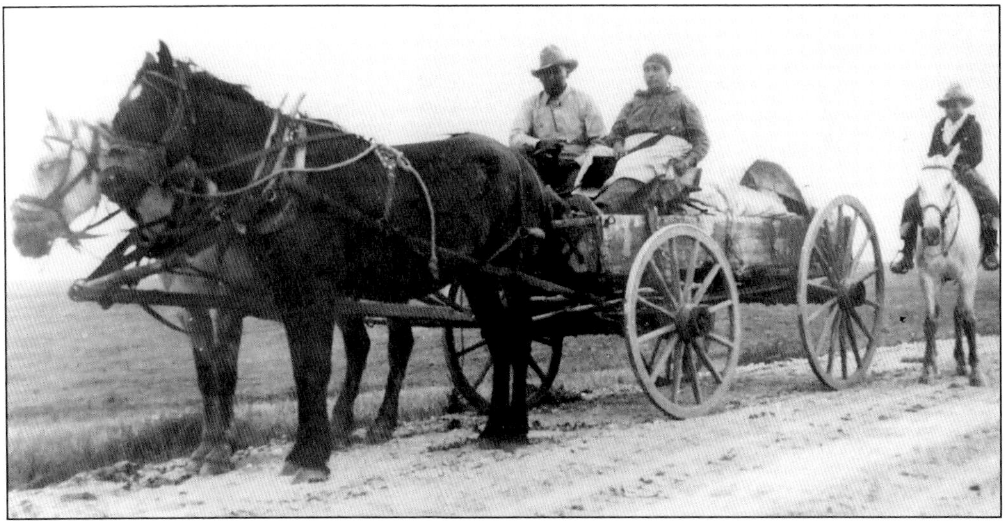

ROBERT DRIVING HAWK, FLORA CLAIRMONT-DRIVING HAWK, AND JAMES DRIVING HAWK (ON HORSE) (SICANGU). This photograph was taken in 1925. Robert and his wife Flora along with son James Driving Hawk are on their way to Frontier Days in White River, South Dakota. Robert was originally from Lower Brule, and Flora's family was from the Ring Thunder Band. Robert and Flora were the grandparents of Virginia and Edward Driving Hawk, and James Driving Hawk was the father of Virginia and Edward. (Photograph courtesy of Virginia Driving Hawk Sneve.)

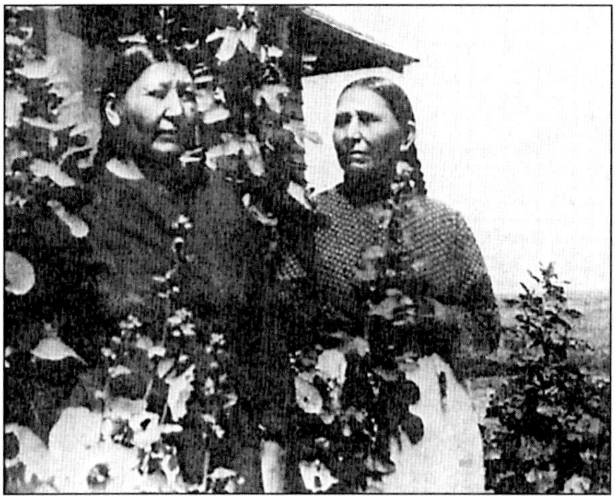

EMILY STANDING BEAR-DILLON AND VICTORIA STANDING BEAR-CONROY (SICANGU/OGLALA). This photograph is undated. Emily married Peter Dillon and Victoria married Frank Conroy. These are the daughters of George Standing Bear pictured at Victoria's home on Pine Ridge Reservation. The Standing Bear family claim a close relationship to Chief Crazy Horse. According to their family records, their link would be from Rattling Stone Woman (Oglala) who they say was a sister to Worm, the father of Crazy Horse. Some Crazy Horse descendants do not agree with this, although several authors have published the Standing Bear records but indicate that little is known about Rattling Stone Woman. She was born about 1815 and married One Horse and they were the parents of Lena Roaming Nation/Hawk/Her Eagle Blanket and Her Eagle Blanket/Roaming Nation. These two sisters were wives of George Standing Bear. One Horse died in 1877 and Rattling Stone Woman settled at Rosebud with her two daughters at the Salt Wearers Camp. Emily and Victoria would be maternal cousins to Crazy Horse. (Photograph courtesy of Donovin Sprague.)

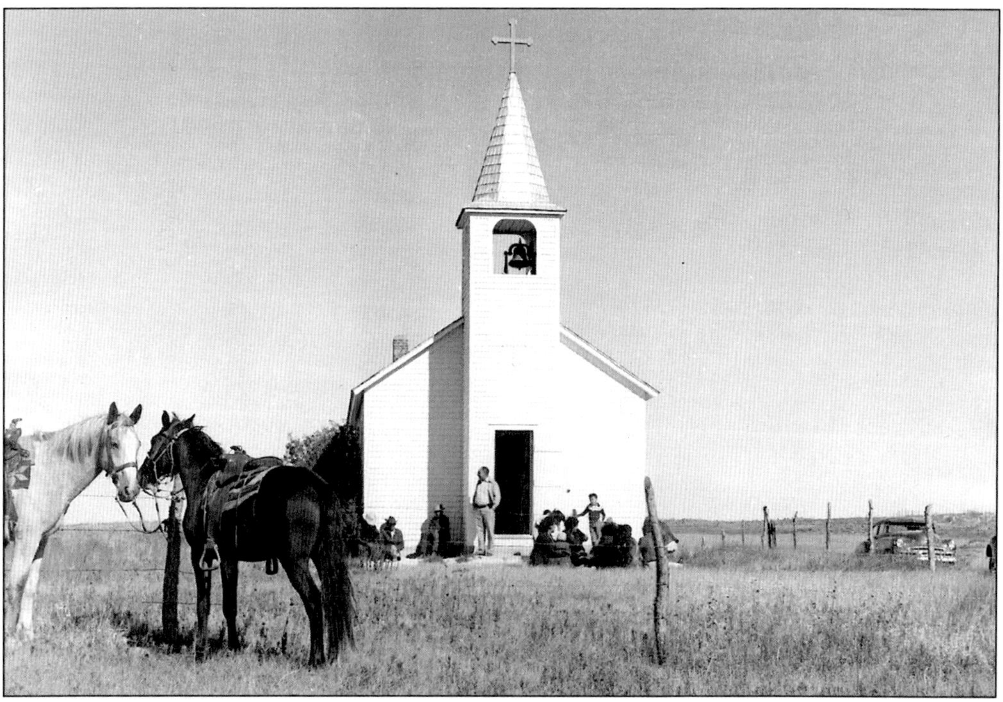

SPRING CREEK CONGREGATION WITH ALBERT GUERUE (LAKOTA). This photograph was taken in 1952. This is the church at Spring Creek with Albert Guerue standing by the door at the church steps. (Postcard courtesy of Red Cloud Heritage Center and Brother Simon, S.J.)

JEFF BRUSHBREAKER (SICANGU) AND PHYLLIS MARTIN. This photograph is undated. This picture was taken at Norris, South Dakota. Jeffery Brushbreaker was born about 1886 and married Eliza Bear Shield. Jeffery lived until about 1925. One of their daughters was Angeline Brushbreaker, who was born in 1908 and lived until 1995. (Photograph courtesy of Jackson Washabaugh County Historical Society.)

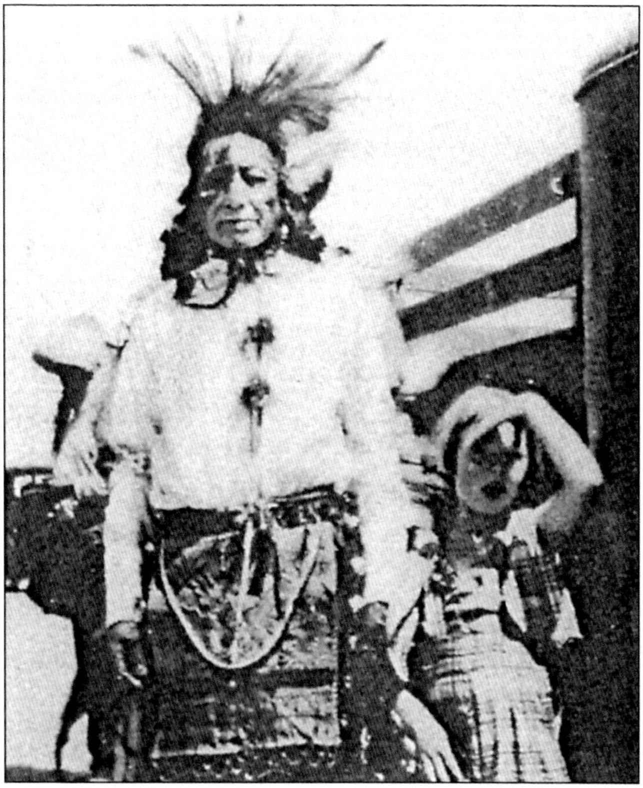

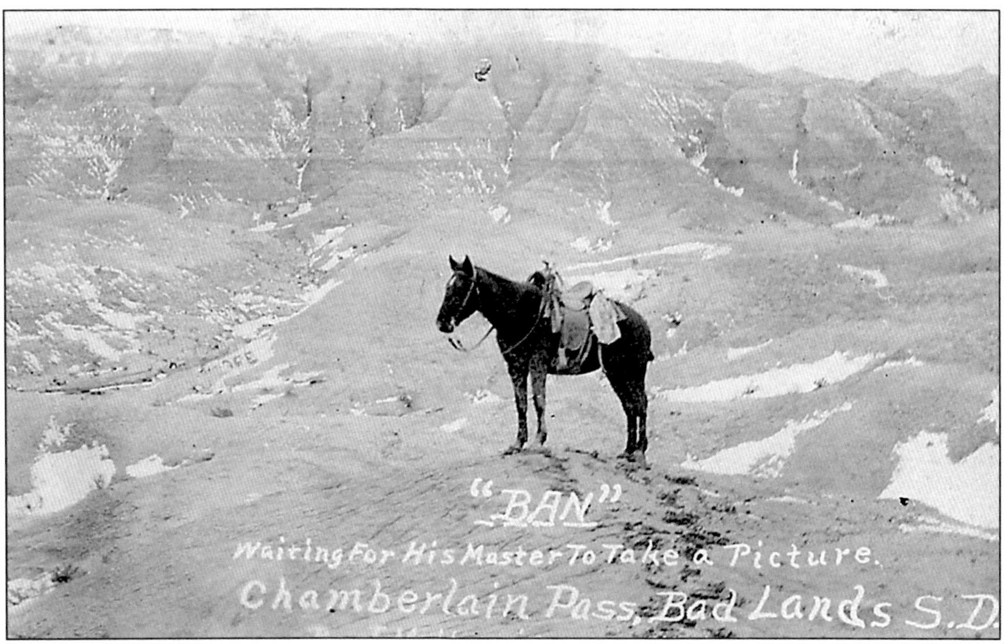

BADLANDS, SOUTH DAKOTA. This photograph was taken by Hamilton, and is undated. This scene is at "Chamberlain Pass" and this sunka wakan is named "Ban." (Photograph courtesy of DeVries and Sleep.)

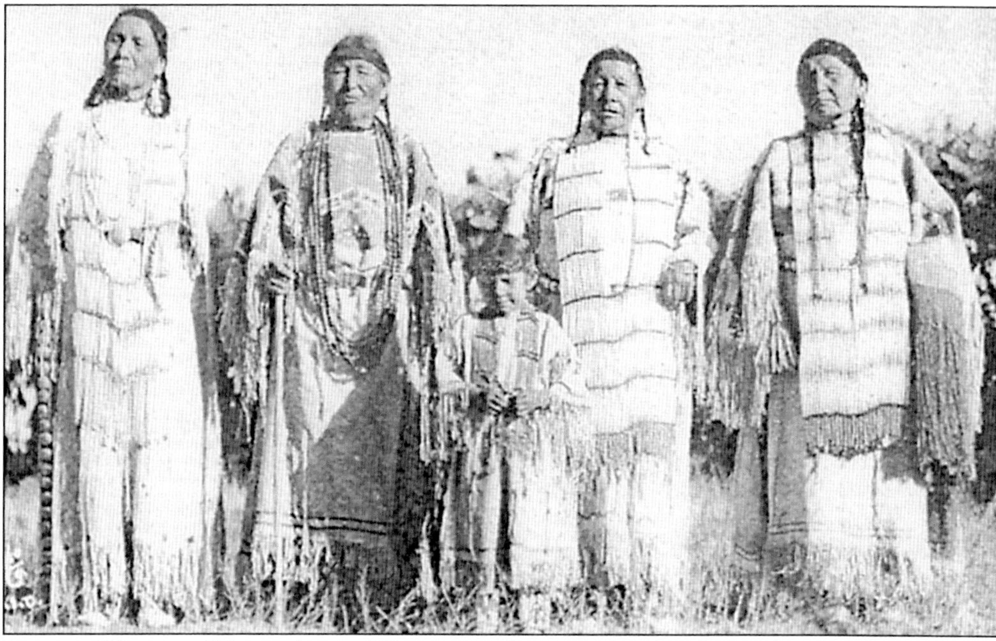

Lakota Winyan (Women) and Wicincila (Young Girl). This undated photograph was taken on or near the Rosebud Reservation. (Photograph courtesy of Jackson Washabaugh Historical Society.)

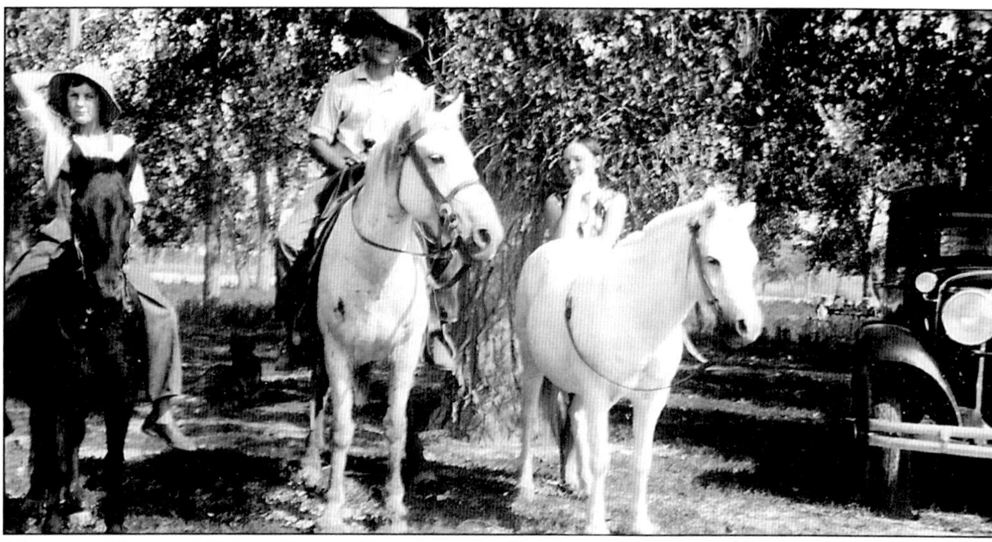

Mildred Thoede Sleep, Frank Luthy, and Ethel Hillmer. Mildred and her sister Ethel are pictured here between 1933 and 1934 with their cousin Frank Luthy at the north crossing into the Rosebud Reservation. Mildred and Ethel's family had a house at the community of Stearns which the DeVries family bought later. There was a pulley and rope on the White River and a cable from the south side for crossing. Stearns had a Post Office and store just west of the family home, before the town of Belvidere was started. Another settlement in the area was Stamford, and Wanamaker village was between Long Valley and Norris. Other White River crossings from west to east were Cavite Crossing, Olson Rock Crossing, Blunck Crossing, Edna Crossing, and Theisen Crossing. (Photograph courtesy of DeVries and Sleep.)

NANNIE DORINE BORDEAUX "WICAKPI OUMINI" (SICANGU). Nannie Dorine Bordeaux was the wife of William Bordeaux and the great-granddaughter of Chief White Thunder of the Sicangu. Mrs. Bordeaux assisted her husband with the book *Custer's Conqueror*, providing historical information on the life of her great-grandfather White Thunder. Mrs. Bordeaux drew a sketch for the book of what they thought Chief Crazy Horse looked like, since there is no proven photo of him. For the sketch she used descriptions provided by Louis Bordeaux, the father of William Bordeaux, and by Julia Clown "Iron Cedar Woman," sister of Crazy Horse. She also used the descriptions from "other close associates" of Crazy Horse. Their accounts describe him as "about 5'11," weight 175, complexion rather light for an Indian, eyes light brown, hair long dark brown, facial expression, firm and determine(d) mouth, manner, winning personality. Very seldom heard in public debates. Character calm and reserved, scar on left cheek." The sketch is described as a "near image," but some family of Crazy Horse wonder about the artist's ability to draw what people described. It is known, however, that he did wear just one feather, had a scar on his left cheek, and his complexion was light for a Lakota. (Photograph courtesy of Bureau of Ethnology.)

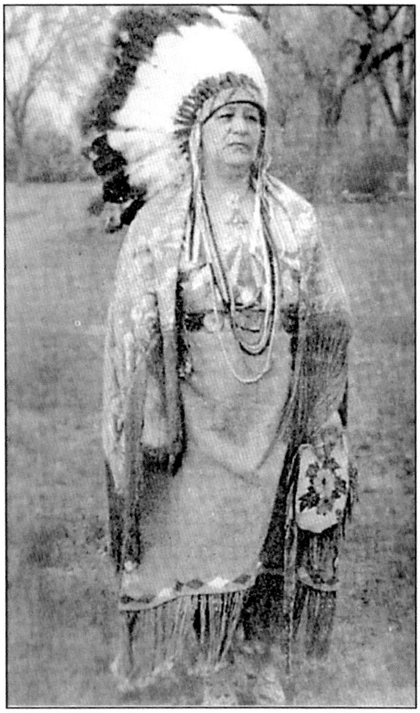

WILLIAM J. BORDEAUX "PTE KASOTELA" (FRENCH/SICANGU). William was born about 1884 on the Rosebud Reservation, attended Haskell Institute in Lawrence, Kansas. William's father was Louis Bordeaux and his grandparents were James Bordeaux (French) and Huntkalutawin, a Sicangu. William wrote *Custer's Conqueror*, covering Bordeaux family history, Lakota history, and interviewing participants in the Battle of the Little Bighorn. The book is a good insight by an early Lakota author, taking interviews from beyond the Rosebud and Pine Ridge Reservations to include the northern Lakota. William recorded history of Touch The Cloud mistakenly identifying him as "Brule." Touch The Cloud was Minnicoujou, first cousin to Crazy Horse. Bordeaux recorded a valuable interview with Julia Clown "Iron Cedar Woman," identifying her as sister of Chief Crazy Horse. Julia was a Minnicoujou and the interview took place at Thunder Butte on Cheyenne River Reservation. Touch The Cloud was son of Chief Lone Horn of the Minnicoujou. Lone Horn's sister was the mother of Crazy Horse, Rattling Blanket Woman. Rattling Blanket Woman was half-sister to Minnicoujou Chief Hump (High Back Bone) by blood (same father but different mother). (Photograph courtesy of Bureau of Ethnology.)

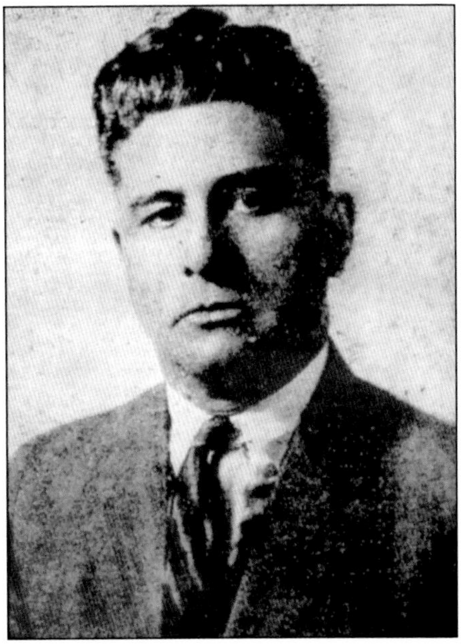

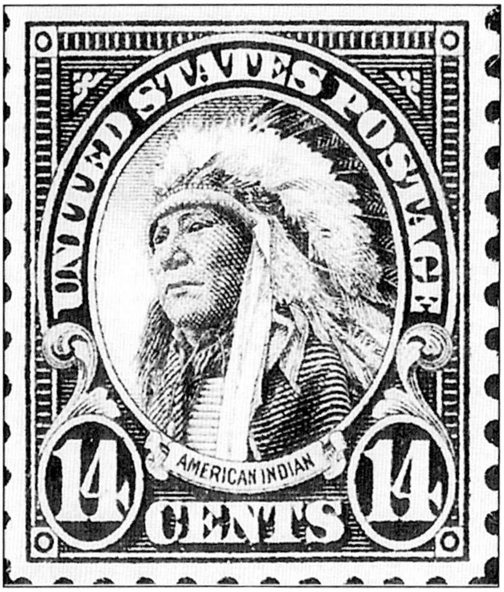

1922 U.S. Stamp of Hollow Horn Bear. The image of Chief Hollow Horn Bear of the Sicangu was chosen to be used on the 1922 14¢ U.S. stamp. The image was from a portrait of Hollow Horn Bear taken in 1905 by DeLancey Gill. Hollow Horn Bear was also on the old $5 U.S. currency bills. (Photograph courtesy of Donovin Sprague.)

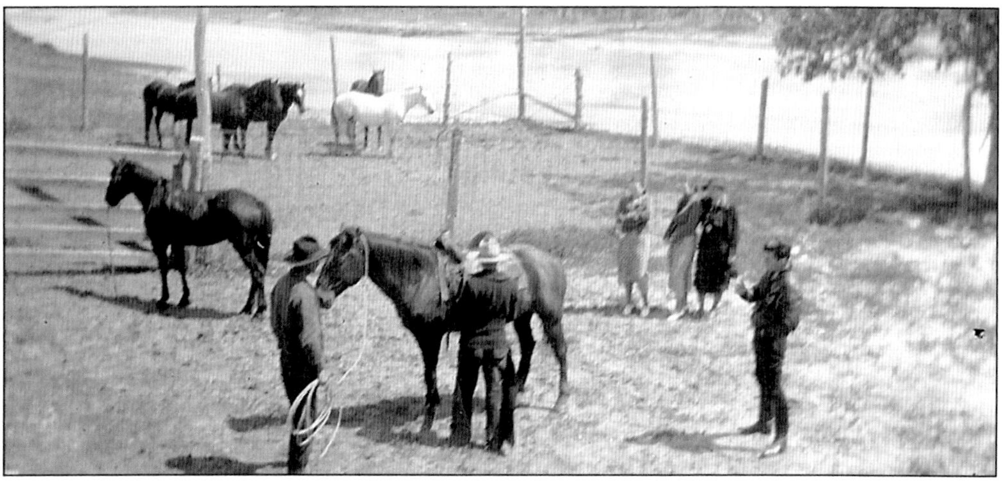

White River Crossing into Rosebud. This was the first crossing into the Rosebud Reservation from the north. There was only one place to cross which had a rock bottom. Nearby was an area known as Sand Point which had excellent drinking water and everyone went there to get water. When the reservation was established it originally was fenced and at this point the fence was across the White River on the south side. The Sicangu were instructed to stay on the south side and the non-Indian homestead settlers were to stay on the north side. Mildred Thoede Sleep knew the Standing Bear family well and they worked for her family. Bear Heels also lived in the area. When daughter Lizzie Standing Bear died Mildred's parents, E.W. "Hans" and Francis "Fanny" Thoede, buried Lizzie. Mildred recalled that at that time the White River was flooded and the Standing Bear family needed help to bury Lizzie because they could not get to town. Mildred's parents and brothers took lumber from their hay racks and wagons and Mrs. Thoede lined the coffin with clothes and a funeral was held. When Mr. Thoede died he wanted to also be buried next to his friends, the Standing Bear family and his request was honored. Other communities in the area which were recalled were the village of Patricia near Hisle, South Dakota, and the Larmers Post Office which was named for the Larmers family. (Photograph courtesy of Mildred Thoede Sleep.)

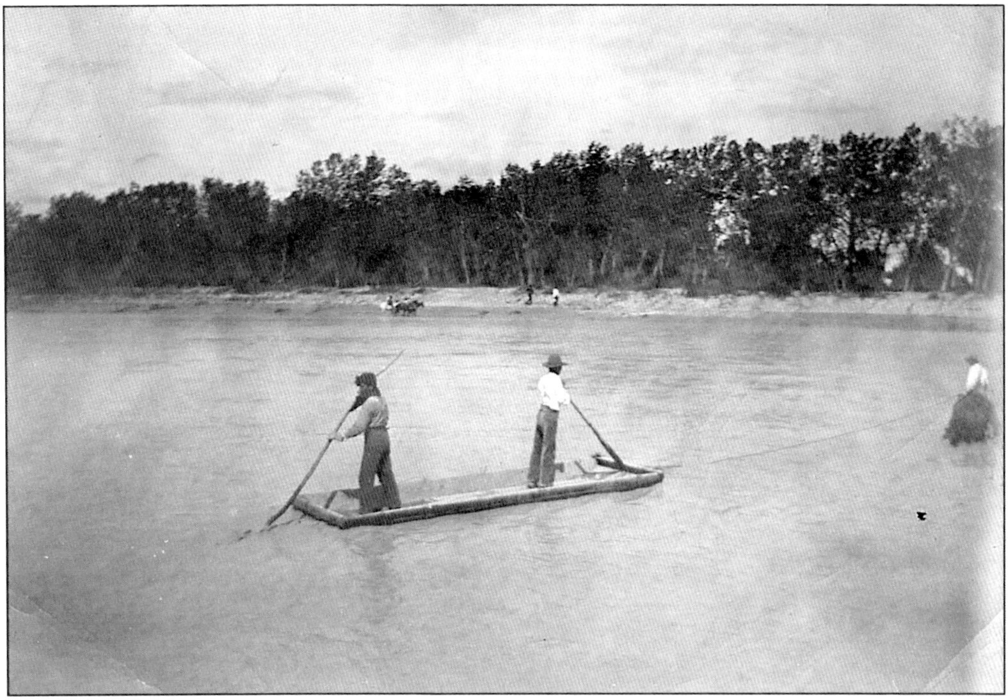

BIG WHITE RIVER FLOODING. This photograph shows the flooding at Rosebud Crossing on the White River near the Thoede Ranch. This area is south of Belvidere, South Dakota, on Highway 63. (Photograph courtesy of Mildred Thoede Sleep.)

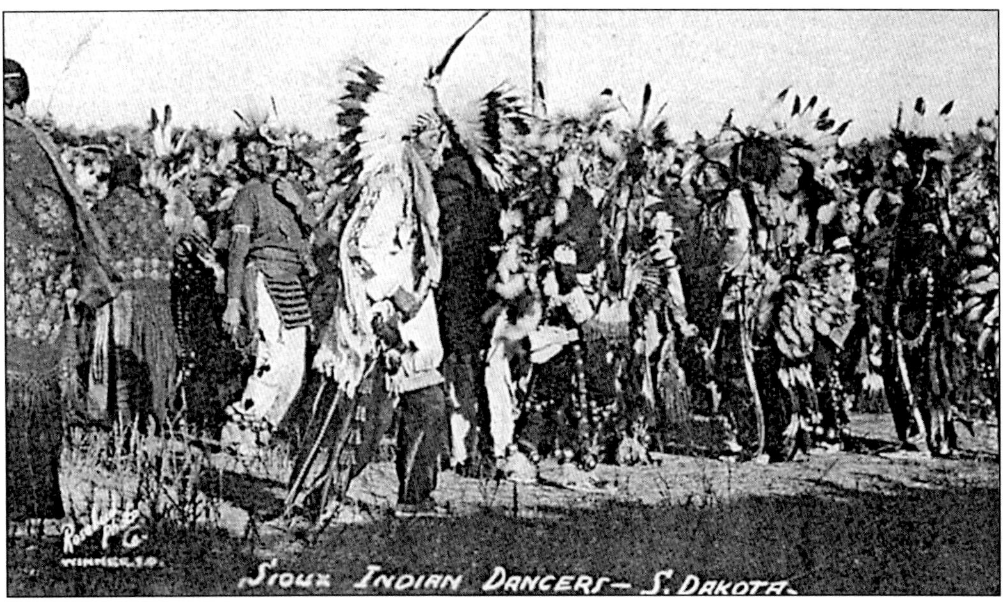

SICANGU DANCERS AT WINNER, SOUTH DAKOTA. This photograph is by Rosebud Photo Co., and is undated. This picture was taken at a Winner celebration. (Postcard courtesy of Donovin Sprague.)

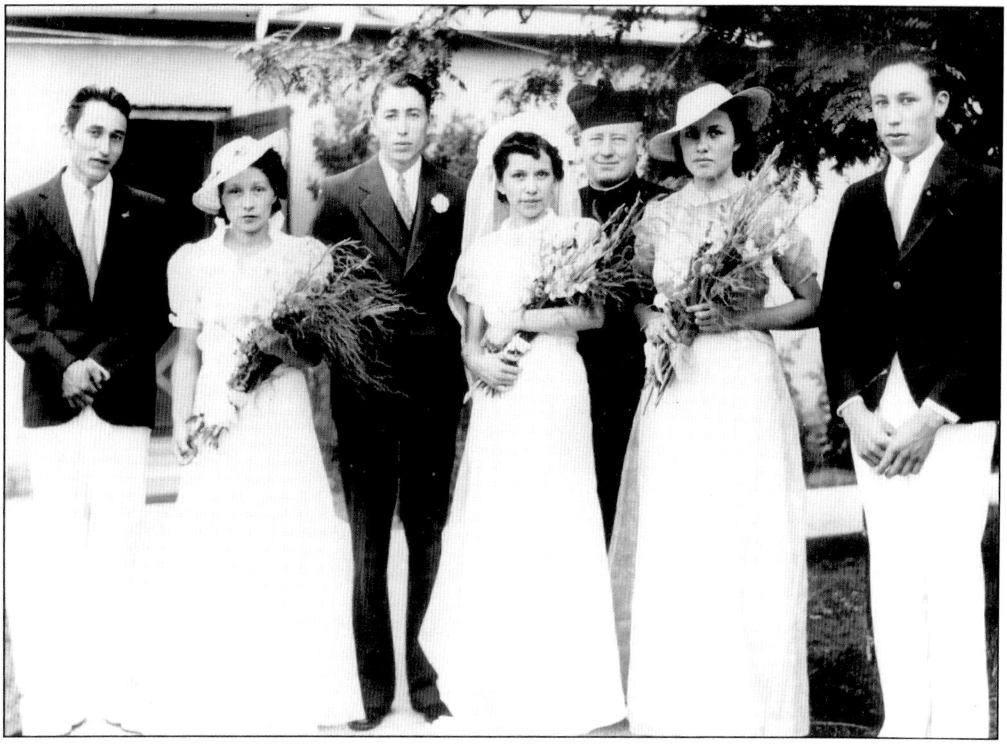

THE WHITING-HUDSON WEDDING PARTY. Pictured, from left to right, are Henry Leon Hudson, Mary Ellen Whiting-Hudson, Donald Francis Hudson, Harriet Whiting-Hudson, Father Fallon, Fauniel Hudson, and Paul Adrian Hudson (Sicangu). This photograph was taken on July 16, 1938. This is the wedding picture of Harriet Whiting and Donald Hudson taken in front of St. Francis Mission. (Photograph courtesy of James and Lenora Hudson.)

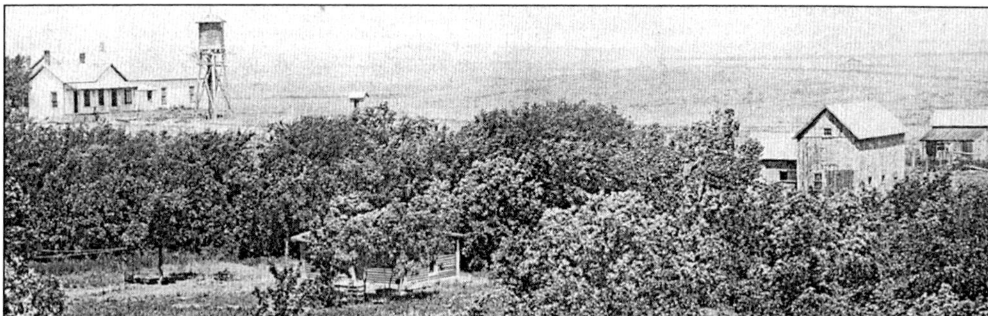

WOOD, SOUTH DAKOTA, ISSUE STATION. This photograph is undated. The community of Wood is the oldest town and was a location for the issue of beef and supplies to the Lakota. There was a boss farmer in charge of the station. This picture shows the buildings at the beef issue station. Wood was named for A. K. Wood, who operated an Indian trading post before Mellette County was opened for settlement. (Photograph courtesy of the Mellette County Historical Society.)

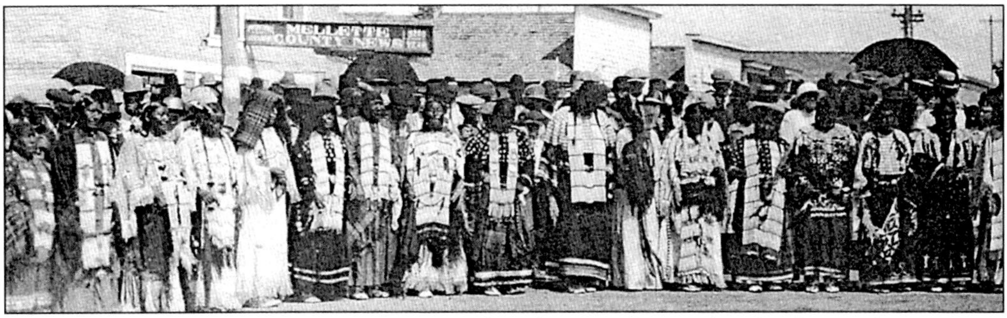

MARTIN, SOUTH DAKOTA, CELEBRATION. This photograph is undated. These Lakota women are dancing at the Frontier Days celebration with spectators in the background. The dancing was held on main street in front of the *Mellette County News* office. (Photograph courtesy of Mellette County Historical Society.)

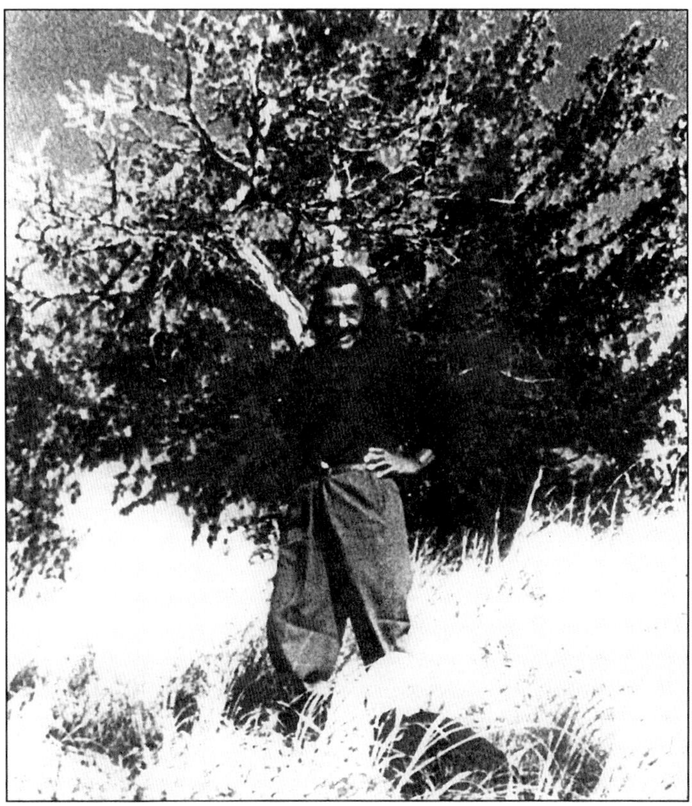

HENRY CROW DOG (SICANGU). This photograph is undated. Leonard Crow Dog is from Grass Mountain. His son is Leonard Crow Dog and Diane Crow Dog is his daughter. (Photograph courtesy of Oglala Lakota College Archives.)

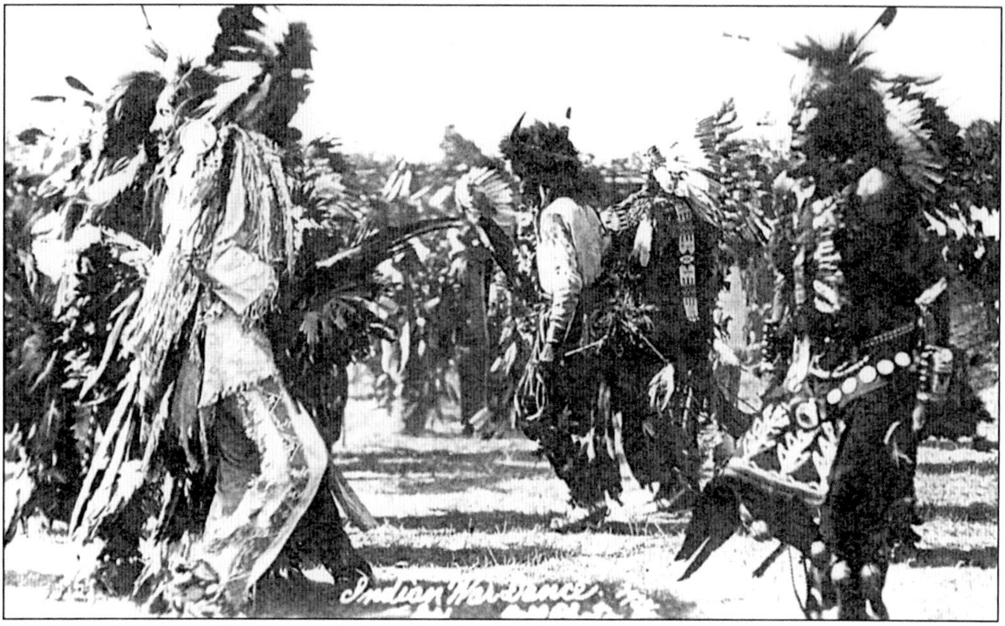

MALE DANCERS AT ROSEBUD (LAKOTA). This photograph was taken in 1928 by Bell. The dancers are depicting a war dance and were photographed by Bell Photo at the Rosebud Indian Fair celebration in 1928. (Postcard courtesy of Donovin Sprague.)

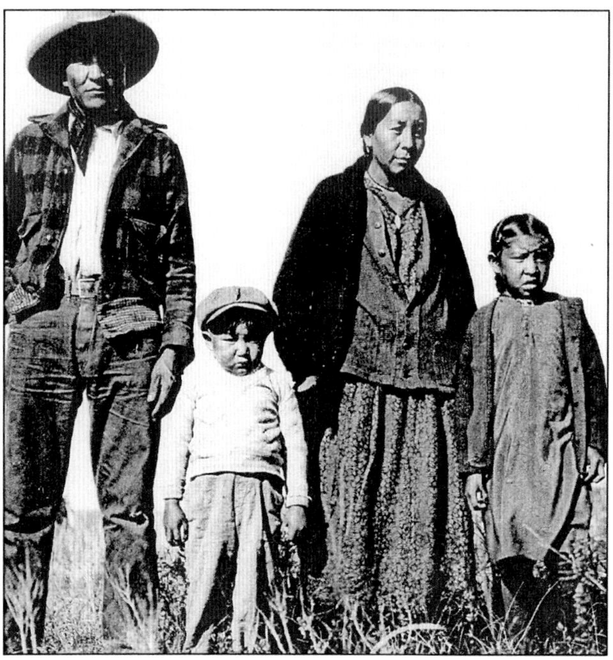

THE SPOTTED WAR BONNET FAMILY. Pictured, from left to right, are Sam Spotted War Bonnet, Sam Spotted War Bonnet Jr., Beatrice Attack Him, and Birdie Beatrice Spotted War Bonnet (Sicangu). This photograph was taken on October 16, 1929. Sam Spotted War Bonnet Sr. was married to Attack Him sisters at different times. Howard Spotted War Bonnet was a son of Sam's, and Howard married Anne Florence Williams. The children of Howard and Anne are Wayne Howard, Duane "Skip", Etta E., Garry Lee, Lawayne "Lolly," John Samuel, and Duana Lynn. Anne Williams Spotted War Bonnet's parents were John "Jack" Williams and Fannie Greenwood. Birdie Spotted War Bonnet is Howard's sister and a son of Birdie's is Eddie Cutgrass. Beatrice, wife of Sam Sr., was the mother of Johnny Attack Him. Johnny Attack Him and Howard Spotted War Bonnet were half brothers by blood. Eddie Cutgrass of Rapid City identified the young boy as Sam Spotted War Bonnet Jr., who died young of an ear infection. (Photograph courtesy of Spotted War Bonnet family.)

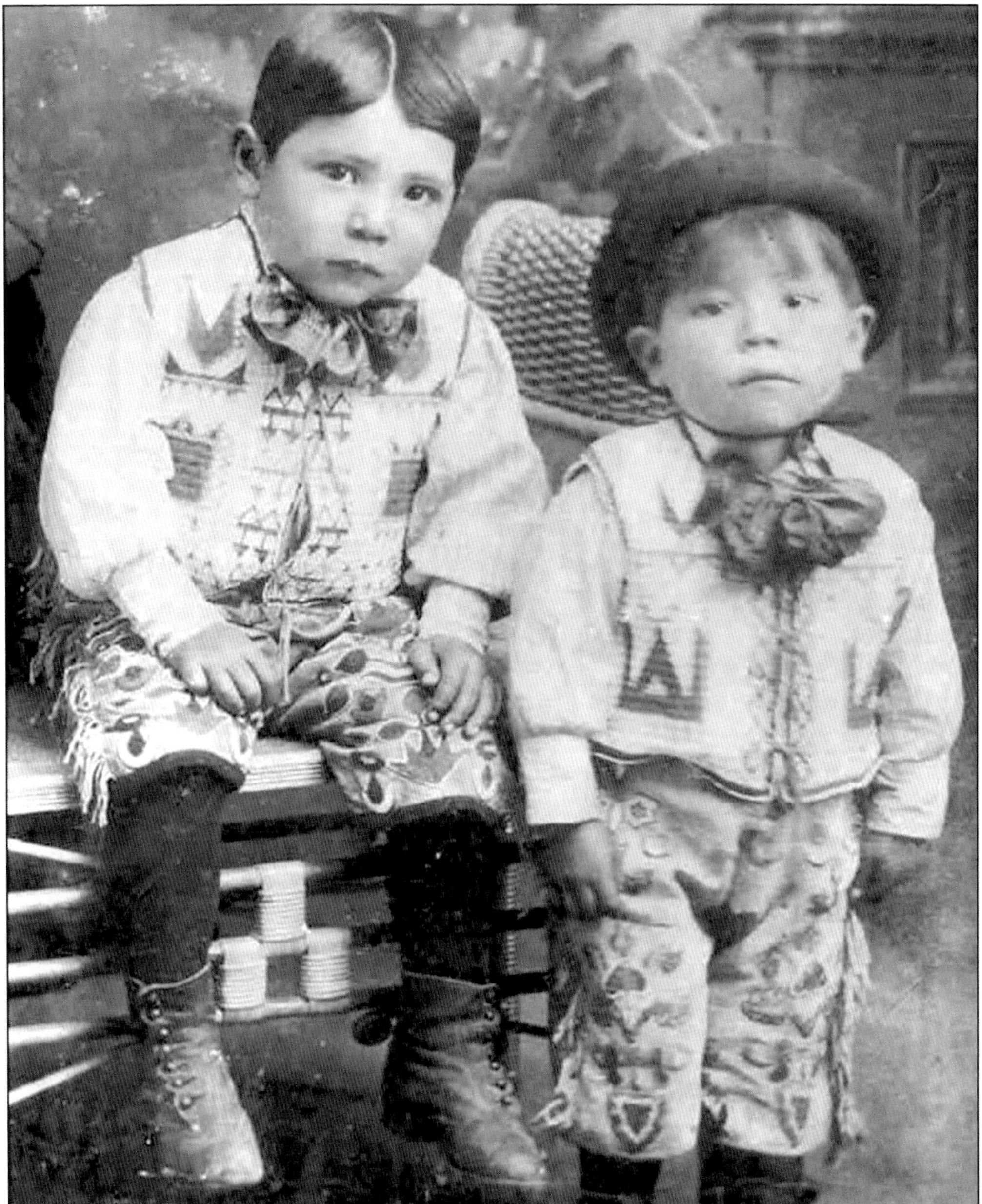

CHOICE AND TAKES THE WAR BONNET (LAKOTA). This photo was taken *c.* 1905. This photograph was in the home of Victoria Standing Bear Conroy. It appears on a mantle within Victoria's home at the State Soldiers Home where she lived in later years. Other photographs on the shelf are clearly family members but this one may have been some little friends of hers. (Photograph courtesy of Luther Standing Bear Collection and Crazy Horse Memorial Foundation.)

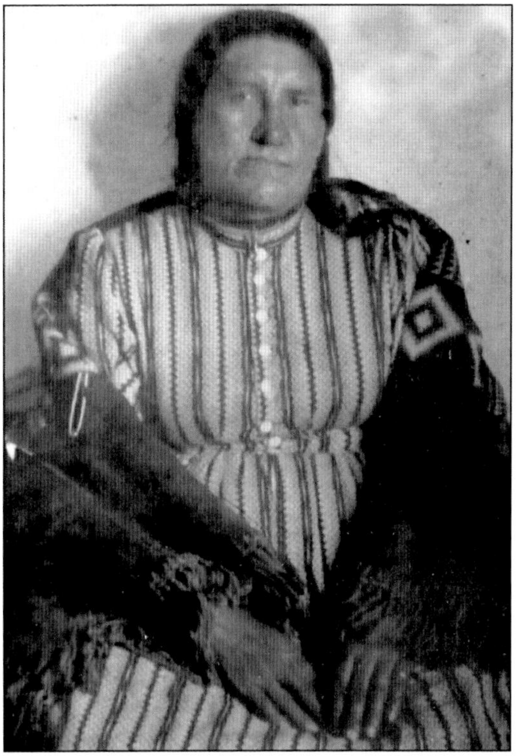

GRANDMA PAWNEE (SICANGU). This photograph is undated. (Photograph courtesy of James and Lenora Hudson.)

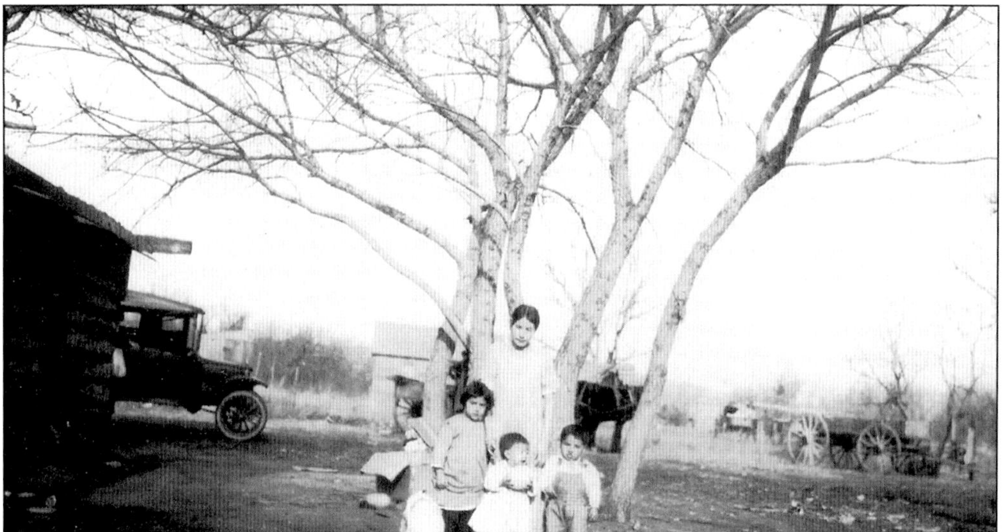

MOORE FAMILY AT OKREEK, SOUTH DAKOTA. This photograph was taken December 26, 1923. Pictured from left to right are Ramona Moore-Casillis, Marrles Moore, Noble Moore Jr., and Elizabeth McCloskey-Moore. Grandpa Noble Moore Sr. is partially hidden behind the tree. This picture was taken at the family homestead at Okreek when a survey was done by the Bureau of Indian Affairs. The Moore family later had a total of eight children. Okreek was named for the many oak trees near a stream in the area, and was originally named Oak Creek, but the U.S. Postal Service would not accept a town name with two words so it was changed. (Photograph courtesy of Jack Moore.)

Six

SAPUNTI TIPI WAKAN NA OWAYAWA EL' TIPI
(WHERE THE BLACK ROBES LIVE/ST. FRANCIS MISSION AND BOARDING SCHOOLS)

WAYAWA ANPETU
(DAY SCHOOL)

Sicangu Lakota attended early boarding schools, such as the Hampton Institute, founded for African Americans. Richard Henry Pratt founded the Carlisle School in Pennsylvania following the model at Hampton. In September 1879, Pratt recruited Dakota Territory students. Today, students can attend Sinte Gleska University at various centers throughout the reservation. President Lionel Bordeaux is recognized nationally for his contributions in tribal higher education.

CARLISLE INDIAN SCHOOL. Pictured in 1883 on their arrival at Carlisle Indian School are, from left to right, Richard Yellow Robe, Henry Standing Bear "Mato Najin," and Chauncey Yellow Robe "Tasinagi" (Sicangu). Richard and Chauncey (b. 1869) were sons of Yellow Robe and "Tahcawin" (Fawn/Deer Woman), also listed as Catch Bear Yellow Robe. Richard's Lakota name was Search The Enemy and Chauncey was known as Kills In The Woods (their classmates nicknamed them "Wounded" and "Timber"). Their father was first known as White Thunder and acquired the Yellow Robe name for heroic war deeds against a Yellow Robe family of Crow Indians. He was the son of Chief Stabber and they participated in the Battle of the Little Bighorn. Yellow Robe's first wife was Her Robe "Tasina;" they had three children, who all died young. He then married Slow Bear, who Chauncey always referred to as "Tahcawin." Yellow Robe and Tahcawin had seven children and Yellow Robe had eight more children with Tahcawin's sister Grabbing Bear. Some of Chauncey's brothers and sisters are listed as Plenty Brothers Yellow Robe, Louis Isaac Yellow Robe, Kate Bear Yellow Robe, Susan Bear Yellow Robe, Joseph Rosebud Sioux Nation South Dakota, and John Yellow Robe and Richard (Search The Enemy). Chauncey Yellow Robe married Lillian "Lillie" Belle Springer, of Swiss-German heritage. Richard Yellow Robe left Carlisle to join the U.S. Army and died in 1893. (Photograph courtesy of Cumberland County Historical Society, Carlisle, Pennsylvania.)

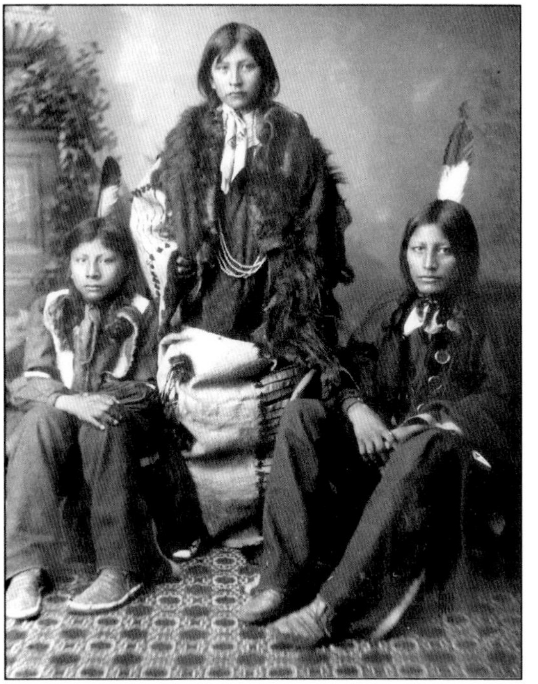

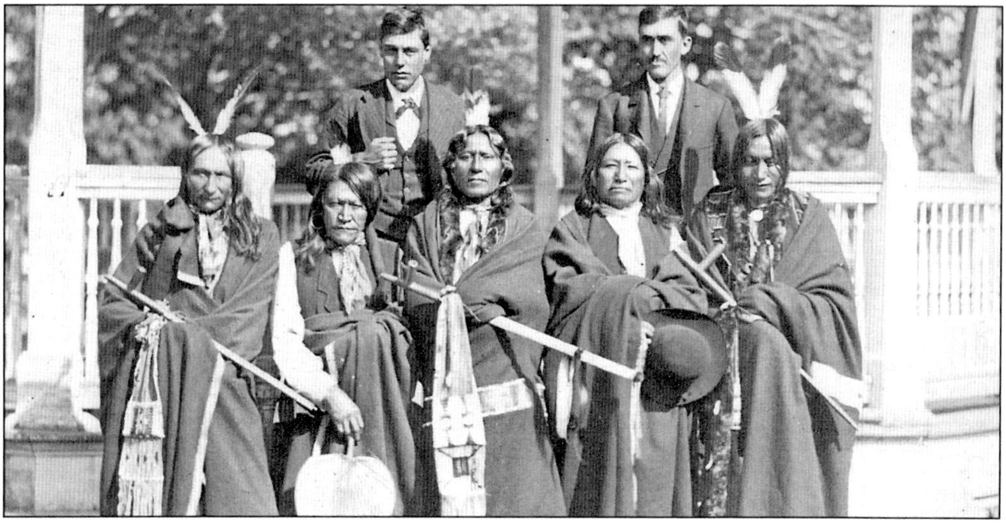

BLACK CROW, TWO STRIKE, WHITE THUNDER, SPOTTED TAIL, IRON WING (SICANGU), AND INTERPRETERS. This photograph was taken by John N. Choate, and is undated. This is a delegation of leaders from Rosebud Reservation visiting the Carlisle Indian School in Carlisle, Pennsylvania. The group was en route to Washington, D.C. Most all of these leaders had sent their children to the Carlisle Indian School. Two Strike did not send his children to the school. The following is a list from the National Archives of Spotted Tail's children/family sent to Carlisle in September 1879: Red Road (Mrs. Charles Tackett) age 18; Stays At Home (William) age 18; Talks With Bear (Oliver) age 14; Bugler (Max) age 12; Little Scout (Pollock) age 9; Running Horse (Hugh Standing Soldier, grandson of Spotted Tail) age 8; and Black Crow (granddaughter of Spotted Tail and daughter of Chief Black Crow). Carlisle School listed these names as Rosebud students in 1879 who were children and relatives of Black Crow: Plenty Aunt, Strikes The Enemy, Passes Through The Enemy, and Rain Water. (Photograph courtesy of Princeton Collections of Western Americana.)

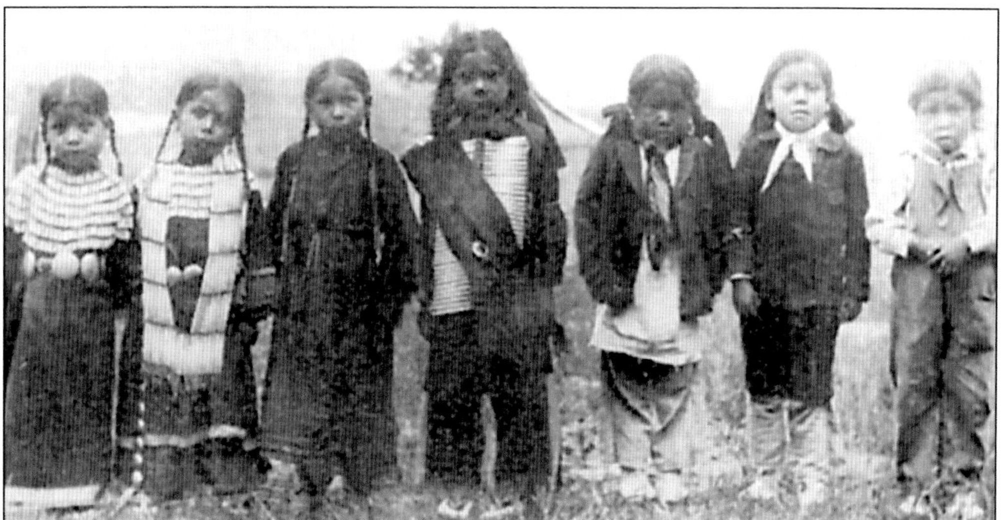

CORA SEARCH THE ENEMY (?), GOOD KILL, LUCY KILLS PLENTY, JOHN UNDER THE WATER, WILLIE GOOD BIRD, PAUL GREY EAGLE TAIL, AND ALLEN OTTERMAN (SICANGU). This photograph was taken in 1897. (Postcard courtesy of Donovin Sprague.)

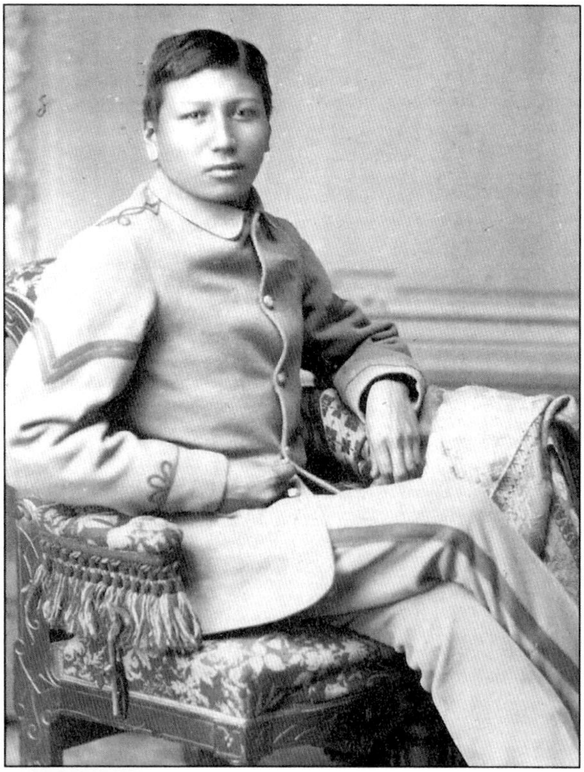

ERNEST WHITE THUNDER (SICANGU). This photograph was taken before 1902. This is Ernest White Thunder at the Carlisle Industrial School, where he was a student. He was the son of Chief White Thunder and the school lists White Thunder's son as Knocks Off, and White Cow is listed as White Thunder's sister-in-law. This list is from 1879 and Knocks Off could be Ernest. There are students listed at Hampton from the Sicangu at Lower Brule and all the other Lakota/Dakota/Nakota reservations except for Rosebud and Pine Ridge. Rosebud and Pine Ridge students would enter Carlisle Indian School the next year in 1879 when it opened. (Photograph courtesy of Princeton Collections of Western Americana.)

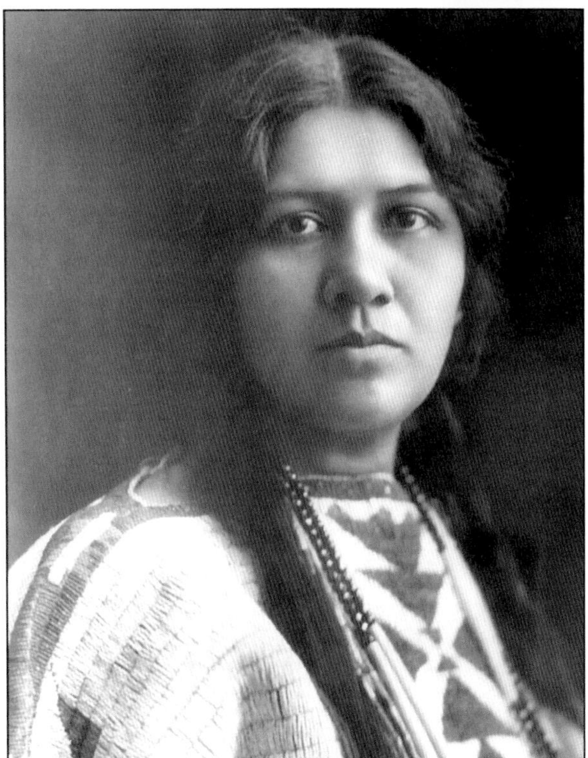

ANGEL DECORA DIETZ (HO-CHUNK AKA WINNEBAGO). This photograph was taken between 1907 and 1916. Angel DeCora Dietz was an instructor of Native American art at Carlisle Indian School and befriended students from Rosebud. She was born in 1871 at Winnebago Reservation in Nebraska, the daughter of David DeCora "Hagasilikaw." The photographer was not recorded. (Photograph courtesy of Cumberland County Historical Society, Carlisle, Pennsylvania.)

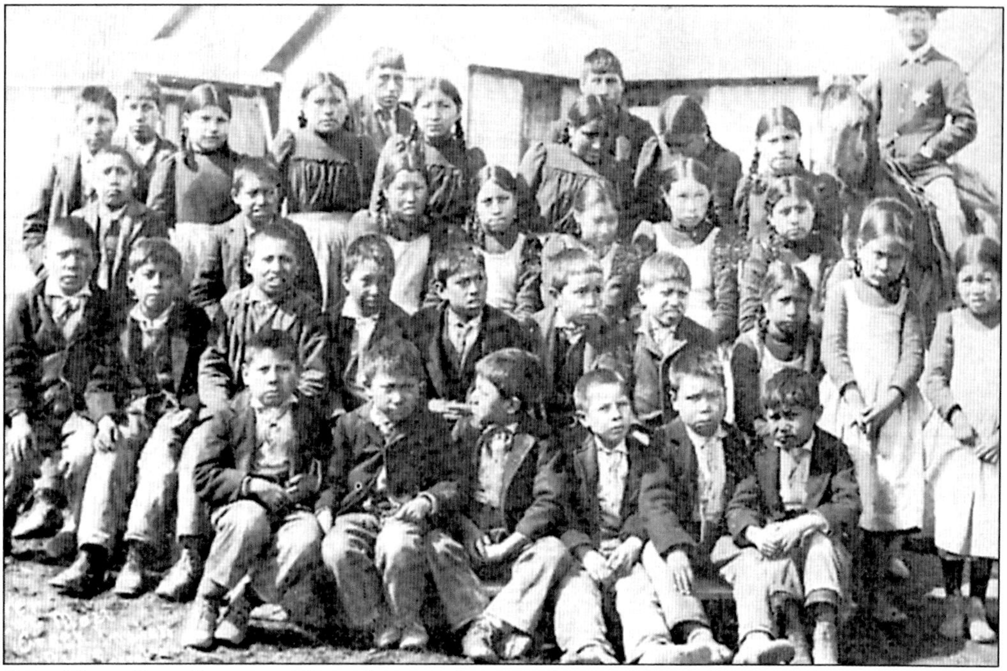

CUT MEAT DAY SCHOOL. This photograph was taken 1895-1896. Pictured are, from left to right: (front row) Sam Slow Fly, Silas Plenty Holes, Charles Black Calf, George Kills Plenty, Sam Yellow Robe, and Nat Elk Teeth; (second row) Charles Little Dog, Freddie Sitting Bear, David Elk Looks Back, Eddie Foot, Lee Wood, Tommy Otterman, Willie Elk Teeth, Stella Good Bird, Hattie With Horns, and Alice Slow Fly; (third row) Charley New, Claudie Blue Horse, Nellie Foot, Maudie Plenty Holes, Gracie Good Bird, Maggie Otterman, Rosa Elk Teeth, and Helen Search The Enemy; (back row) Joe Yellow Robe, Turning Wood, Kitty Turning Eagle, Julia Broken Legs, Henry Good Bird, Emma Looks Back, Eliza Sleeping Bear, Frank Sleeping Bear, Edith Otterman, Jennie Greyhound and John Search The Enemy (policeman). (Photograph courtesy of Donovin Sprague.)

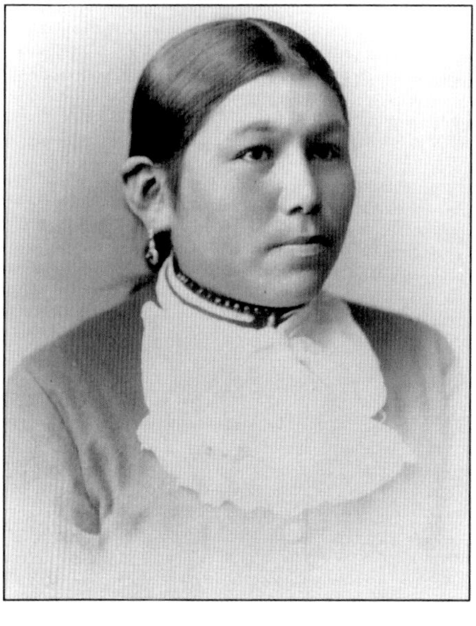

ROSA WHITE THUNDER (SICANGU). This photograph is undated. Rosa is pictured here at the Carlisle Indian School where she was a student. (Photograph courtesy of U.S. Army Military History Institute and Carlisle Indian School.)

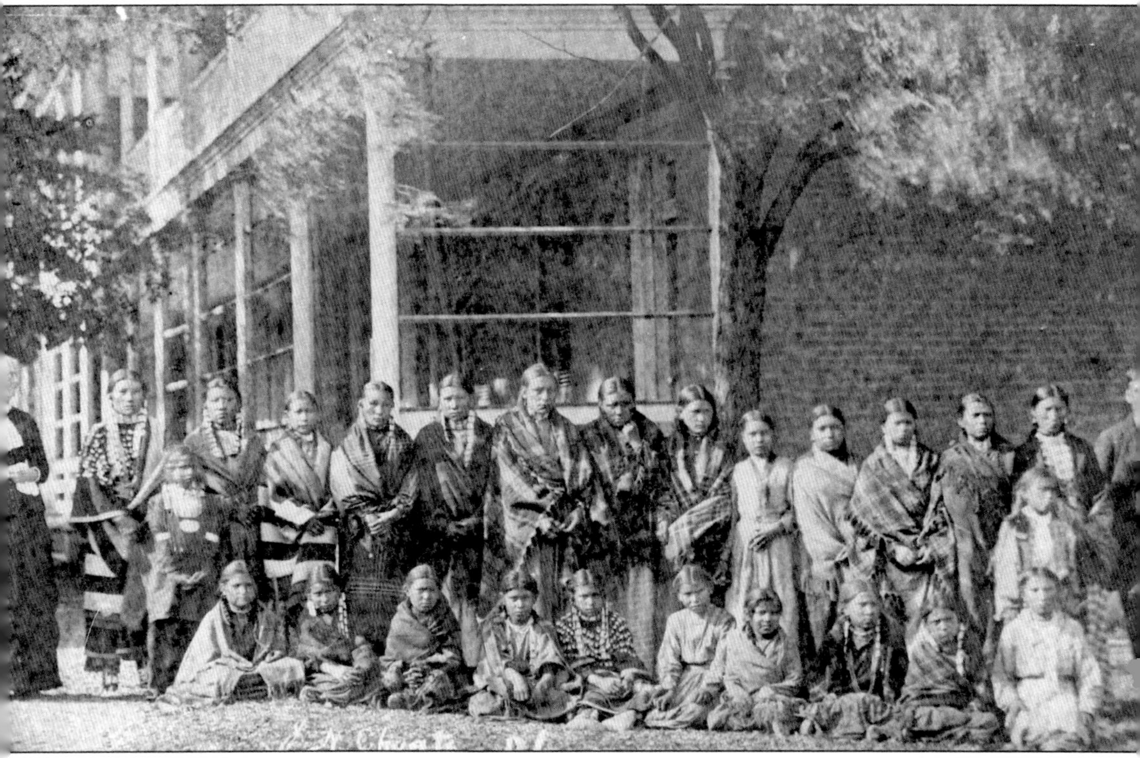

LAKOTA GIRLS FROM ROSEBUD AND PINE RIDGE AT CARLISLE INDIAN SCHOOL (SICANGU AND OGLALA). This photograph was taken by John N. Choate at Carlisle, PA, on October 6, 1879. Pictured, from left to right, are Ms. S. A. Mather (of St. Augustine, Florida), Emma Black Crow, Horace Black Crow, Maggie American Horse, Rebecca Big Star, Ida Kills Plenty, Ruth Big Head, Dora Brave Bull, Zonie McKenzie, Nellie Black Twin, Hattie Long Wolf, Rose Long Face, Nancy Shooting Cat, Agnes White Cow, Julia Good Voice, Lulu Bridgeman, Lizzie Glode, Alice Lone Bear, Mary Iron On The Head, Winnie Pawnee, Hope Blue Teeth, Stella Chasing Hawk, Maud Swift Bear, Pollock Spotted Tail, Lucy Day, Sarah Tackett, Charles Tackett (Interpreter). (Photograph courtesy of Cumberland County Historical Society, Carlisle, Pennsylvania.)

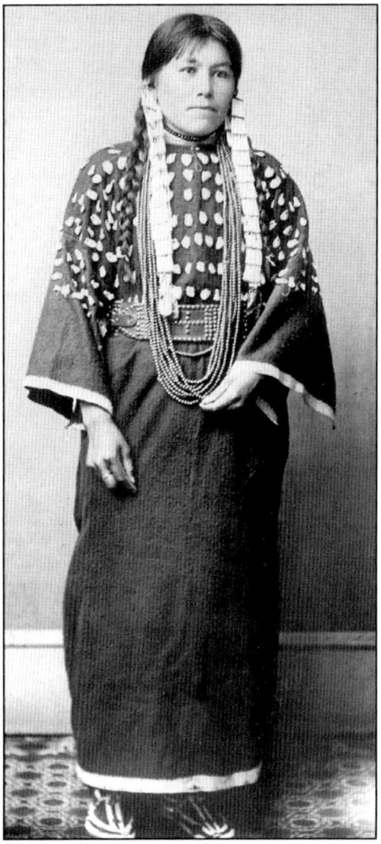

ROSA WHITE THUNDER (SICANGU). This photograph was taken *c.* 1890. Rosa "Rosy" White Thunder was a student at Carlisle Indian School. In 2001, the author visited with a family descendant, Tony White Thunder, who was told by his aunt that Rosa was also in Canada at one time with Sitting Bull's group. (Photograph courtesy of Cumberland County Historical Society, Carlisle, Pennsylvania.)

LOWER CUT MEAT CREEK CAMP INDIAN DAY SCHOOL STUDENTS. This photograph was taken by Jesse Hastings Bratley in 1897. These unidentified girls are in the sewing room at this school on Rosebud Reservation. The photograph was taken by the teacher at this school. Another school was known as Upper Cut Meat School and was located about 14 miles southwest of White River in what became known as Robert Adrian's pasture. When the school was no longer in use, Olaf Nelson of the Circle M Cattle Company used it as his headquarters. (Postcard courtesy of Donovin Sprague.)

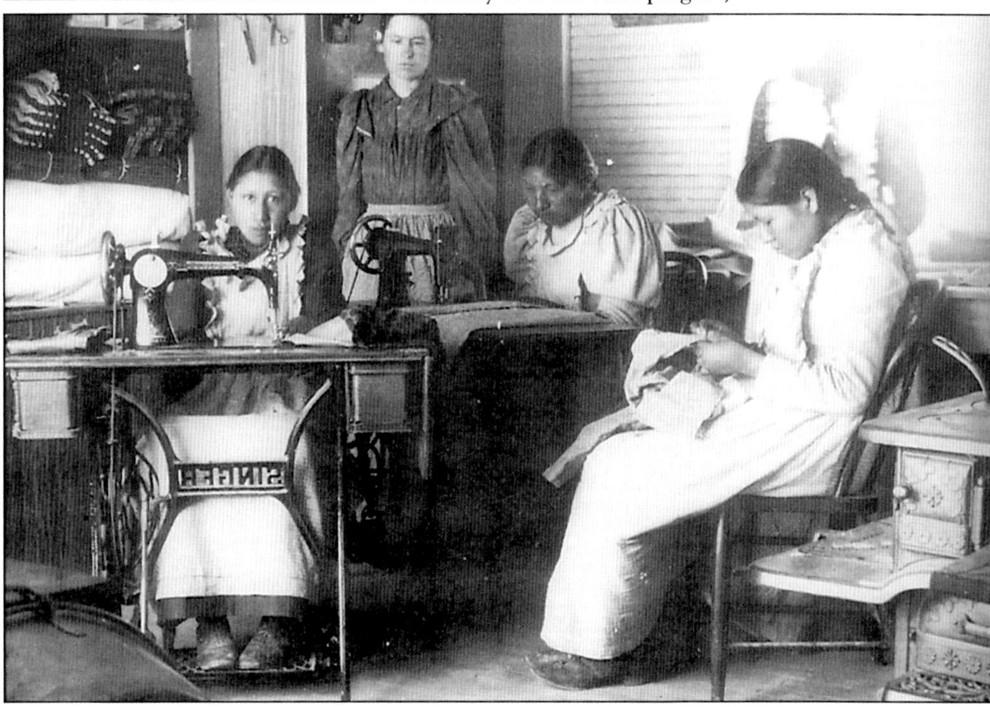

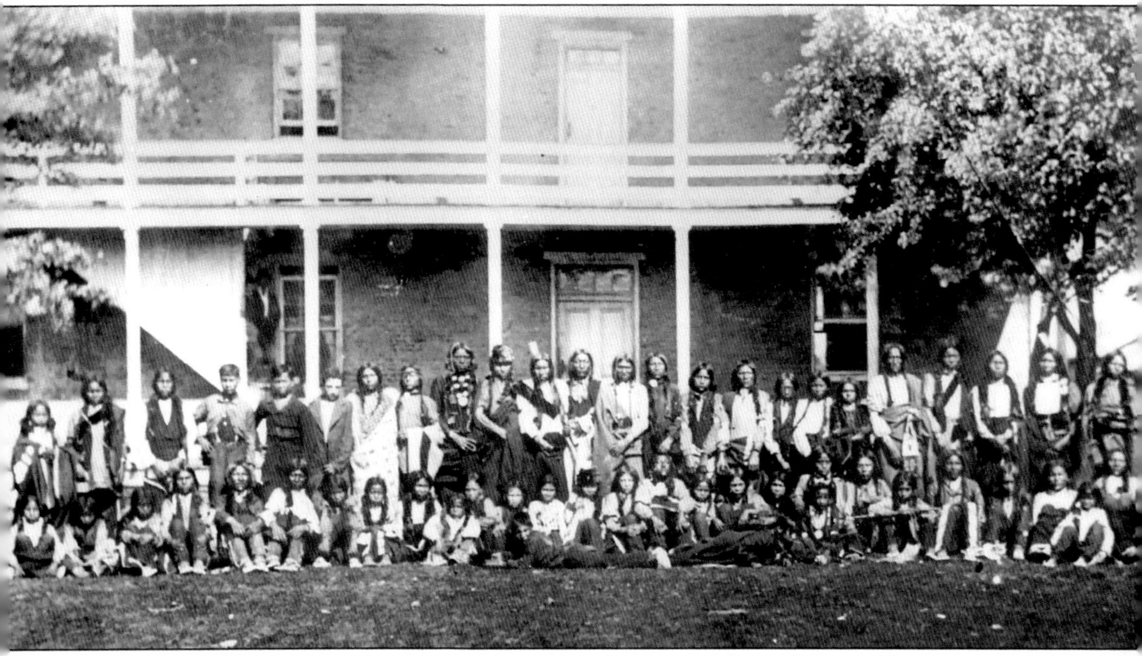

CARLISLE INDIAN SCHOOL STUDENTS FROM ROSEBUD AND PINE RIDGE (SICANGU AND OGLALA). This photograph was taken by John N. Choate at Carlisle, PA, on October 6, 1879. Pictured, from left to right, are Captain Pratt, Austin Wind Blows, Dennis Blue Tomahawk, Geoffrey Chips, Norman Thunderhawk, Horace Coarse Voice, Max Spotted Tail, James Goose Quiver, Joseph Hollow Bear, Ralph Eagle Feather, Valentine McKenzie, Thomas Roaster, Frank Twiss, Conrad Kills Alive, Lawrence War Bonnett, Marshall Bad Milk, Edgar Fire Thunder, Alvin Roaster, Frederick Cloud Bull, Clarence Whirlwind, Arthur Two Strike, Cecil Iron Wings, Theron Two Strike, Lewis Eagle Dog, Nathan Standing Cloud, Robert American Horse, Amos Lonehill, Reuben Quick Bear, Bennett Singer, Luther Standing Bear, Walter Red Face, Guy Burt, Andrew Short Bear, Arnold Iron Shell, Gilbert Iron Shell, George Hollow Horn, Moses Broken Leg, Duke Windy, David Blue Teeth, Cyrus Windy, Paul Black Bear, Rufus Black Crow, Harrison Cloud Shield, Clarence Three Stars, Julian Whistler, Bernard Hawk, Phillip Good Voice, Edward Little, William Spotted Tail, Stephen Murray, Ernest White Thunder, Herbert Kills, Pollock Spotted Tail, Morgan Big Star, Samuel High Bear, Raymond White Bear, Henry Thigh, Daniel Milk, Baldwin Blue Horse, Vincent Stranger Horse, Oliver Spotted Tail, and Charles Tackett (Interpreter). The front row and back row are not specified in this photograph. Information provided stated this was the first group of students to arrive at the Industrial School. (Photograph courtesy of Cumberland County Historical Society, Carlisle, Pennsylvania.)

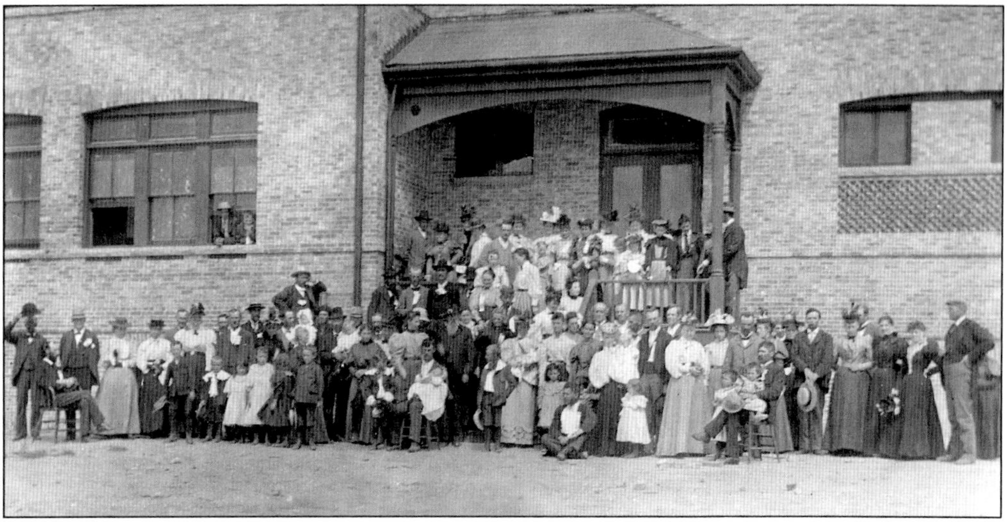

PINE RIDGE AND ROSEBUD INTER-RESERVATION TEACHER'S ASSOCIATION. This photograph was taken in 1897. (Photograph courtesy of Oglala Lakota College Archives.)

YELLOW ROBE AND STANDING BEAR BOYS AT CARLISLE INDIAN SCHOOL (SICANGU). This photograph was taken by John N. Choate at Carlisle, Pennsylvania, *c.* 1887. Pictured, from left to right, are Chauncey (Timber) Yellow Robe, Henry Standing Bear, and Richard (Wounded) Yellow Robe. Henry Standing Bear was the son of Chief George Standing Bear but earlier had been known as Spotted Horse when he was young. Henry's mother was Roaming Nation, the second wife of Chief George Standing Bear. The third wife of the Chief, was Lena Roaming Nation, sister of Roaming Nation. Lena may have also used the name Her Eagle Blanket and Hawk. Henry's sisters were Feather Weaver "Wanbli Koyakewin," Two Staffs "Ta Wahukeza Nunpawin," and Yellow Bird "Zintkazawin." His brothers were Willard "Never Defeated" and Ellis "Totola Wopotapi." These Lakota names came from statements of the family, and they may not have made a distinction between full or half siblings. In Lakota culture they would be your brother or sister. (Cyrus is also another half brother, and Sarah is a half sister although her Lakota name may be listed above. Roaming Nation is also sometimes referred to as One Horse). Henry's Lakota name was Sorrel Horse and he stated that Chief Crazy Horse was a brother in law to his father, Chief George Standing Bear. (Photograph courtesy of Cumberland County Historical Society, Carlisle, Pennsylvania.)

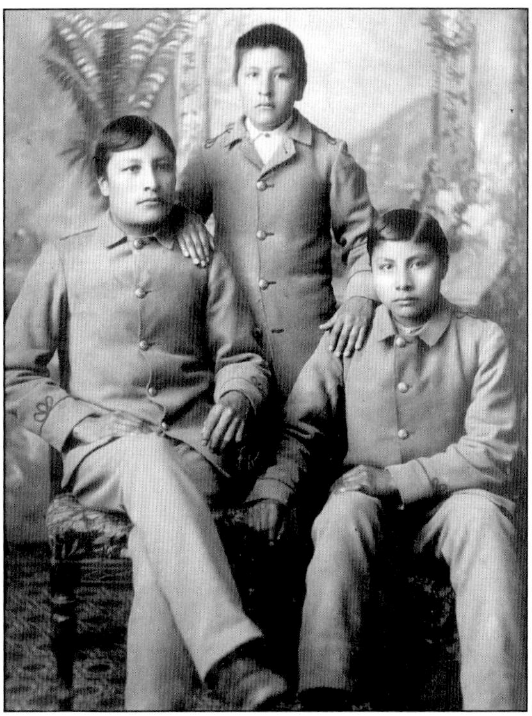

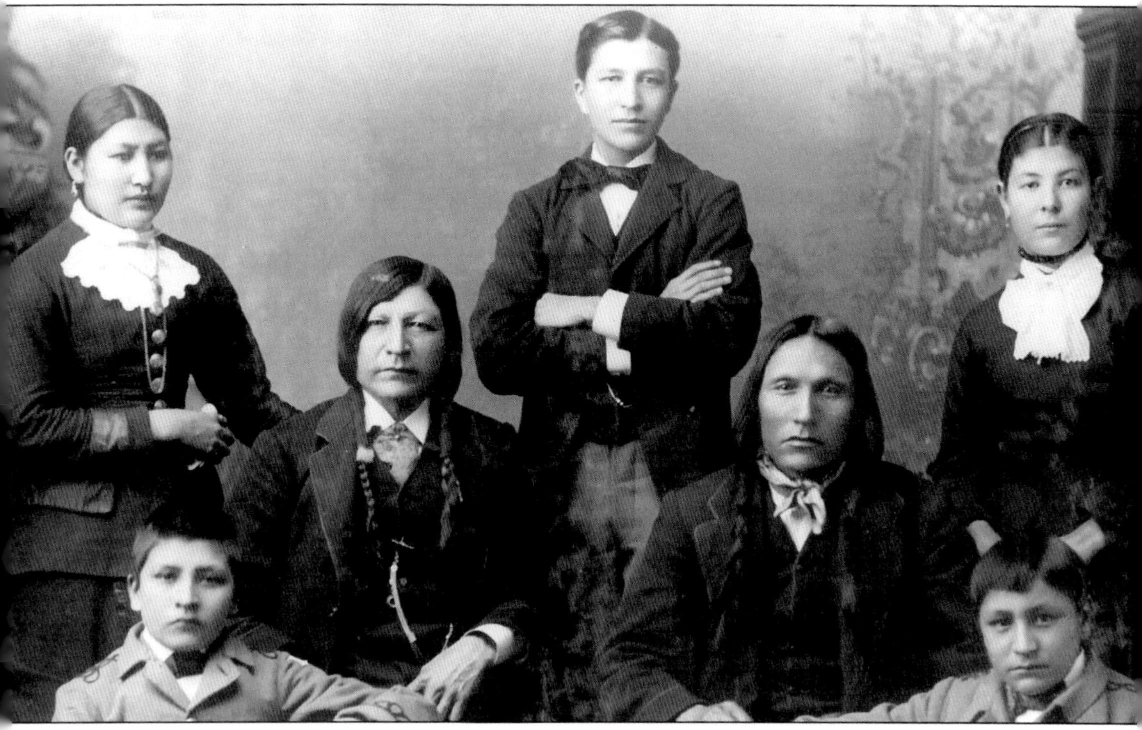

Standing Bear Family and Red Fish at Carlisle Indian School (Sicangu). This photograph was taken by John N. Choate at Carlisle, Pennsylvania, *c.*1887. Pictured, from left to right, are: (back row) Victoria Standing Bear, Luther Standing Bear, Red Fish's Daughter; (front row) Henry Standing Bear, George Standing Bear, Red Fish, and Willard Standing Bear. The elder Standing Bear and Red Fish were visiting their children at the school at this time. Luther Standing Bear was the son of Chief Standing Bear and Pretty Face. Henry and Willard were sons of Chief Standing Bear and Roaming Nation/Her Eagle Blanket, while Victoria was the daughter of Chief Standing Bear and his third wife, Lena Roaming Nation. His other children with Lena Roaming Nation were Emily (m. Peter Dillon), Alfred (married Julia Red Bear and later to Olga Cielfeldt of Sweden), Lucy (m. Henry Hunter), and Anna "Annie." Victoria later married Frank Conroy. Other children of Standing Bear and Roaming Nation/Her Eagle Blanket were Sarah and Cyrus. Henry Standing Bear later attended school in Chicago and taught at both Rosebud and Pine Ridge. Henry is credited with the idea to have Chief Crazy Horse carved in stone in the Black Hills of South Dakota at the Crazy Horse Memorial. He contacted sculptor Korczak Ziolkowski to do the work, which began in 1948. (Photograph courtesy of Cumberland County Historical Society, Carlisle, Pennsylvania.)

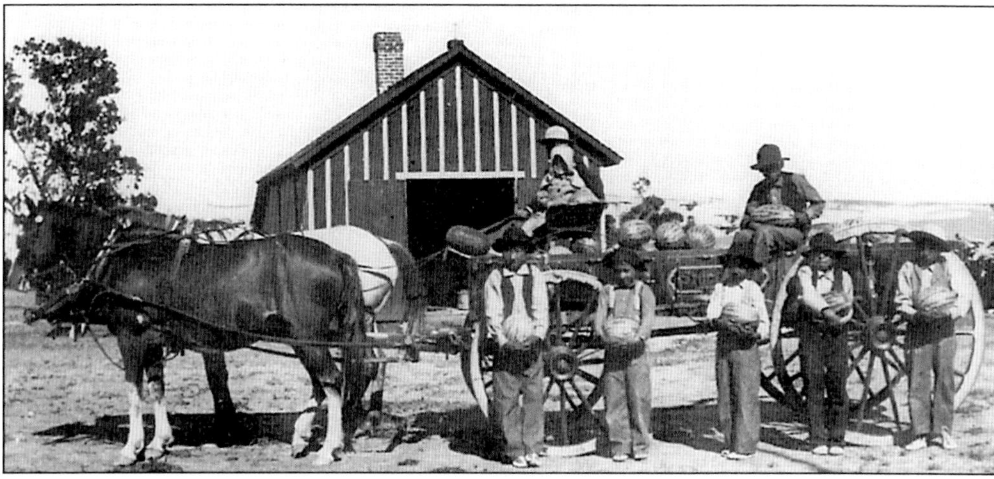

LOWER CUT MEAT CREEK CAMP INDIAN DAY SCHOOL STUDENTS. This photograph was taken by Jesse Hastings Bratley between 1895-1899. These boys are displaying watermelons grown at this day school at Rosebud Reservation. The photographer was a teacher at this school. Notable facts about the Lower Cut Meat School include that it was located in Surprise Valley Township, an area which became the pasture of Earl Adrian. Students who attended included Sam Yellow Robe, Tom and Clyde Otterman, and Mrs. Ed Eagle Bear. By 1918, Indian land allotments had moved and the school was sold to Frank Eloe, who moved it to Parmelee, South Dakota. Then Frank Halligan bought the place and used it as his house. (Postcard courtesy of Donovin Sprague.)

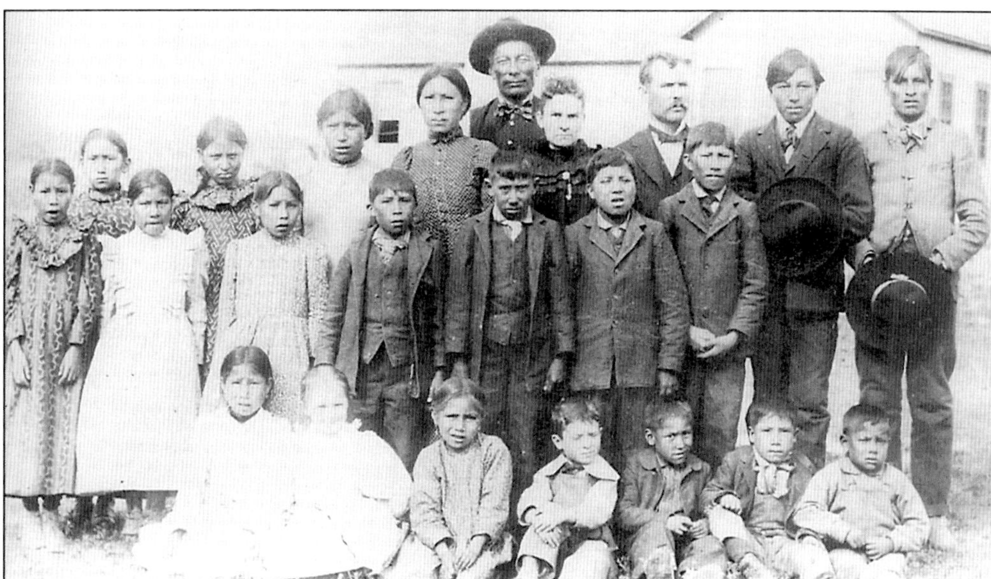

HE DOG CREEK SCHOOL STUDENTS AND TEACHERS. This photograph was taken by Jesse Hastings Bratley, a teacher at Lower Cut Meat Creek Camp Day School, between 1895-1899. These unidentified students stand outside the He Dog Creek School on Rosebud Reservation. The two non-Indian teachers are Mr. and Mrs. Arthur E. McFatridge. (Postcard courtesy of Donovin Sprague.)

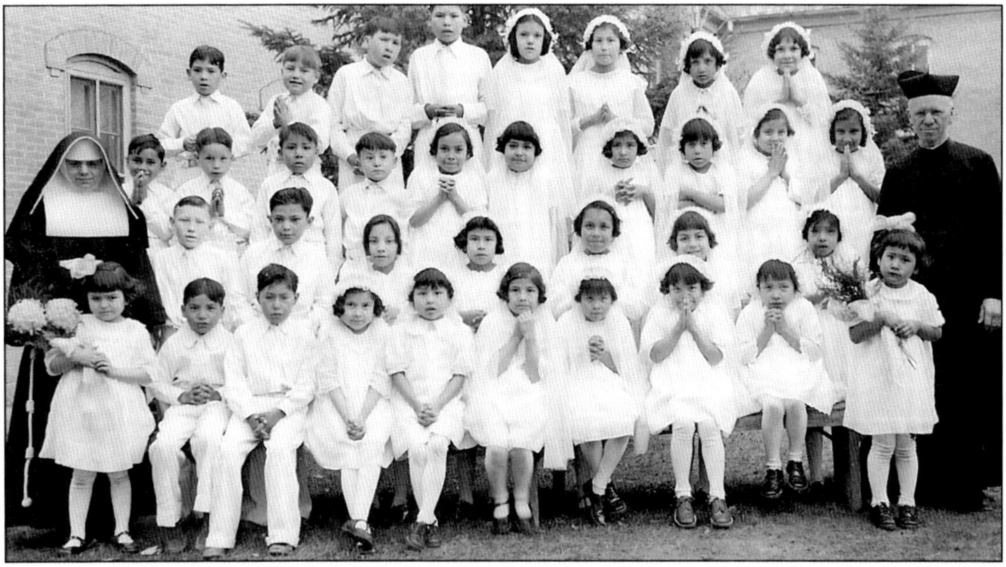

First Communion Class at Holy Rosary Mission, 1940. This photograph was taken in 1940. This is the first communion class at Holy Rosary Mission at Pine Ridge Reservation. Most of the students in the early class pictures from Holy Rosary Mission and St. Francis Mission are unidentified. This photograph is typical of many that the author viewed at St. Francis Museum Archives on Rosebud Reservation where they house 42,000 pictures. At left is Sister Ann and at right is Father Martin Schiltz, S.J. (Photograph courtesy of Red Cloud Heritage Center and Brother Simon, S.J.)

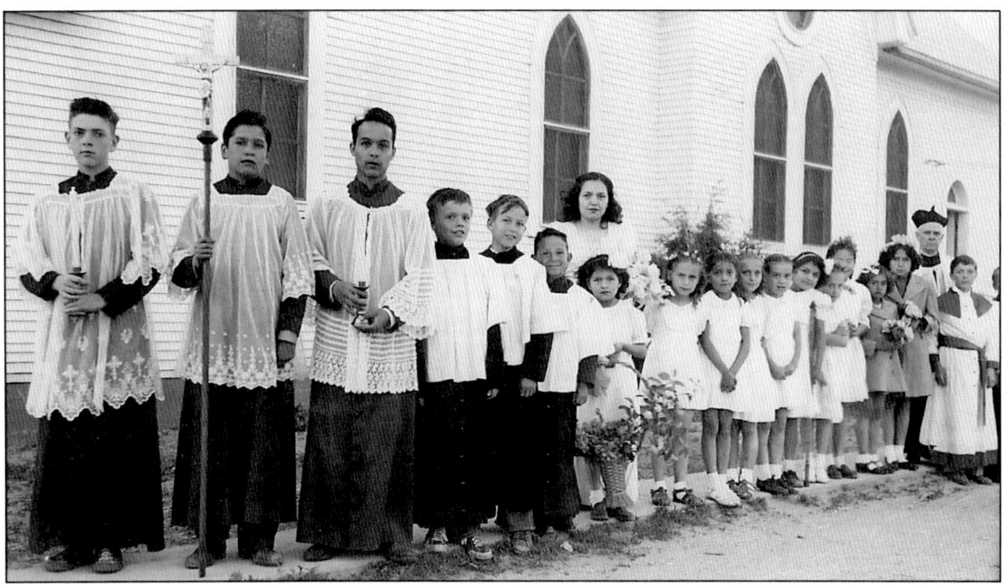

First Communion Class at Holy Rosary Mission, 1947. Photograph taken in 1947. This is the first communion class for this group of boys and girls at Pine Ridge Reservation. Some students from Rosebud attended the Holy Rosary Catholic Mission, but St. Francis Mission at Rosebud had the largest number of Sicangu students. (Photograph courtesy of Red Cloud Heritage Center and Brother Simon, S.J.)

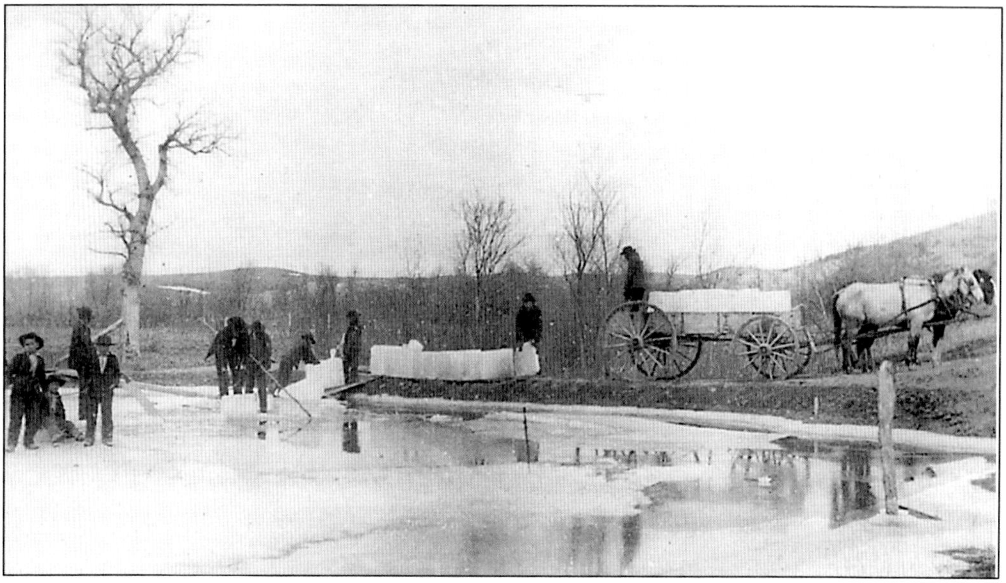

Lower Cut Meat Creek Camp Indian Day School Students. This photograph was taken by Jesse Hastings Bratley in 1898. The students are cutting and loading ice onto the wagon to be delivered to an ice house which was built by the students. The ice was used to preserve milk and butter. The photograph was taken by their teacher at Rosebud Reservation. (Postcard courtesy of Donovin Sprague.)

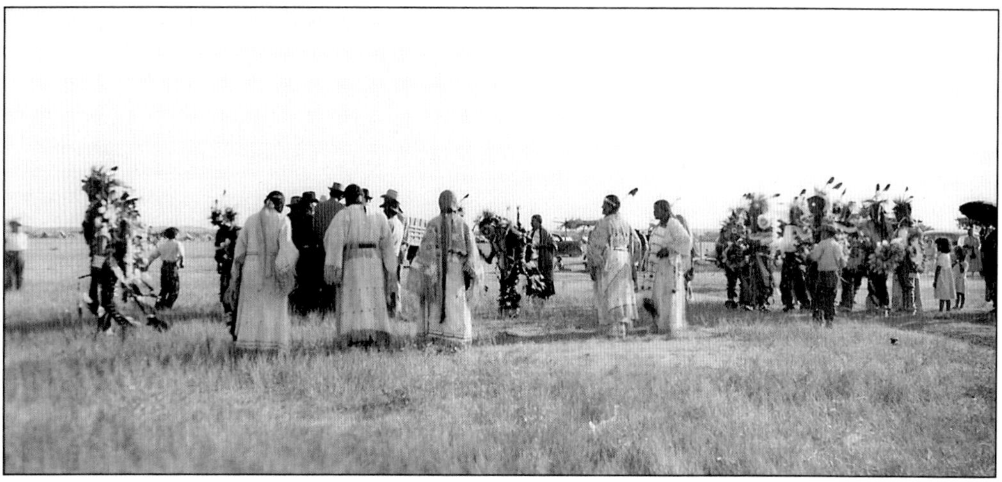

Lakota Dance and Ceremony. This photograph is undated. The people are gathered here for a traditional dance and ceremony. A drum group is performing at left center in a small circle wearing hats, while the dancers in the larger circle begin to perform. (Photograph courtesy of Red Cloud Heritage Center and Brother Simon, S.J.)

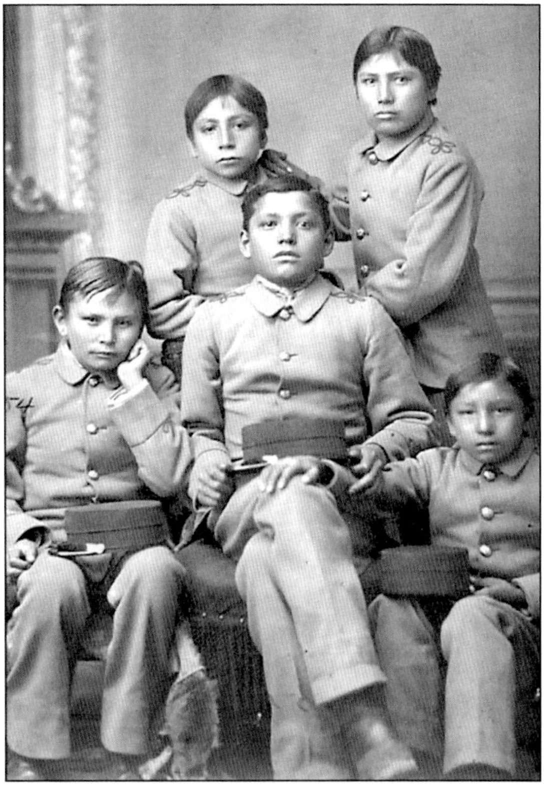

STUDENTS AT CARLISLE INDIAN SCHOOL. This photograph was taken by John N. Choate in 1881. Shown are Reuben Quick Bear (Sicangu), Bernard Ring Thunder (Sicangu), John Renville (Sisseton Dakota), Horace Coarse Voice (Sicangu). This photograph was taken at the Carlisle Indian School. The school recorded these names of the children and relatives of Coarse Voice in 1879: Little Wolf, One That Kills Seven Horses, Wind Blows, White Whirlwind, Negut, Chitsetshe, and Passon. (Photograph courtesy of Princeton Collections of Western Americana.)

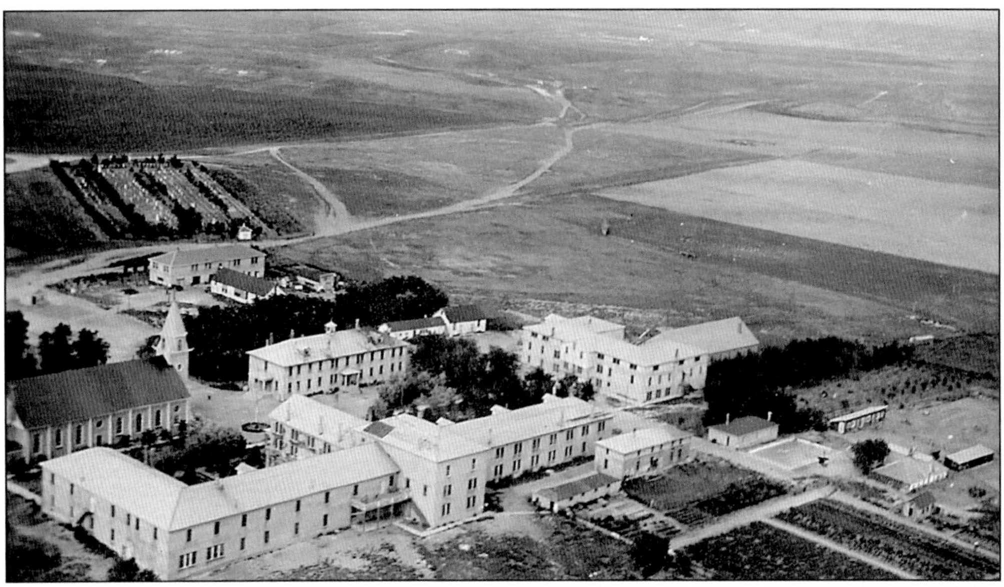

ST. FRANCIS MISSION INDIAN SCHOOL. This undated photograph is an aerial view of the Mission School at St. Francis, South Dakota. Father Eugene Buechel was at St. Francis Mission at Rosebud Reservation and also at Holy Rosary Mission at Pine Ridge Reservation. Brother Simon, S.J., of Holy Rosary Mission and Red Cloud Heritage Center assisted the author and noted that Father Buechel spent nine years at Holy Rosary Mission in 1907, 1908-1916, and 1926-1928. (Postcard courtesy of Red Cloud Heritage Center and Brother Simon, S.J.)

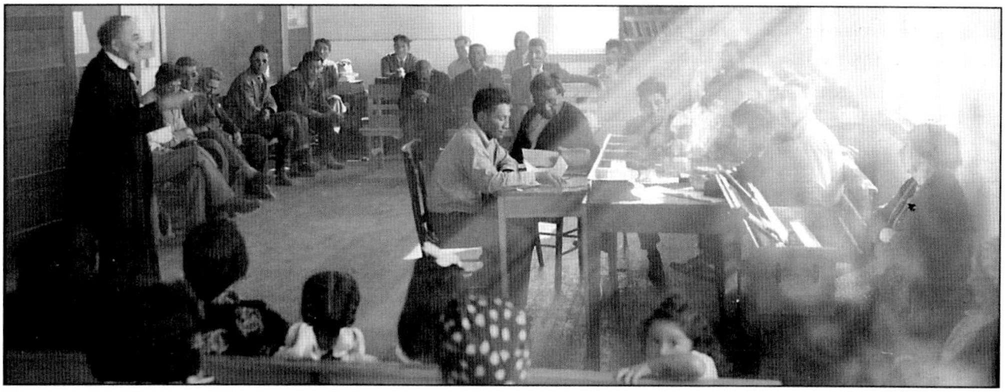

REVEREND EUGENE BUECHEL, S.J., AT A ST. JOSEPH'S-ST. MARY'S SOCIETY MEETING. Father Buechel was born in Schleida, Germany, in 1874. He entered the Jesuit Order in Holland in 1897, came to the United States in 1900, and was ordained in 1906. In 1907, he was at Holy Rosary Mission at Pine Ridge and was at St. Francis Mission at Rosebud until 1923. He conducted prayer meetings in the Lakota language in chapels and homes and began cataloging Lakota words for a dictionary, a project he started in 1910 (it became the largest and most complete collection of its kind). He died before the project could be finished but he did publish a "Bible History" in 1923 and a "Grammar of Lakota" in 1939. Father Buechel received the Lakota name of Wanbli Sapa (Black Eagle). When Buechel died in 1954, Rev. John F. Bryde, S.J., took his work and completed a "Teton Dictionary." Bryde was granted leave to move the manuscript from St. Francis Mission to Holy Rosary Mission at Pine Ridge. Through efforts of various people, the "Lakota-English Dictionary," which Father Buechel started was published and is the largest Lakota dictionary today. (Photograph courtesy of Red Cloud Heritage Center and Brother Simon, S.J.)

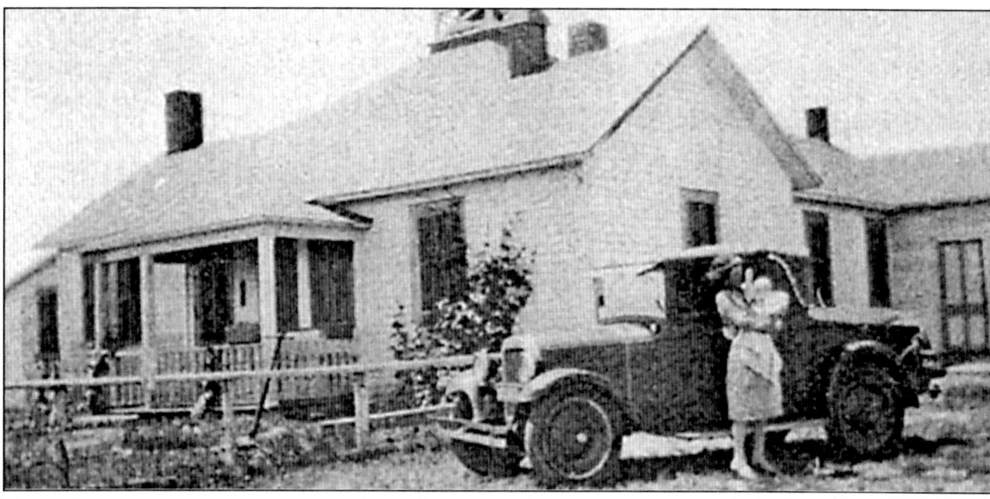

RING THUNDER DAY SCHOOL. This school was located on the Little White River Hill near a large Indian camp. The area is named for the itancan (leader/headman) Ring Thunder "Cangleska Wakinyan," who was born in 1841. Dave Blue Thunder was a student at the school. Two other area schools were Blackpipe Day School and Corn Creek School. Blackpipe was north of Norris on Blackpipe Creek. Ed Eagle Bear and Quick Bear were among the students who attended the school. Students at Corn Creek School included Abbie Chasing Horse-Red Fish, Alex Dog Eye, A. C. Long Warrior, Henry and Jennie Medicine Bear, and Luke Leading Cloud. Corn Creek School was seven miles north of Norris and later moved into Norris. (Photograph courtesy of Mellette County Historical Society.)

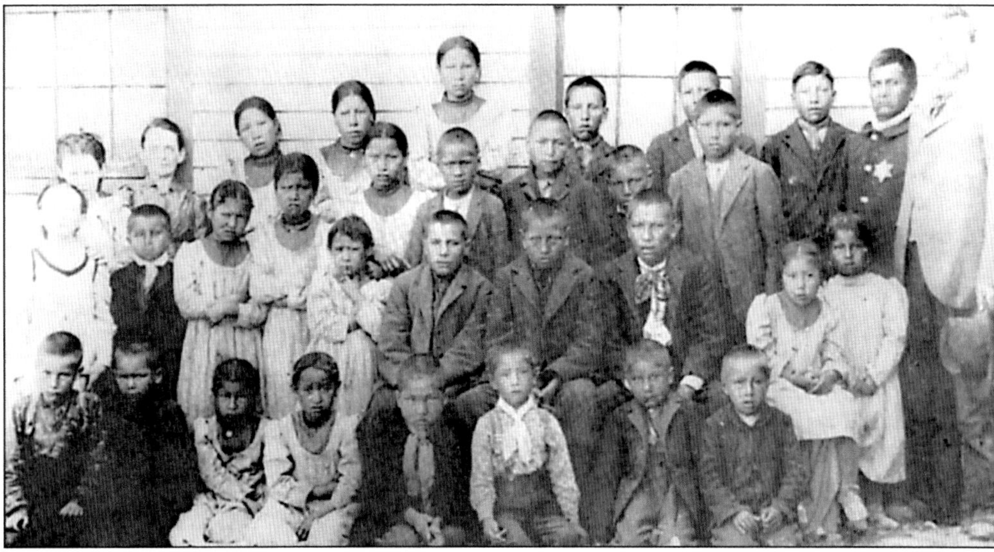

BLACKPIPE CREEK DAY SCHOOL. Pictured in 1894, from left to right, are: (front row) Albert Punch Him, Earnest Quick Bear, Ruth Little Chief, Mollie Blue Bird, Abram Horned Antelope, Jesse Charging In The Timber, Henry Eagle Bear, and Joe Weeds Father; (second row) Myra Good Thunder, Frank Eagle Horn, Rex Charging Bear, John Bull Walks Behind, Jenny Porcupine, and Hattie Charging Bear; (third row) unidentified girl, Charles Weeds Father, Mary Eagle Bear, Lucy Charging Bear, Allie Skunk, Henry Charging Bear, James Red Weasel, Patrick Yellow Bird, and Emmet Eagle Bear; (back row) Anna Tripp, Mrs. Emelina Tripp (housekeeper), Ida Charging In The Timber, Annie Little Chief, Mittie Quick Bear, Grover Red Weasel, Silas Quick Bear, Zander Big Crow, unidentified policeman, and John B. Tripp Sr. (teacher). The names Joe and Charles Weeds Father are complete names and their father was named Weeds Father. (Photograph courtesy of Donovin Sprague.)

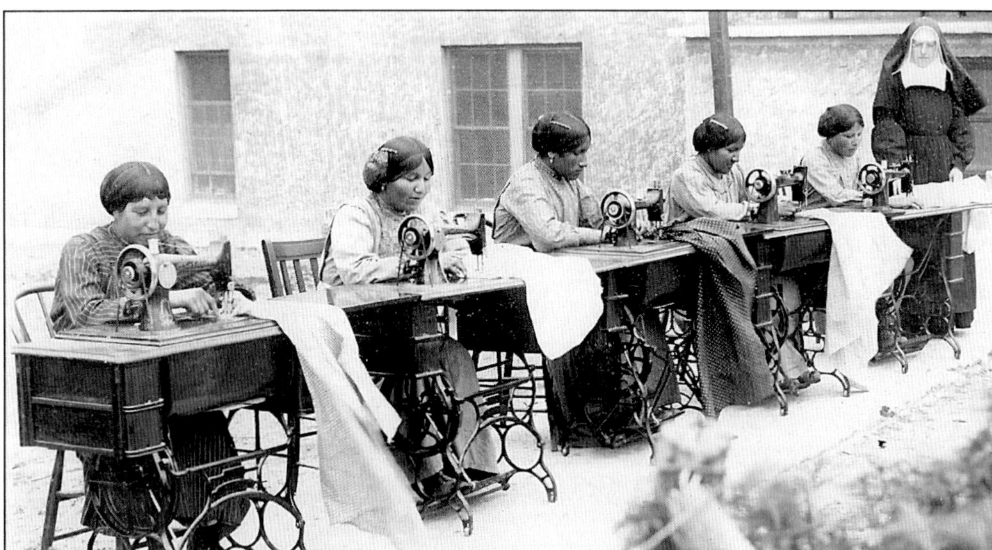

ST. FRANCIS MISSION SEWING CLASS. This photograph is undated. (Postcard courtesy of Red Cloud Heritage Center and Brother Simon, S.J.)

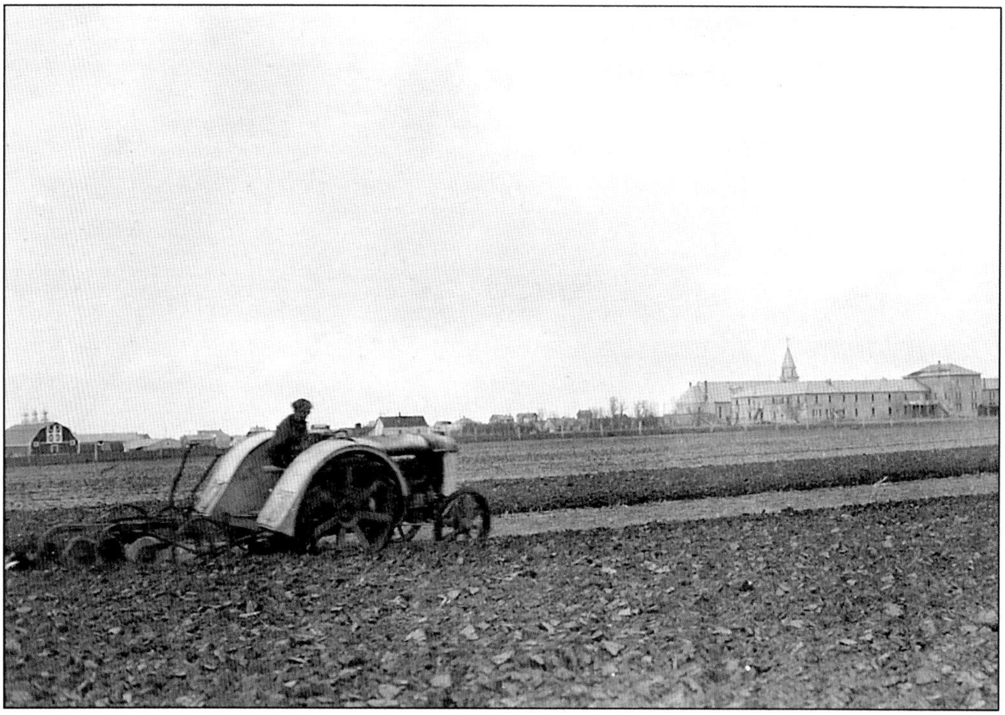

ST. FRANCIS MISSION FARMING SCENE. This photograph is undated. This boy on the tractor is plowing the field to prepare for a crop to be planted, with St. Francis Mission in the background. Earlier, Swift Bear's winter count depicted how his crops failed and how he was shot in his own field. Corn planted at that time was called Ree (Arikara) corn, which produced roasting ears in about eight weeks. Crops of corn, pumpkins, squash, and field beans were often wiped out by drought and grasshoppers. (Postcard courtesy of Red Cloud Heritage Center and Brother Simon, S.J.)

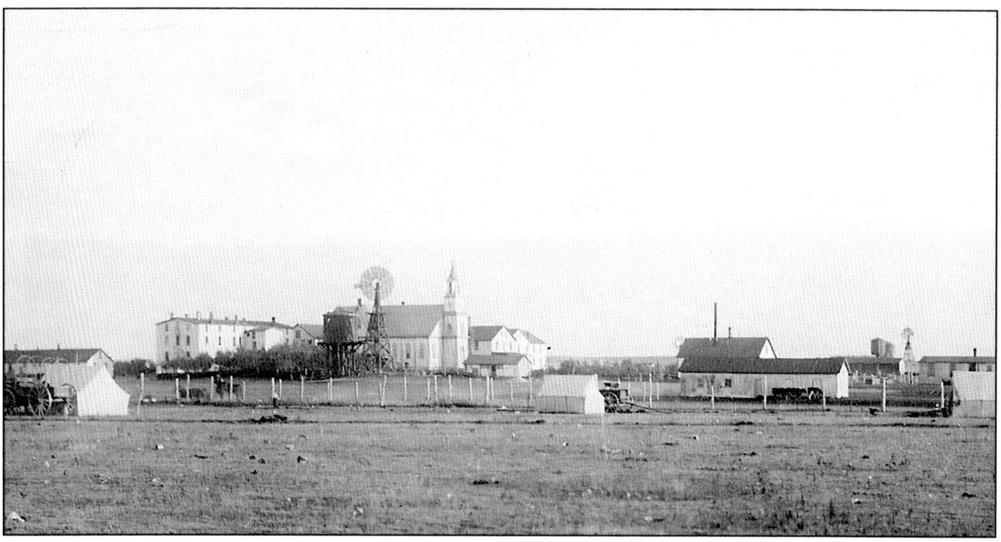

ST. FRANCIS MISSION. This photograph is undated. (Postcard courtesy of Red Cloud Heritage Center and Brother Simon, S.J.)

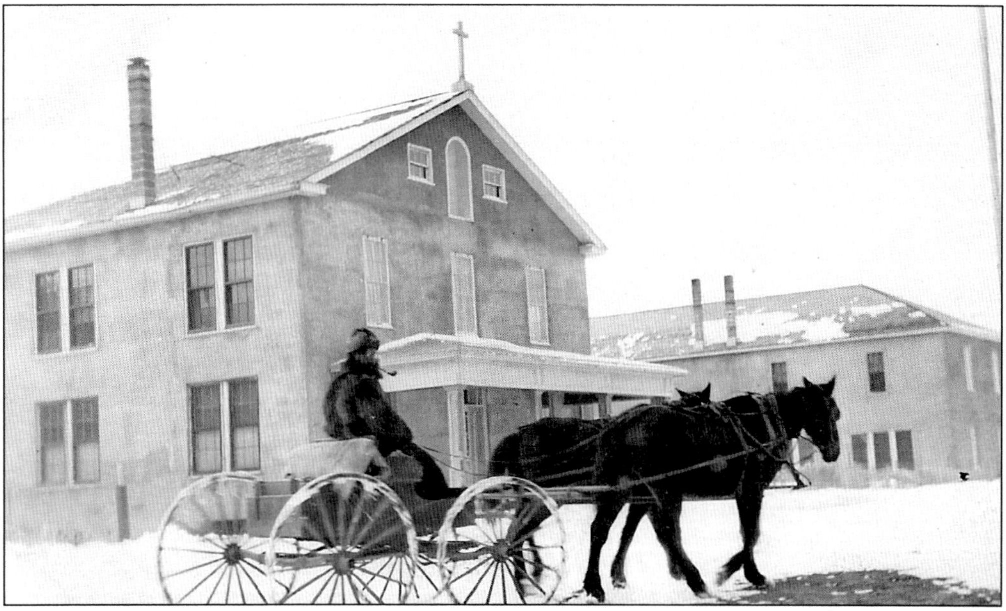

FATHER GROTHE AT ST. FRANCIS MISSION. This photograph is undated. Father Grothe is pictured with a team of horses and wagon in the winter. As early as 1885, Two Strike and others chose a location, and St. Francis Mission School opened on January 1, 1886. The St. Francis Indian School was later formed around 1971. (Postcard courtesy of Red Cloud Heritage Center and Brother Simon, S.J.)

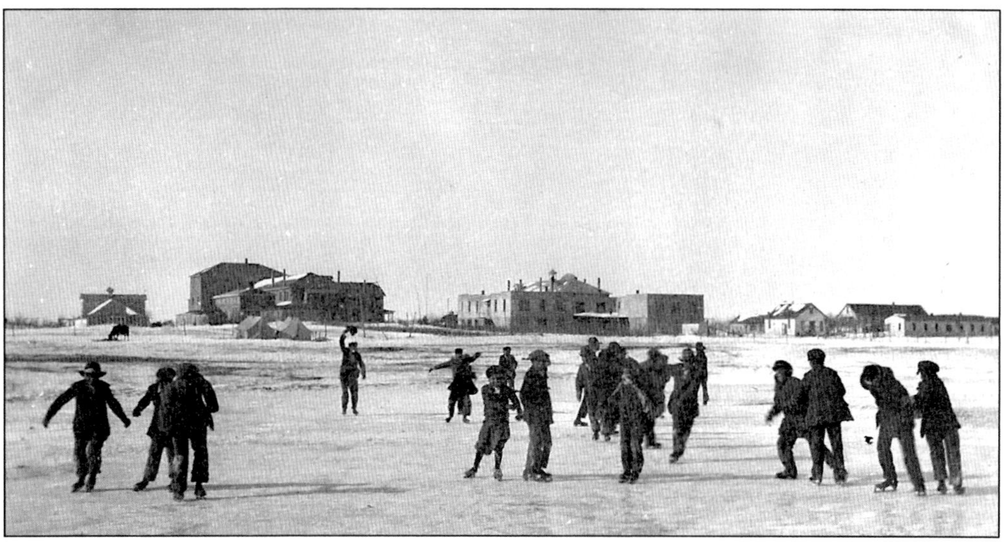

BOYS ICE SKATING AT ST. FRANCIS MISSION SCHOOL. This photograph is undated. The boys are having an ice skating party with St. Francis Mission in the background. (Postcard courtesy of Red Cloud Heritage Center and Brother Simon, S.J.)

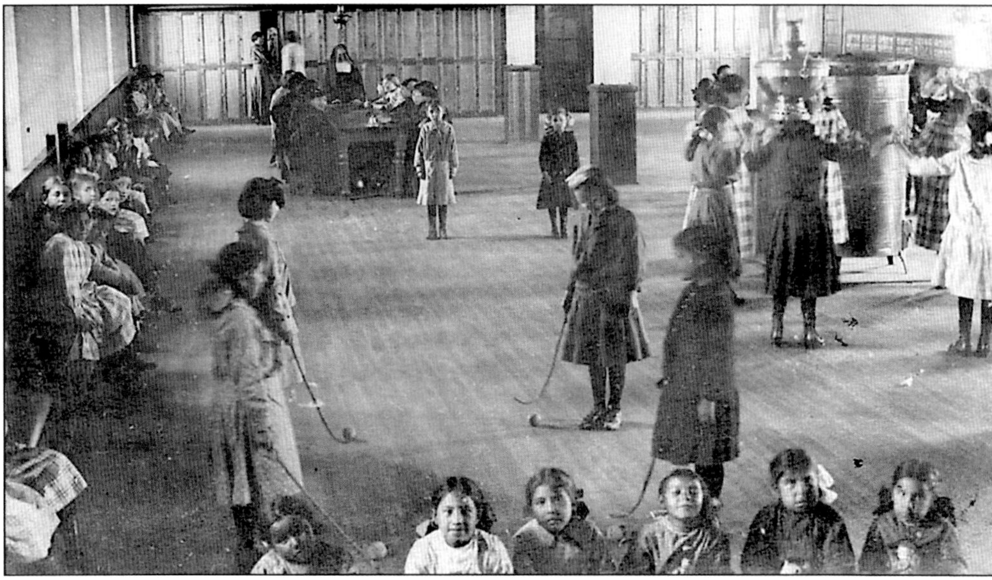

GIRLS SHINNY GAME AT ST. FRANCIS MISSION SCHOOL. This photograph is undated. The girls are playing the Lakota shinny ball game at St. Francis Mission School. The school was originally named Owl Feather Bonnet "Hinhan Sunwapa," though the name was later changed to honor St. Francis of Assisi. "Sapunti" means "where the black robes live," referring to the robes worn by the priests. (Postcard courtesy of Red Cloud Heritage Center and Brother Simon, S.J.)

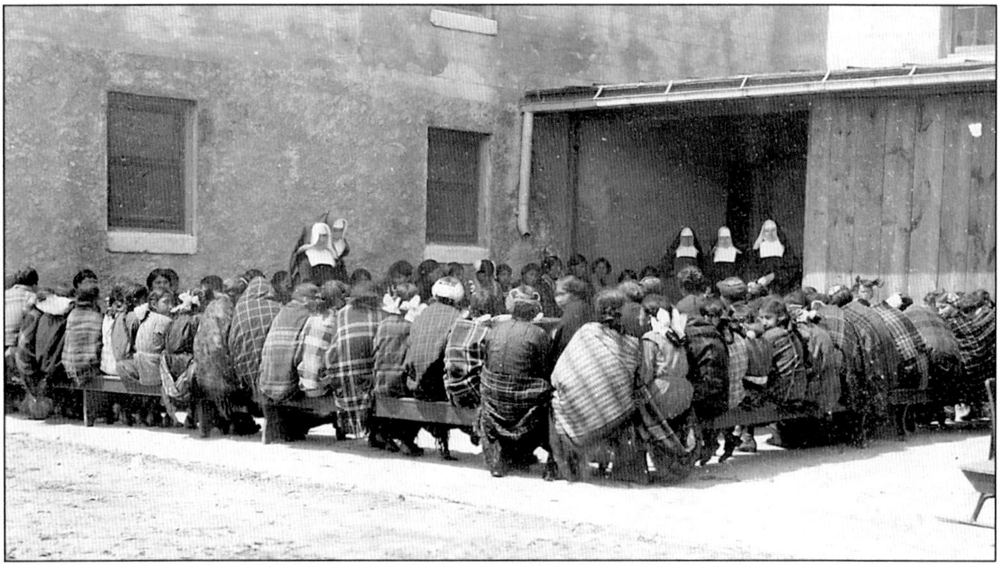

GIRLS AT ST. FRANCIS MISSION SCHOOL. This photograph is undated. The girls are seated on benches wearing shawls at St. Francis Mission School. (Postcard courtesy of Red Cloud Heritage Center and Brother Simon, S.J.)

ST. FRANCIS MISSION SCHOOL. This photograph is undated. This girl is in the classroom at St. Francis Mission School. (Postcard courtesy of Red Cloud Heritage Center and Brother Simon, S.J.)

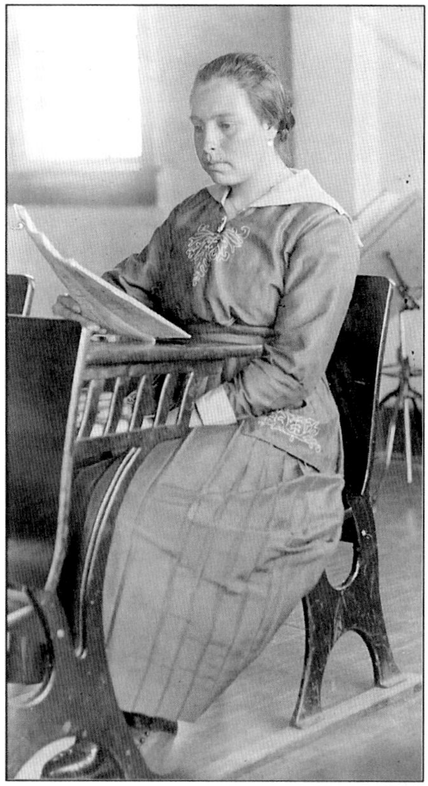

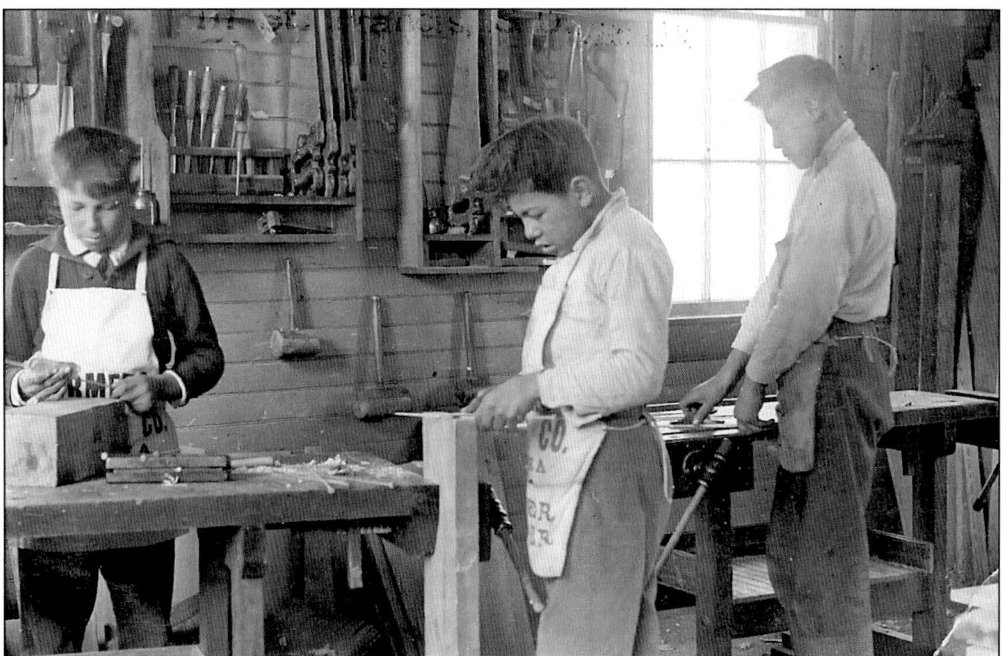

CARPENTRY STUDENTS AT ST. FRANCIS MISSION SCHOOL. This photograph is undated. These boys are learning the trade of carpentry at St. Francis Mission School. (Postcard courtesy of Red Cloud Heritage Center and Brother Simon, S.J.)

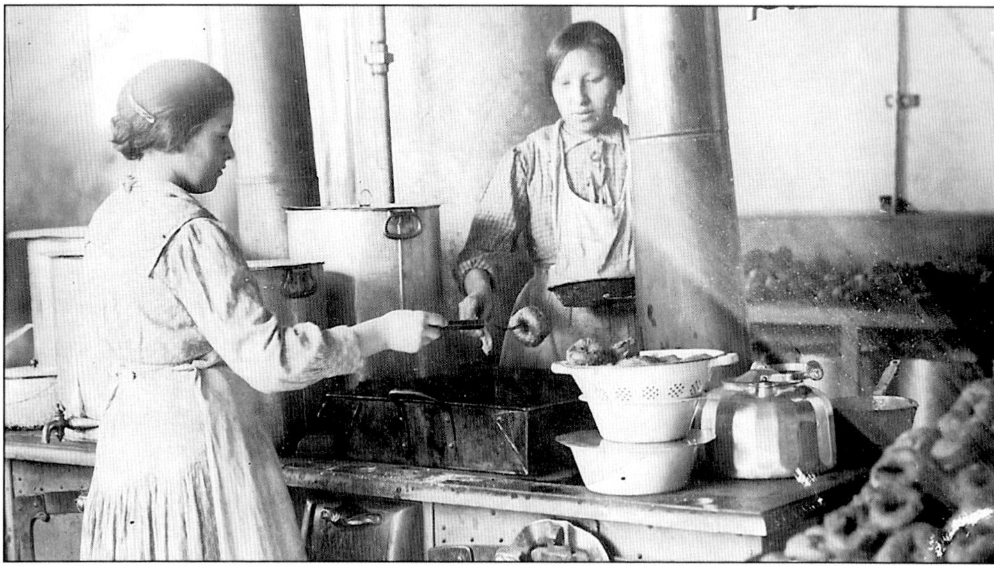

GIRLS COOKING AT ST. FRANCIS MISSION SCHOOL.. This photograph is undated. These two girls are making donuts in the kitchen at St. Francis Mission School. (Postcard courtesy of Red Cloud Heritage Center and Brother Simon, S.J.)

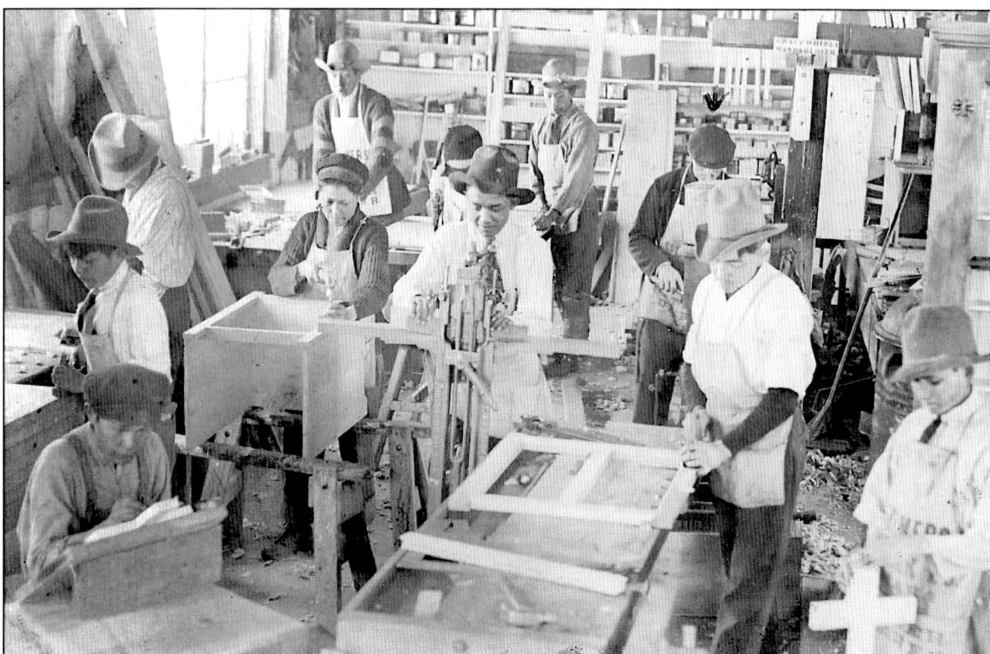

CARPENTRY CLASS AT ST. FRANCIS MISSION SCHOOL. This photograph is undated. This is the boys carpentry class at work at St. Francis Mission School. Brother Hartmann is identified with a dark cap and an ink arrow marks him in the back, to the right. (Postcard courtesy of Red Cloud Heritage Center and Brother Simon, S.J.)

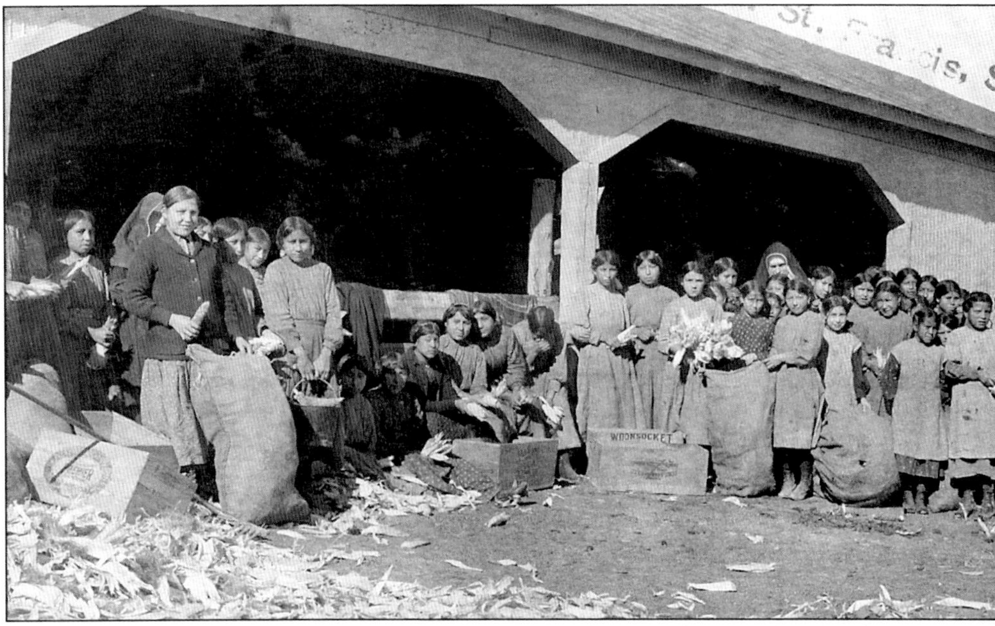

CHORES AT ST. FRANCIS MISSION SCHOOL. This photograph is undated. These girls are gathering corn husks to sack them up and to be used as padding in bed mattresses. (Postcard courtesy of Red Cloud Heritage Center and Brother Simon, S.J.)

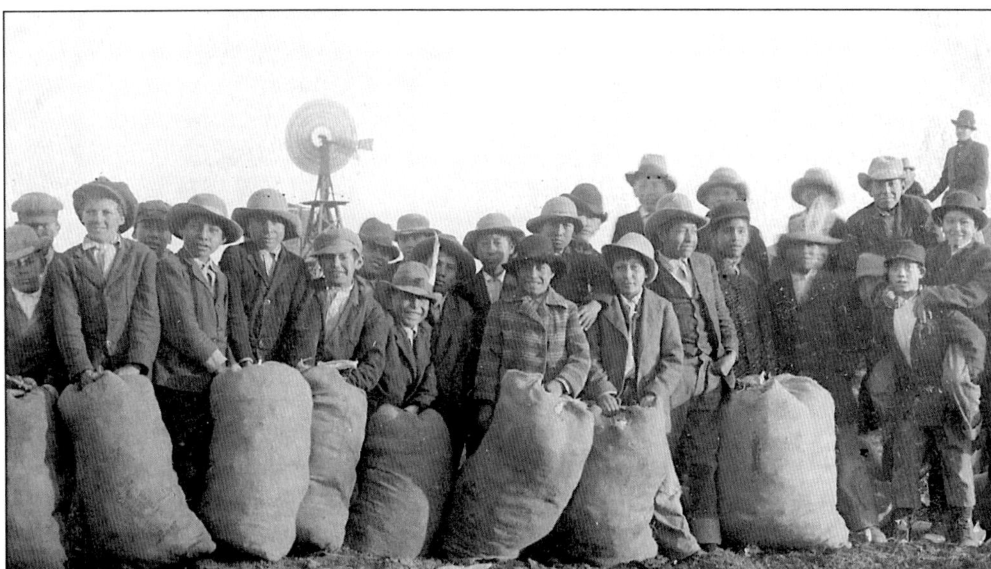

MORE CHORES AT ST. FRANCIS MISSION SCHOOL. This photograph is undated. These boys have sacked up corn husks to fill bed mattresses at the school. (Postcard courtesy of Red Cloud Heritage Center and Brother Simon, S.J.)

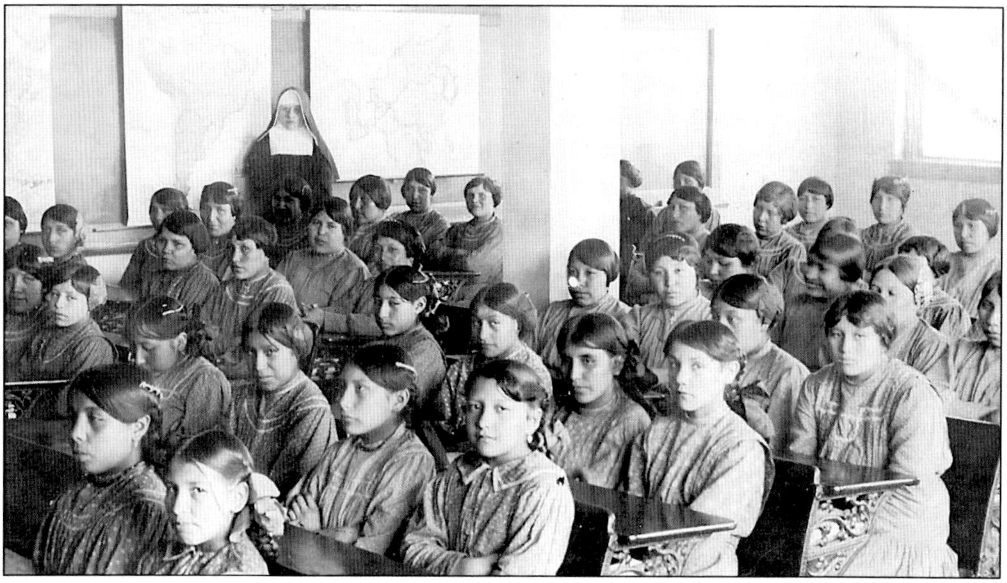

A CLASSROOM AT ST. FRANCIS MISSION SCHOOL. This photograph is undated. This picture shows the inside of a classroom at St. Francis Mission School. (Postcard courtesy of Red Cloud Heritage Center and Brother Simon, S.J.)

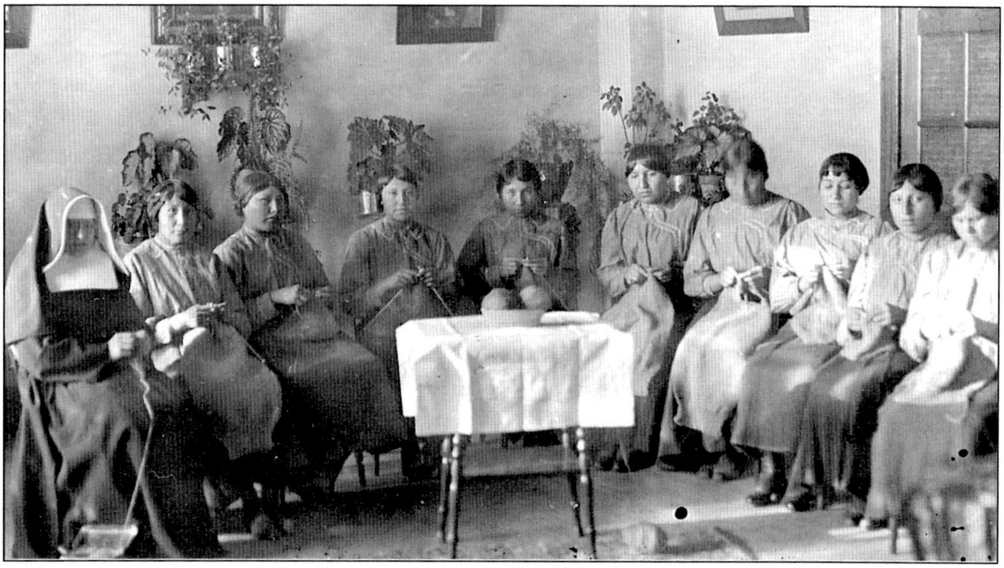

GIRLS SEWING AT ST. FRANCIS MISSION SCHOOL. This photograph is undated. These girls are sewing at the mission school. (Postcard courtesy of Red Cloud Heritage Center and Brother Simon, S.J.)

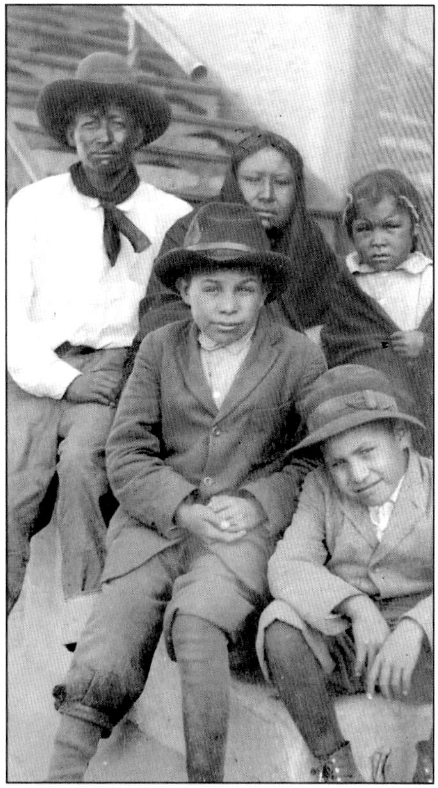

ROSEBUD RESERVATION FAMILY. This photograph is undated. This family is unidentified. (Postcard courtesy of Red Cloud Heritage Center and Brother Simon, S.J.)

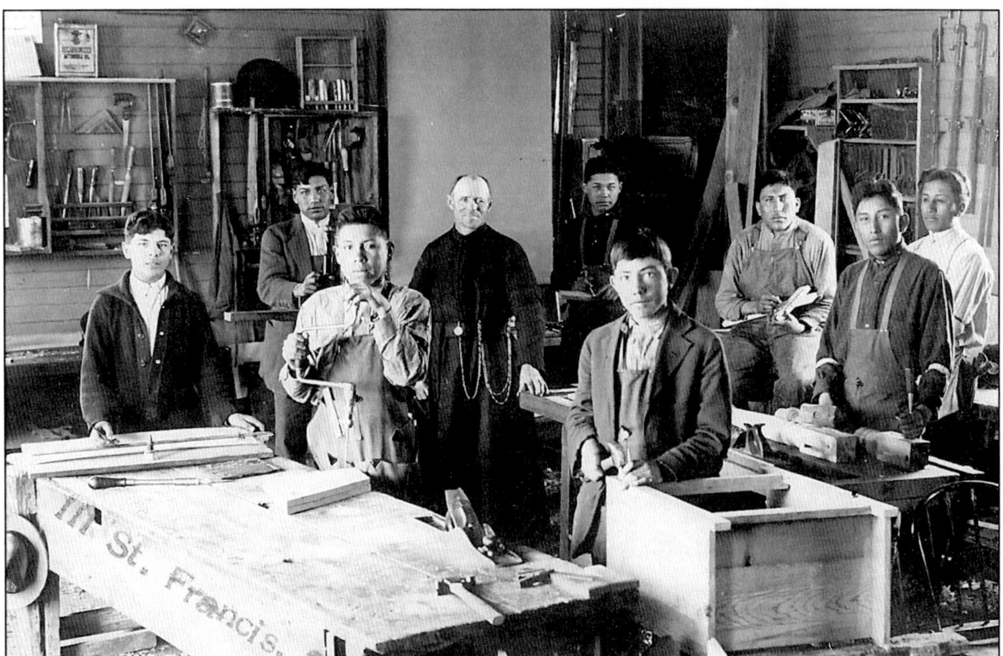

CARPENTRY CLASS AT ST. FRANCIS MISSION SCHOOL. This photograph is undated. This is Brother Hartmann pictured with another of the boy's carpentry class at St. Francis Mission School. (Postcard courtesy of Red Cloud Heritage Center and Brother Simon, S.J.)

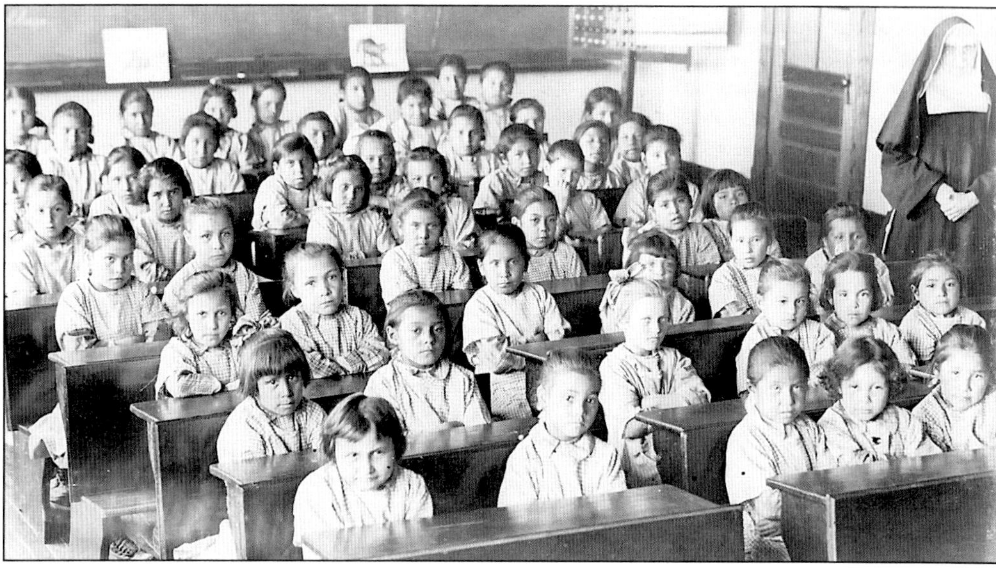

St. Francis Mission School Class. This photograph is undated. Boys and girls are pictured in this early class photograph at St. Francis Mission School. (Postcard courtesy of Red Cloud Heritage Center and Brother Simon, S.J.)

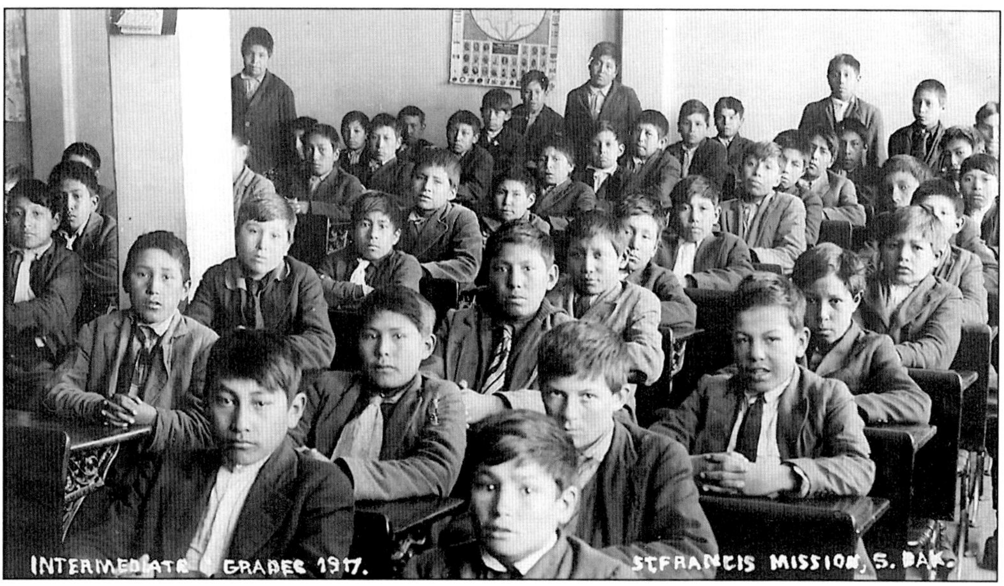

St. Francis Mission School Intermediate Grades. Photograph taken in 1917. This is the intermediate boys' grades at St. Francis Mission School in 1917. (Postcard courtesy of Red Cloud Heritage Center and Brother Simon, S.J.)

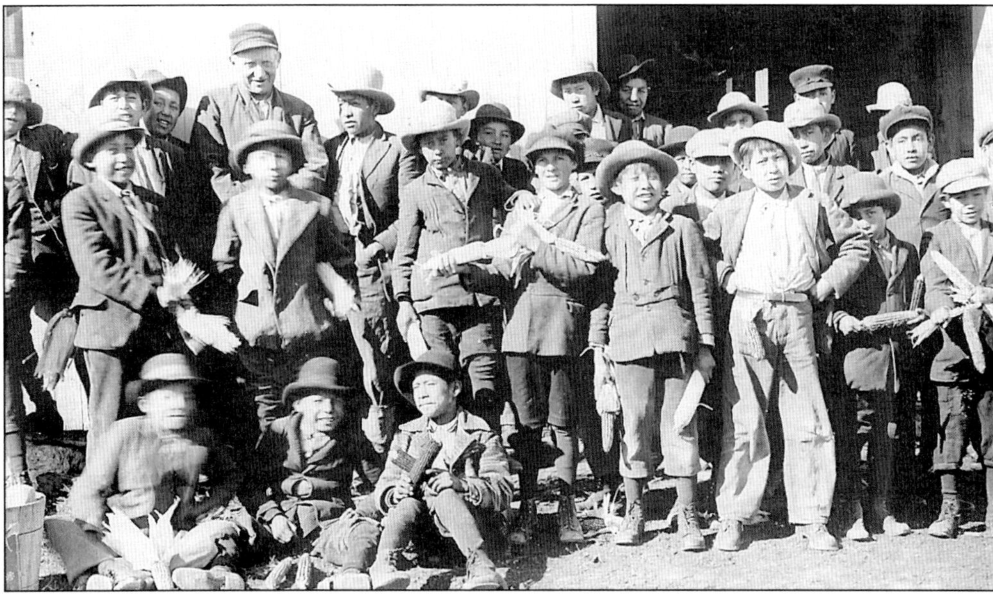

ST. FRANCIS MISSION SCHOOL. This photograph is undated. This group of boys are shown with corn they have picked. (Postcard courtesy of Red Cloud Heritage Center and Brother Simon, S.J.)

REUBEN QUICK BEAR (SICANGU). Reuben Quick Bear's birth year is listed as 1866, but we know that it was later than that from dated pictures of him at Carlisle Indian School. He was born at Fort Laramie (c. 1872) to Chief Quick Bear and Kind Hearted Woman. He was among the first group of students to attend Carlisle Indian School, arriving in 1879. Carlisle School records list the following as children and relatives of Chief Quick Bear: Want to be Chief, Kills Plenty, Kills The Enemy, and Paints Dust. When Reuben returned to Rosebud from Carlisle, he was one of the first county commissioners of Mellette County, served as postmaster at Norris, owned the Norris store, and represented his tribe in Washington, D.C., on affairs related to the Lakota. He also played a role in getting White River, South Dakota, approved as a town site and county seat location. He felt that education was a priority and helped start a school at Norris. Reuben died in 1918 and his wife Mary Quick Bear lived on her land allotment until about 1950 when she moved to White River. She lived until 1953 dying at the age of 81. A family photograph shows they had at least five children. (Photograph courtesy of Donovin Sprague.)

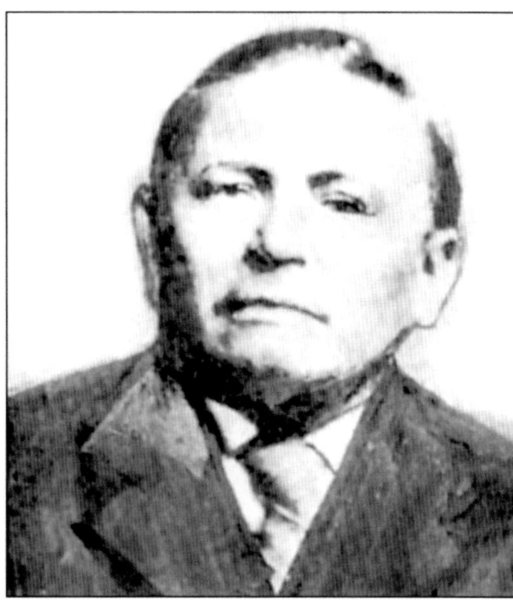

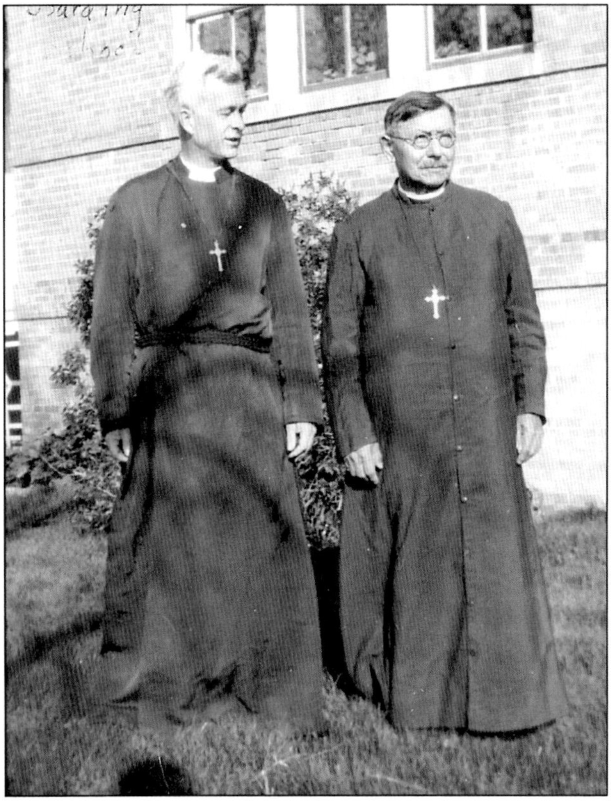

REV. BARBOUR, LEFT, AND REV. DECORY, RIGHT, (SICANGU). This photograph was taken in 1935 at the St. Francis Mission School at Rosebud Reservation. Ollie Napesni recalled in her book *Salt Camp* that the DeCorys lived south of the town of Lakeview. Other family names she recalled in the Lakeview area were Small Bear, Yellow Robe, White Hat, Search Enemy, Good Voice, Iron Boy, Little Cloud, and Marshall. Early DeCory family members the author found at Rosebud include Peter DeCory (b. 1835) from New York who married Mary Little Willow (b. 1839) at Rosebud. Their children were Julia, John, Rose, Mary, Oliver, Nellie, George, and Ben. Other DeCory family may have used the name "DeCora." (Photograph courtesy of Jace DeCory.)

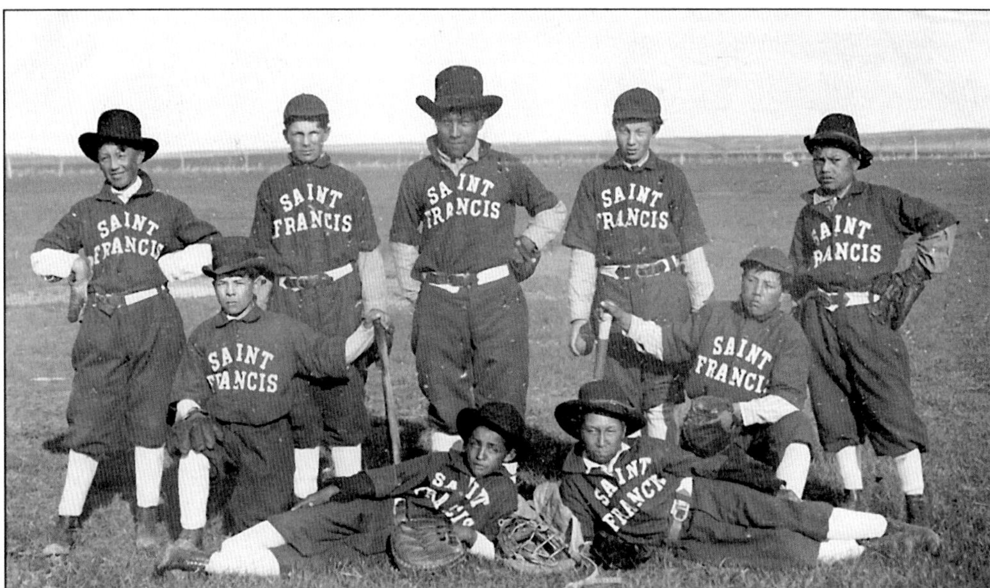

ST. FRANCIS MISSION SCHOOL BASEBALL TEAM. This photograph is undated. This baseball team of nine players is from St. Francis Mission School. (Postcard courtesy of Red Cloud Heritage Center and Brother Simon, S.J.)

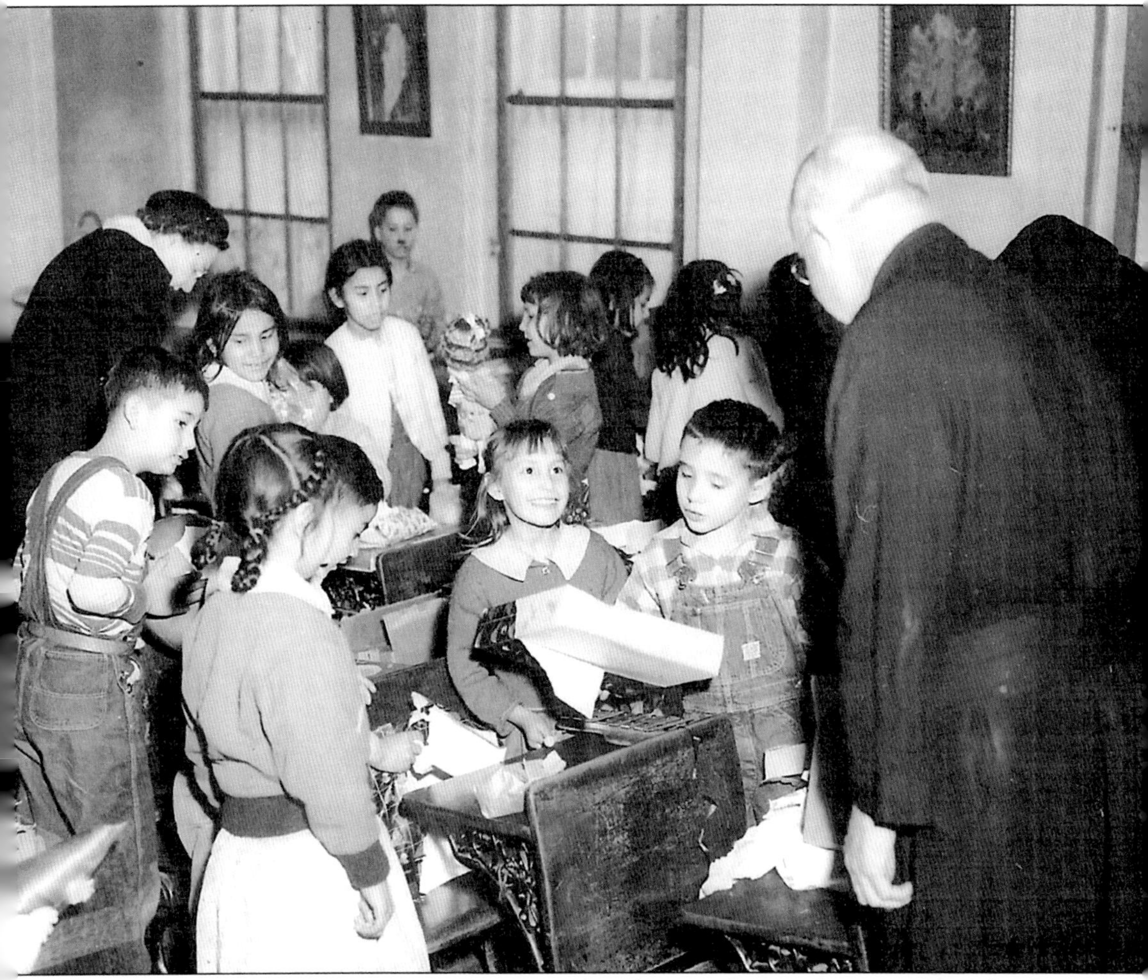

Christmas at St. Francis Mission School. This photograph was taken in 1956. Father J. Zuercher, S.J., is pictured at right with first grade students at the Christmas party at St. Francis Mission School. (Photograph courtesy of Red Cloud Heritage Center and Brother Simon, S.J.)

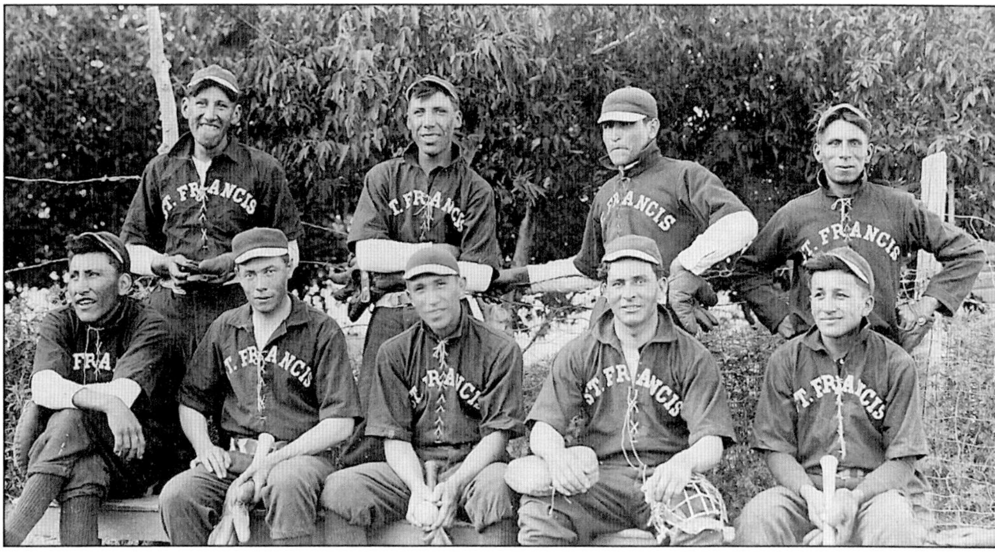

1917 ST. FRANCIS MISSION SCHOOL BASEBALL TEAM.. This photograph was taken in 1917. This baseball team of nine players were known as the St. Francis Reds. (Postcard courtesy of Red Cloud Heritage Center and Brother Simon, S.J.)

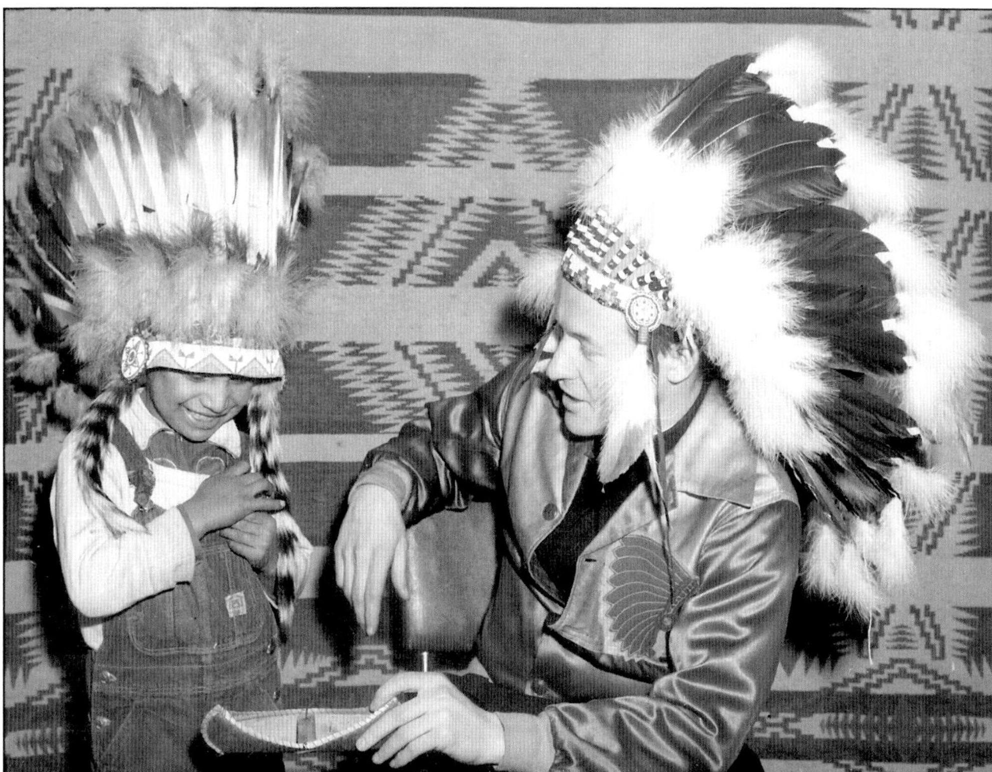

TONY GOOD BUFFALO, AT LEFT, AND FATHER JOSEPH GILL, S.J., RIGHT. This photograph was taken in 1956. Tony Good Buffalo is receiving Christmas presents at St. Francis Mission School from Father Gill. (Photograph courtesy of Red Cloud Heritage Center and Brother Simon, S.J.)

Five

Sicangu Lakota Owakpamni
(Rosebud Sioux Reservation)
1950–2005

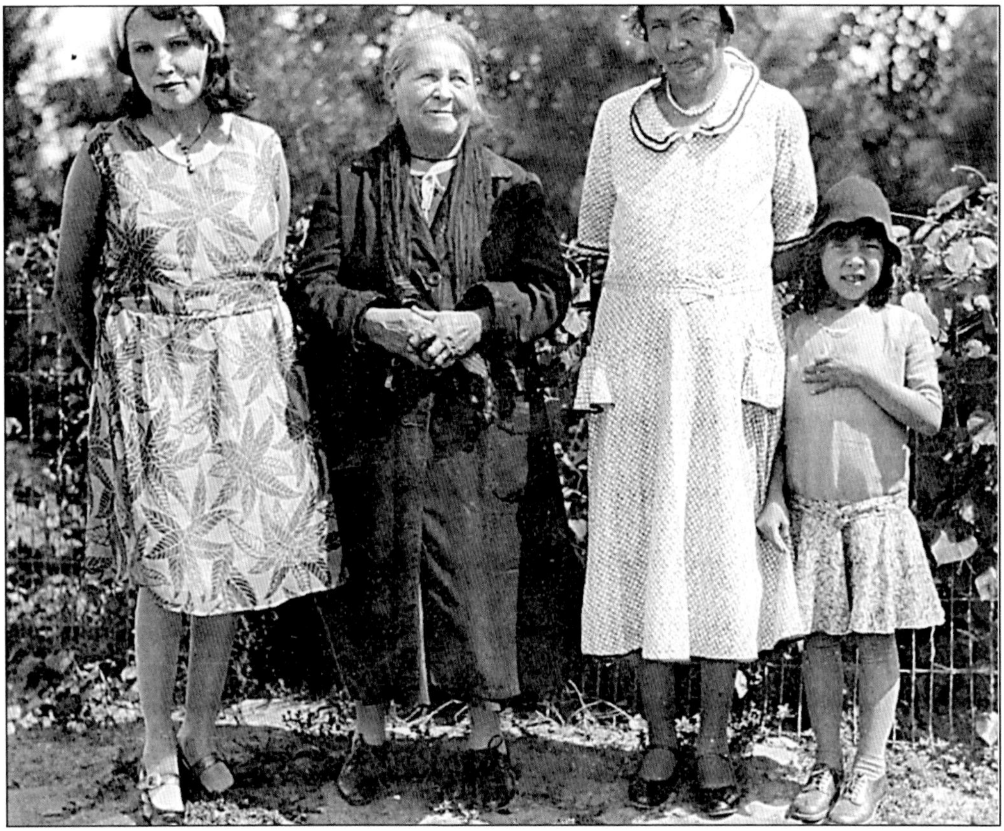

Women of the La Roche-Hudson Family. Pictured, from left to right, are Pauline Hudson, Julie Douville Hudson, Minnie Hudson La Roche, and Mary Louise La Roche Bordeaux (Sicangu). This photograph is undated. This is a three generation picture with Grandmother Julie, mother is Minnie, and her daughter Mary Louise. Pauline is the sister of Minnie Hudson La Roche. The little girl, Mary Louise, had 15 children, 40 grandchildren, and 60 great-grandchildren. Mary Louise worked 40 years at St. Francis Indian Mission and later at KINI Radio. (Photograph courtesy of Rose Two Strike Stenstrom.)

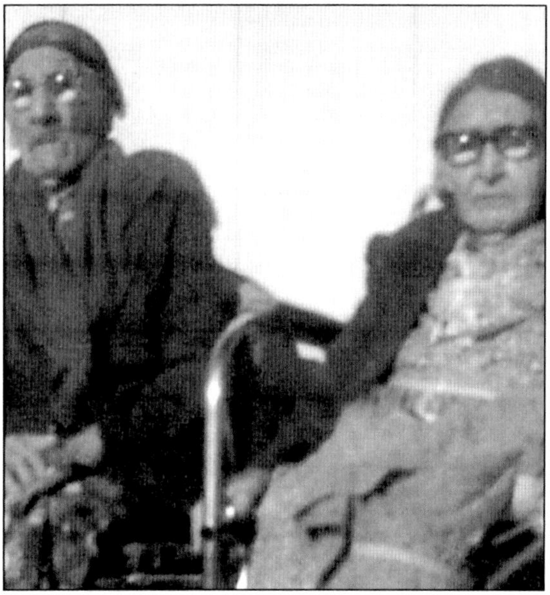

LUCY RATTLING LEAF, LEFT, AND AGATHA WOUNDED FOOT CLAIRMONT, RIGHT, (SICANGU). This photograph is undated. Lucy Rattling Leaf was the wife of Moses Rattling Leaf and they lived in White River, South Dakota. The author visited with her granddaughter Virginia Broncho Bill Broken Leg, also of White River. Virginia married Wilson Broken Leg. Wilson's brothers are Leslie and Simon Broken Leg, and his sister is Corrine. Agatha Wounded Foot was born in 1888 and had an early marriage to Peter Claymore in 1906. There were three different men named Peter Claymore around this time period at Rosebud, Pine Ridge, and Cheyenne River. (Photograph courtesy of Rose Two Strike Stenstrom.)

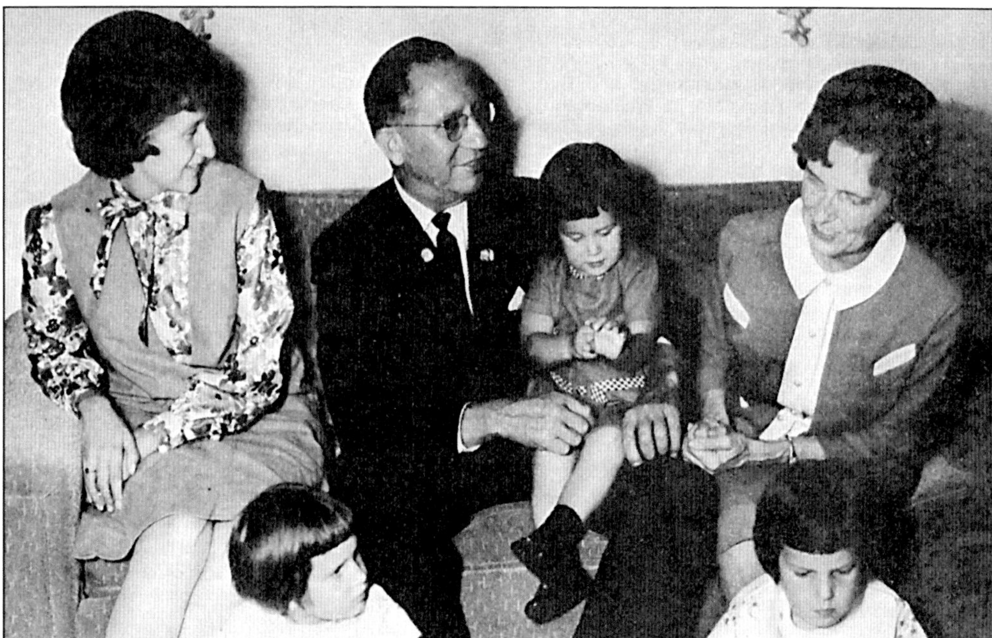

THE BEN REIFEL FAMILY (SICANGU). This photograph is undated. Pictured, from left to right, are Loyce Anderson, Ben Reifel, Valerie Anderson, Mrs. Ben Reifel. Seated in front on floor are Laurie Anderson and Lisa Anderson. Benjamin Reifel was the first American Indian to represent South Dakota in the U.S. Congress. He was born in 1906 near Parmelee and his parents were William Reifel and Lucy Burning Breast. Ben graduated from South Dakota State University, and then served as an advisor at the Episcopal Hare Indian School in Mission. In 1954, he received a Ph.D. from Harvard University and became the first American Indian superintendent of Pine Ridge Reservation, and then was the area director of the Bureau of Indian Affairs office in Aberdeen, South Dakota. In 1960, he was elected to the U.S. House of Representatives. (Photograph courtesy of South Dakota State Historical Archives.)

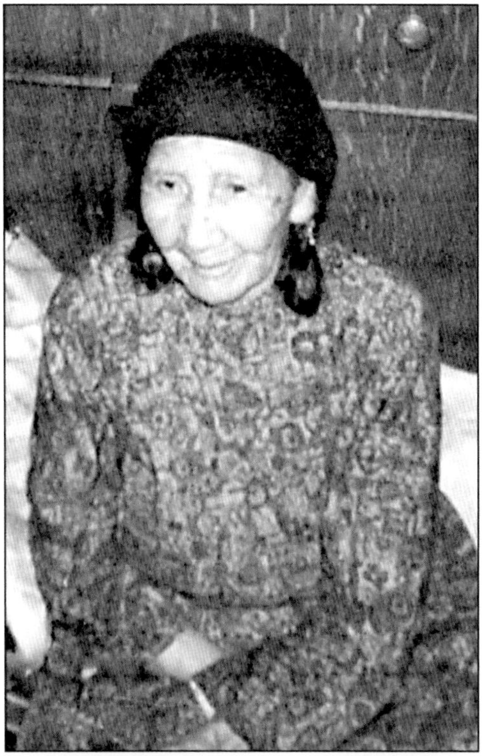

LILLIAN FIRE HEART (SICANGU). This photograph is undated. The Fire Heart family is listed on the 1875 Rosebud census with husband, wife, four sons, and three daughters. The Fire Heart name is also among the Siha Sapa Lakota at Standing Rock and Cheyenne River. At Rosebud some of the Fire Heart's first used the name Fire Heart Bear. (Photograph courtesy of Rose Two Strike Stenstrom.)

LUCY RATTLING LEAF, LEFT, AND SOPHIE SLOW HEART IYOTTE, RIGHT, (SICANGU). This photograph is undated. Ice cream is being served and the other subjects in the picture are unidentified. Lucy Rattling Leaf was born in 1891 and lived until 1978. A brother of Lucy Rattling Leaf was Albert Two Hawk, and Maggie Little Dog was a sister of Lucy's. Maggie married Paul Little Dog who was also known by the name of No Two Horns. (Photograph courtesy of Rose Two Strike Stenstrom.)

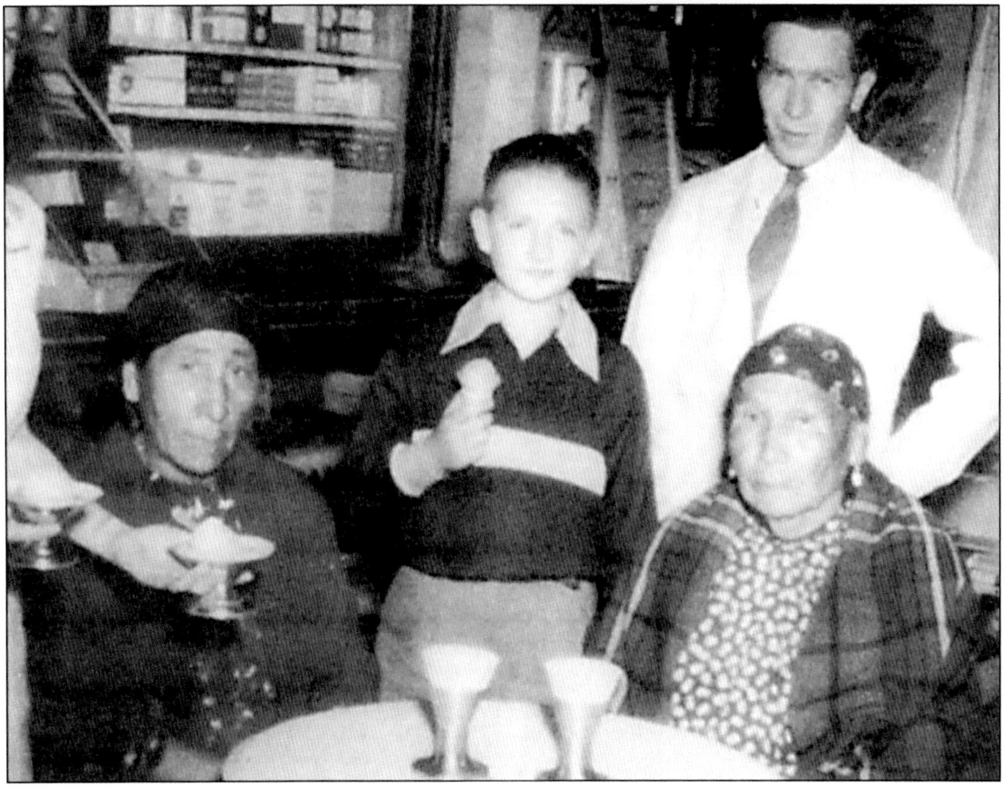

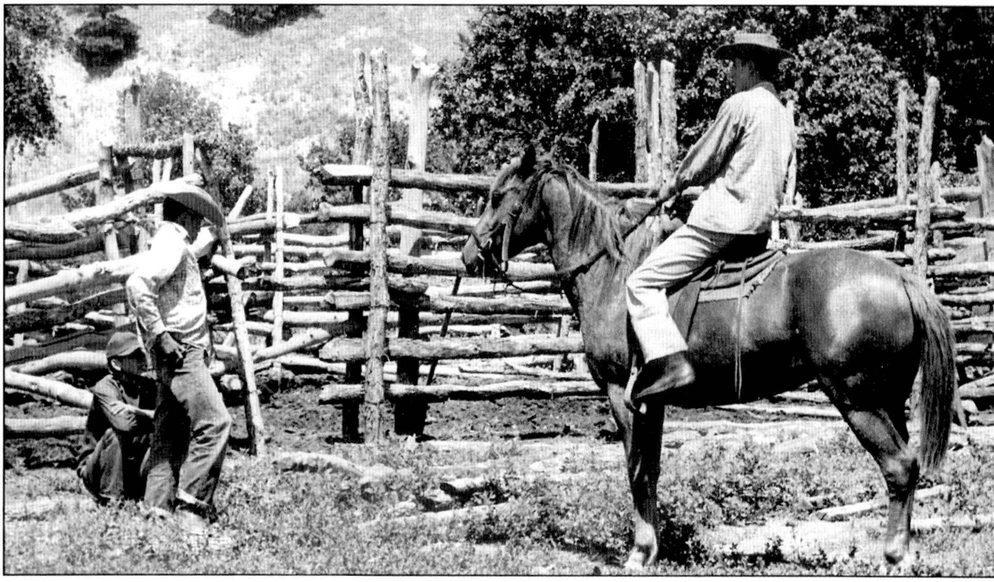

NOAH LITTLE JR. AT SPRING CREEK CORRAL. This undated photograph was taken at Spring Creek Corral. Noah Little Jr. was identified but not specifically. The photograph is from Father G. Pieper, S.J. (Photograph courtesy of Red Cloud Heritage Center and Brother Simon, S.J.)

JOHN (FIRE) LAME DEER "TAHCA USHTE" (MINNICOUJOU/HUNKPAPA). John Fire Lame Deer and Richard Erdoes wrote a book entitled *Lame Deer, Seeker of Visions*. John was a storyteller, rodeo clown, painter, prisoner, and practitioner of Lakota ceremonies. Born at Rosebud Reservation, he began school 12 miles south of Norris. He took back his original Lame Deer name. John's great grandfather was Chief Lame Deer, a Minnicoujou headman who was killed on May 7, 1877 during his flight from surrender on Lame Deer Creek, Montana. The headmen surrendering were Lame Deer, Hump, Crazy Horse, Touch The Cloud, and Dull Knife (Cheyenne). All were separated and Lame Deer was killed. His son Flying By returned to recover his father's body and found that it was decapitated and had 17 bullet wounds. Chief Lame Deer had three wives. His first wife had three sons: Did Not Butcher, Flying By, and Crazy Heart. Crazy Heart "Cante Witko" was John's grandfather. The second wife had one daughter and the third wife had no children. John's other grandfather was Good Fox, who died in 1928, and was at the Battle of the Little Bighorn and the Wounded Knee Massacre. Good Fox's wife was Plenty White Buffalo "Pte Sa Otawin." John's father was from Standing Rock and his name was Wawi-Yohi-Ya "Let Them Have Enough." Missionaries gave him the first name Silas and he became known as Silas Fire. People went to Rosebud and Silas was among them. As they were registering names in a book they told Silas his name was too long and suddenly a fire broke out. They quickly named him Fire and went to battle the blaze. John's mother was Sally Red Blanket and some Red Blankets are from Pine Ridge Reservation and John may be a mixture of all the Lakota bands. He also served in the U.S. Army. (Photograph courtesy of Ed McGaa "Wanbli Wicasa.")

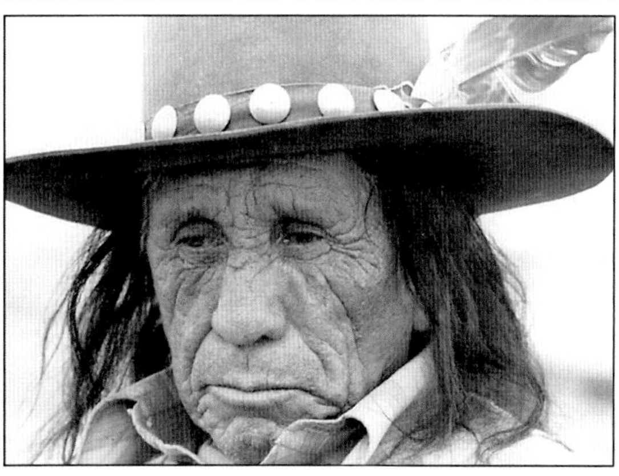

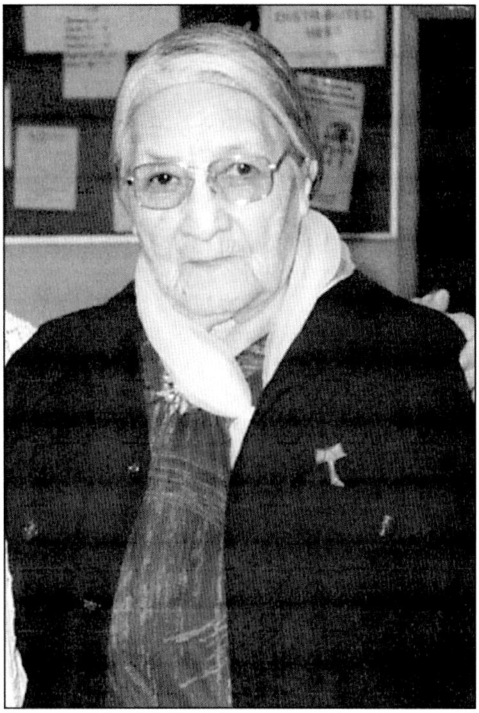

MARY BORDEAUX-HUNGER (SICANGU). This photograph is undated. Mary Bordeaux married Adolph Hunger, who was born in 1909 and was of German descent. Mary is the aunt of Virginia (Broncho Bill) Broken Leg, with whom the author visited with. The Hunger family is from Antelope. (Photograph courtesy of Rose Two Strike Stenstrom.)

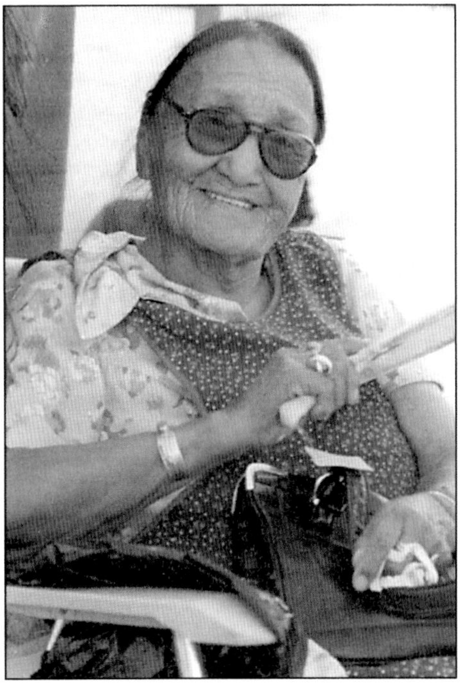

NANCY THIN ELK-WHITE HORSE (SICANGU). This photograph is undated. Nancy Thin Elk was born in 1897 along the Little White River, six miles northeast of present day White River, South Dakota. She had three brothers and two sisters. Her grandmother was Mrs. Alex Bordeaux (Sara). Alex Bordeaux had a large ranch and Nancy's father worked for him. Nancy attended Hare Boarding School and upon completion of the sixth grade they held a graduation for which her great-grandmother made her a beautiful beaded dress and moccasins. Nancy's great-grandfather's Lakota name was Sitting On The Hill, but his land allotment was under the name of Black Rabbit. Nancy later attended Haskell Institute at Lawrence, Kansas, for three years. While at this school an influenza epidemic struck Rosebud in 1917-1918 and many people died, including her younger sister. Nancy married Sam White Horse in 1921 and they had nine children, five of whom were Mrs. Bertha Shaw, Samuel J. White Horse, Albert White Horse, Theresa Guerue, and Lydia Charging Elk. Lydia's husband Raymond died in World War II. Sam White Horse was born in 1897 and his father was Fred White Horse. There were six children in that family, one girl and five boys. Sam attended school at Rapid City in 1910 and also at Pierre, South Dakota. Sam died in 1973 and Nancy lived until 1986. (Photograph courtesy of Rose Two Strike Stenstrom.)

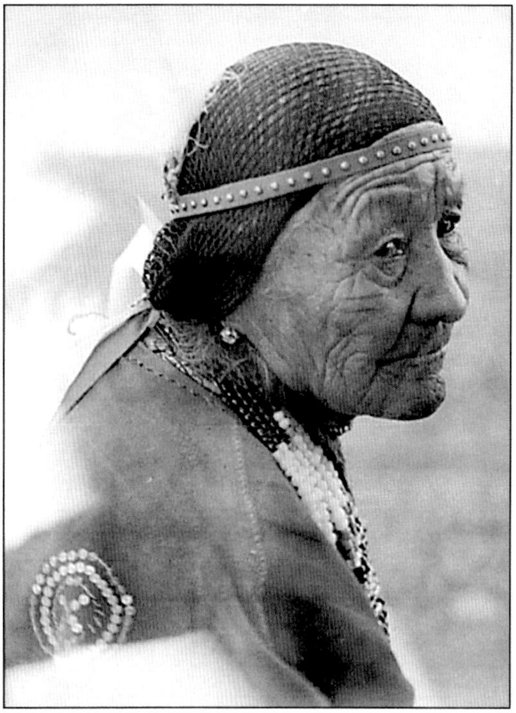

ANNIE KILLS ENEMY-BORDEAUX (SICANGU). This photograph is undated. Annie is the grandmother of Virginia (Broncho Bill) Broken Leg, whom the author interviewed for this book. (Photograph courtesy of Rose Two Strike Stenstrom.)

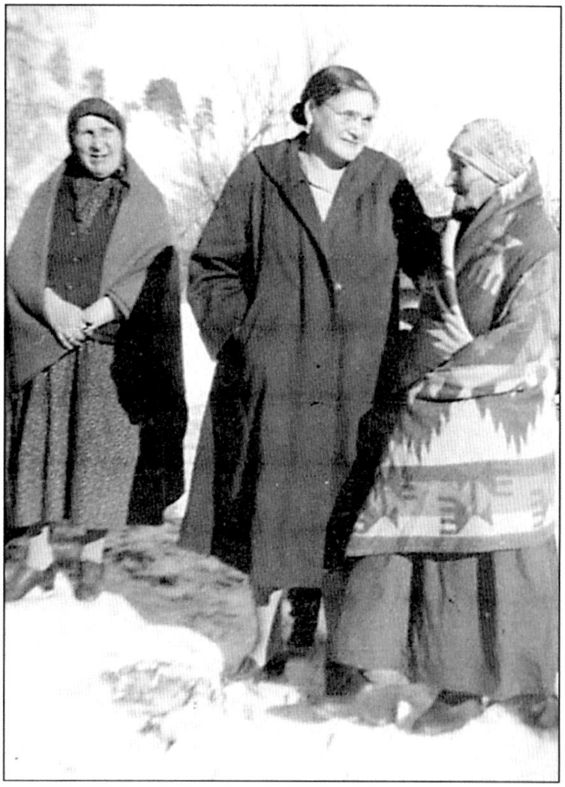

EMILY HOLLOW HORN BEAR-WHITE HAT, MARY KILLS IN SIGHT, LAURA HOLLOW HORN BEAR (SICANGU). This photograph is undated. Emily White Hat was a daughter of Chief Hollow Horn Bear. The Hollow Horn Bear family are from Grass Mountain and there is a bridge there named for them. Mary Kills In Sight was born in 1903 to Charles Kills In Sight and Laura Kills In Sight. (Photograph courtesy of Rose Two Strike Stenstrom.)

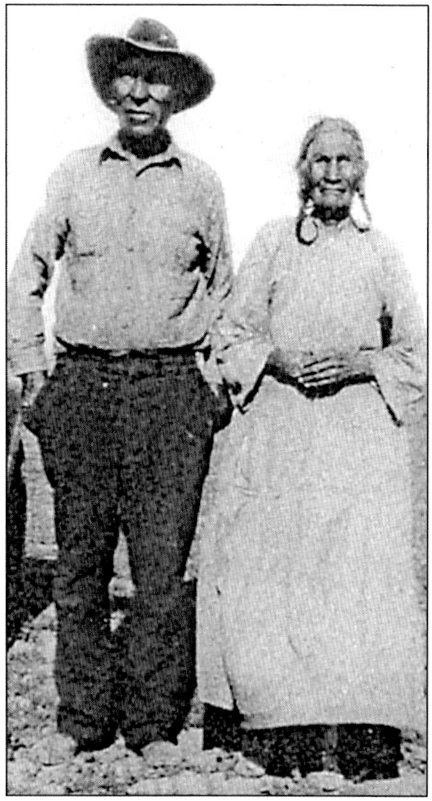

RICHARD AND FANNIE NIGHT CHASE (SICANGU). This photograph is undated. The Night Chase family lived near the Tom Berry ranch. (Photograph courtesy of Donovin Sprague.)

(below) **OLLIE NAPESNI (SICANGU/OGLALA).** This photograph is undated. Ollie Naspesni was born in 1917 at a camp which became part of the cemetery at St. Francis. The family lived at Red Leaf. She is a longtime quilt maker, beader, and well-known storyteller. Ollie's father Paul Napesni died when she was one year old and her mother bought land at Parmalee. Ollie's mother was Sophia Deon from Pine Ridge. The area where Ollie grew up is known as Salt Camp and is between Rosebud and Parmalee, South Dakota. That area is where the Spotted Tail family is from. The older sisters of Ollie were Emily, Alice, and Nellie. Emily and Alice's father was Joseph High Eagle, also from Pine Ridge but he passed away when they were small. There were five children born to Sophia Deon and Paul Napesni, but their children Sally, Joseph, and Owen all died when they were very young. Harry Flying Horse was a good step-father of Ollie's and the only father she knew. Harry's wife had died and they had two daughters. Harry's daughter Louise was remembered by Ollie when she came to their home but Louise also died young. Ollie attended St. Francis Mission School and later married Mike Bordeaux in 1936, and later married Jesse Medel. She is an instructor for Sinte Gleska University and received "Elder of the Year for 2002" by the National Indian Education Association, the 2002 "South Dakota Living Treasure Award" and many other honors. She has made over 600 star quilts and has a quilt at the Smithsonian Institute. Ollie's cousin was John (Fire) Lame Deer. (Photograph courtesy of Rose Two Strike Stenstrom.)

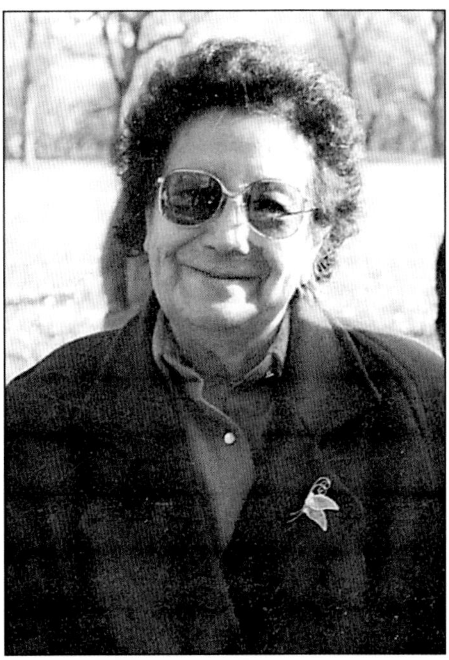

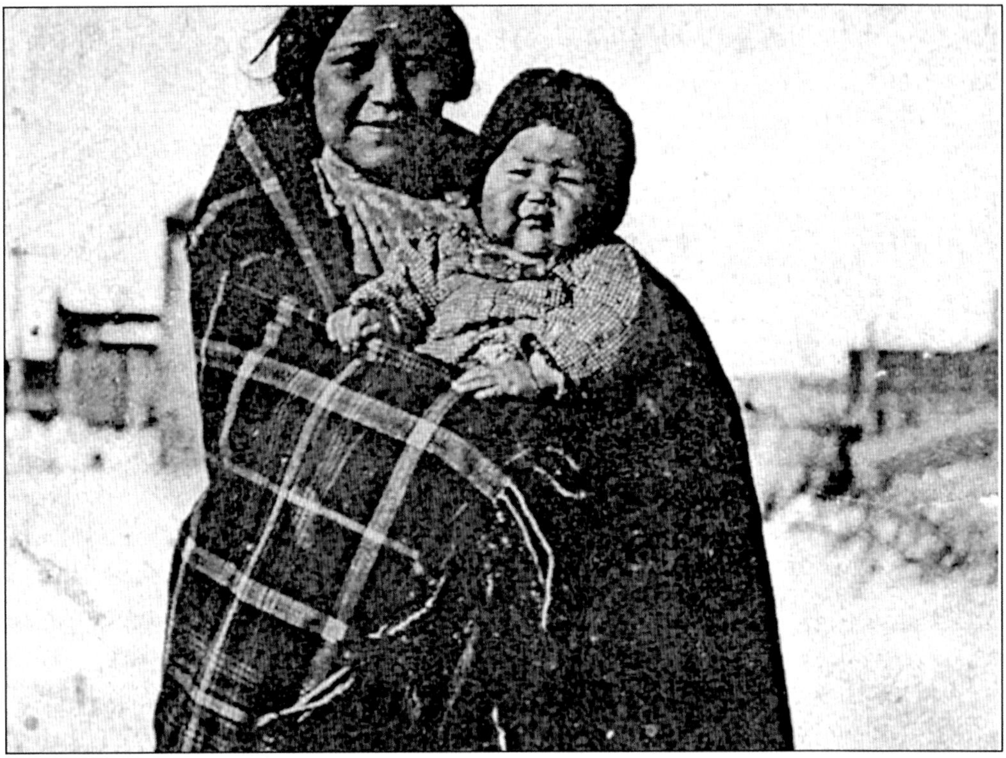

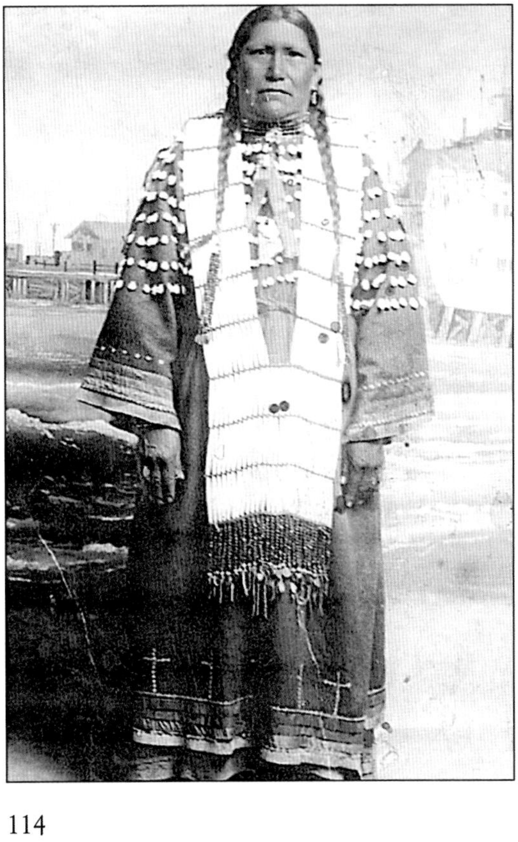

SARAH SHARP BUTTE AND HOWARD SHARP BUTTE (SICANGU). The author visited Howard Sharp Butte, who is an elder at the White River Health Care Center. Howard was raised about 26 miles north of White River, South Dakota, on the Big White River. His parents were William Sharp Butte and Sarah Quick Bear-Sharp Butte. This photograph is undated. (Photograph courtesy of Donovin Sprague.)

MARY SPOTTED TAIL (SICANGU). This photograph is undated. Many of the Spotted Tail family are from Soldier Creek area. (Photograph courtesy of Rose Two Strike Stenstrom.)

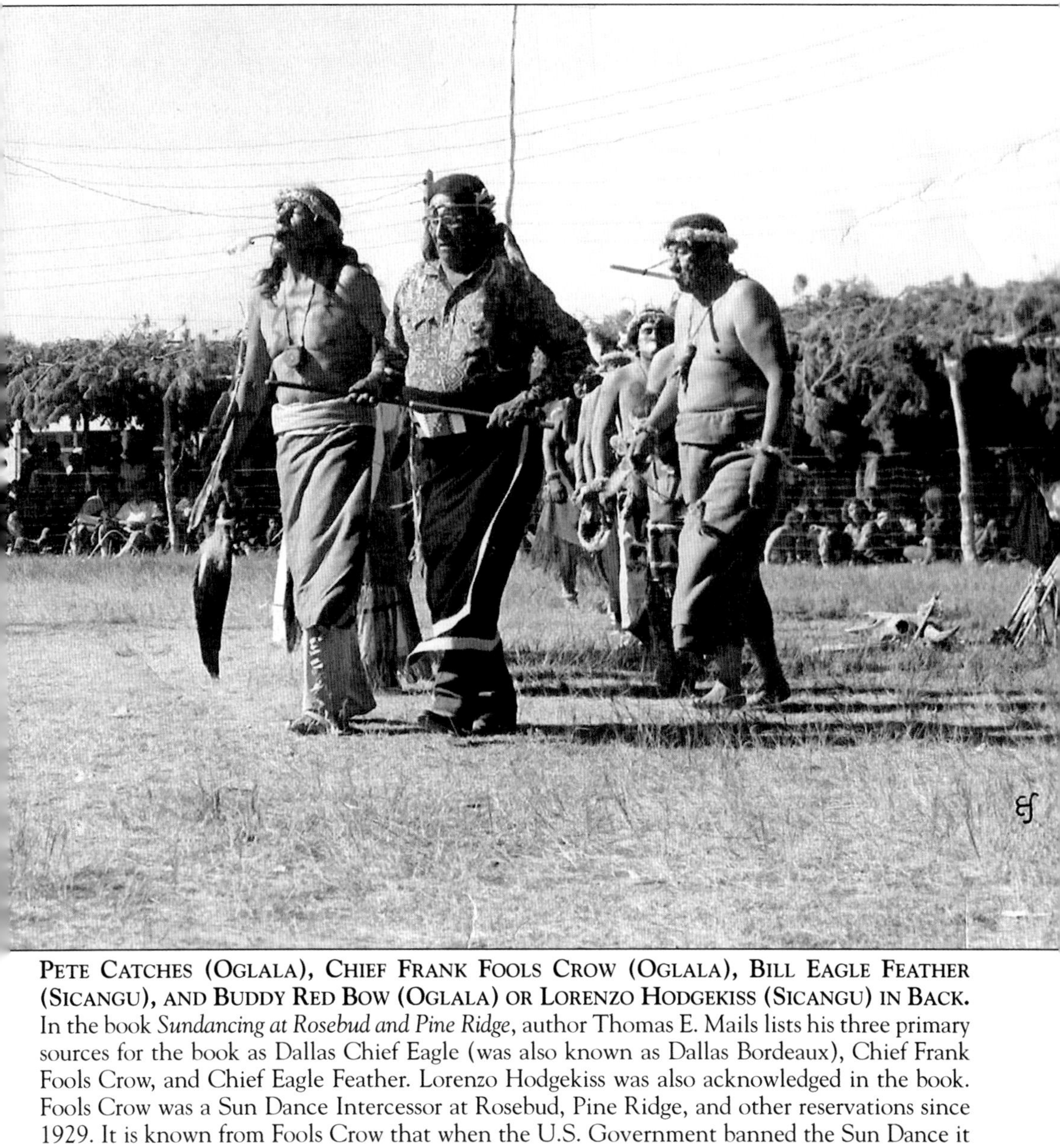

PETE CATCHES (OGLALA), CHIEF FRANK FOOLS CROW (OGLALA), BILL EAGLE FEATHER (SICANGU), AND BUDDY RED BOW (OGLALA) OR LORENZO HODGEKISS (SICANGU) IN BACK. In the book *Sundancing at Rosebud and Pine Ridge*, author Thomas E. Mails lists his three primary sources for the book as Dallas Chief Eagle (was also known as Dallas Bordeaux), Chief Frank Fools Crow, and Chief Eagle Feather. Lorenzo Hodgekiss was also acknowledged in the book. Fools Crow was a Sun Dance Intercessor at Rosebud, Pine Ridge, and other reservations since 1929. It is known from Fools Crow that when the U.S. Government banned the Sun Dance it went underground and was still practiced in the early 1900s, a time period when some thought it was not performed. This Sun Dance is at Pine Ridge Reservation and the photograph is included for its historic value only. (Photograph courtesy of Ed McGaa.)

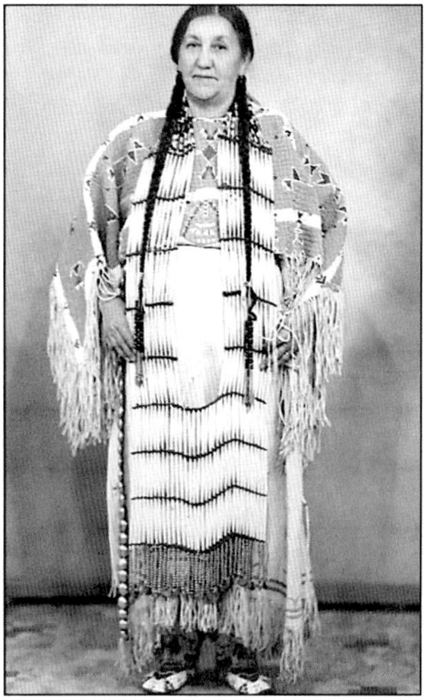

MARY BORDEAUX (SICANGU). This photograph is undated. Mary Bordeaux is from St. Francis. Mary is a name that is handed down by each generation from this family which used the name Bordeau and Bordeaux. One of the early "Mary Bordeauxs" at Rosebud was born in 1864, the wife of William Bordeaux. (Photograph courtesy of Rose Two Strike Stenstrom.)

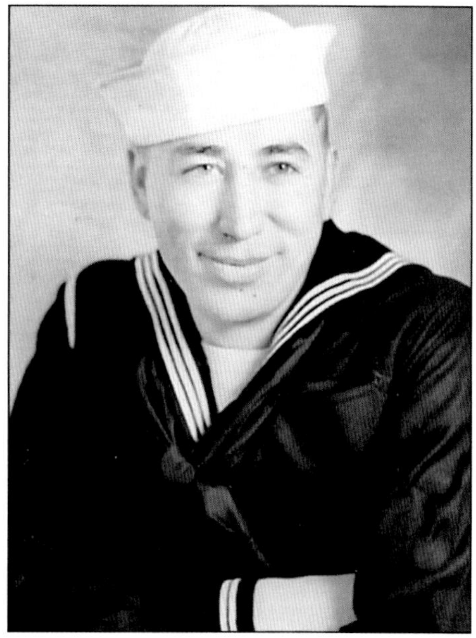

DONALD FRANCIS HUDSON (SICANGU). Donald was born in 1918 at Gregory, South Dakota, and is shown here in his U.S. Navy uniform. He served during World War II from 1943-1945. Donald and his wife Harriet had ten children: James, Thomas (deceased), Michael, Jean Marie, Rose Marie (deceased), Donna, Patricia, Shirley, William, and Mary Josephine. (Photograph courtesy of James and Lenora Hudson.)

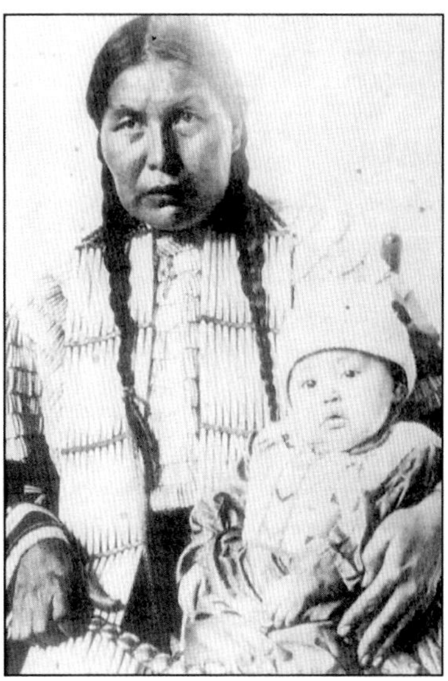

NETTIE LITTLE ELK AND HER DAUGHTER EDNA LITTLE ELK-LEIGHTON (SICANGU). This photograph is undated. The Little Elk name appears on the 1875 Rosebud census and is a common name which also is known at other Lakota reservations. This family is from Grass Mountain. (Photograph courtesy of Rose Two Strike Stenstrom.)

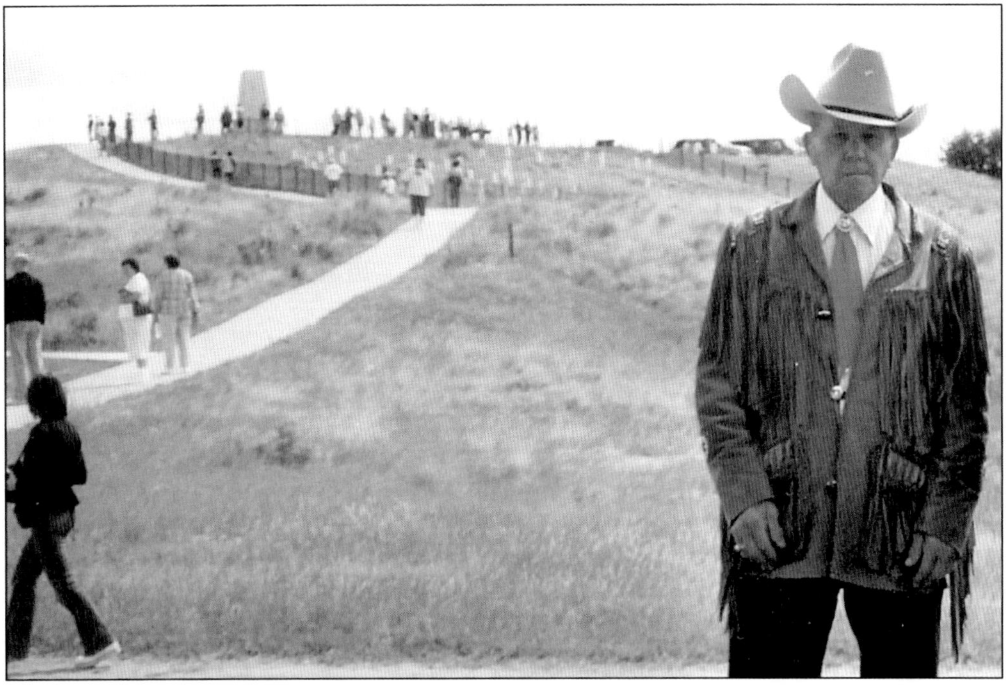

Chester Fuhrman, Jr. (Cheyenne River). This photograph was taken June 25, 2004. Chester is from Hardin, Montana and is a historian and friend of the author. His father was Chester Fuhrman, Sr. and his mother was Mary Rousseau. His grandparents were Paul Rousseau and Julia Boucher Rousseau. This picture was taken at the site of the Battle of the Little Bighorn and in the background is the Last Stand Hill. (Photograph courtesy of Donovin Sprague.)

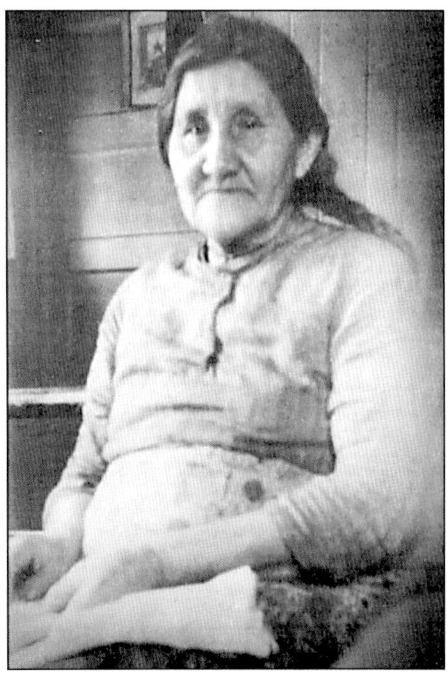

Anne Left Hand Bull (Sicangu). This photograph is undated. The Left Hand Bull family is from Upper Cut Meat area. Annie Left Hand Bull ("Chinapa Win") was born in 1880 and lived until 1959. Her parents were George Left Hand Bull "Tatanka Catka" and Whirlwind Woman "Wamniomni"/ "Wamniomni Win." Annie married Peter Francis Bordeaux about 1899. Peter's parents were William Bordeaux (b. 1860) and Mary Cazeaux (b. 1864). Peter lived until 1969. (Photograph courtesy of Rose Two Strike Stenstrom.)

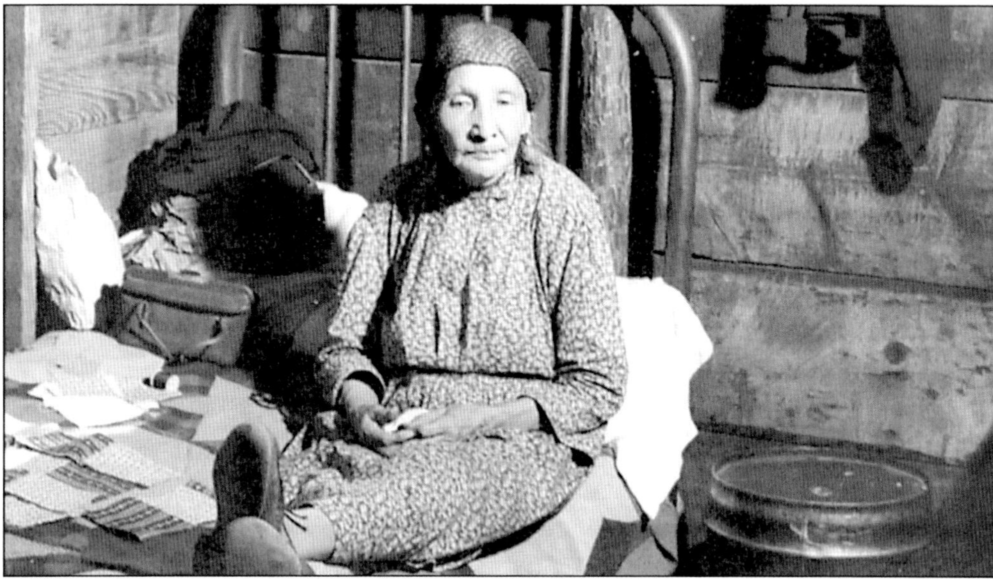

NORA JUMPING THUNDER (SICANGU). This photograph is undated. Nora was born in 1883 and is pictured here relaxing at her home. The Jumping Thunder name appears on the 1875 Rosebud census with a husband, a wife, one son, and three daughters for a family household total of six people. (Photograph courtesy of Rose Two Strike Stenstrom.)

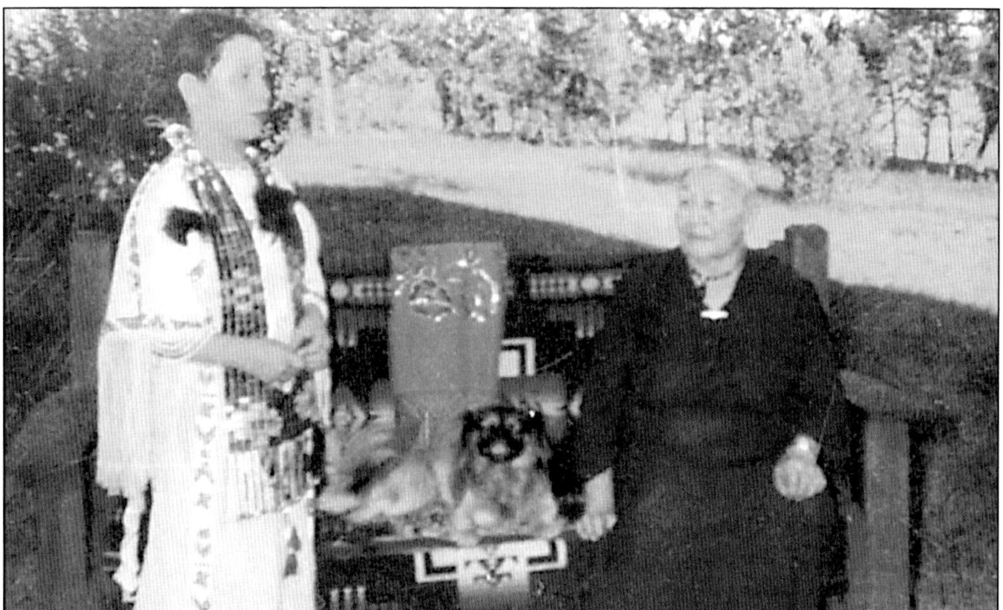

MARIE YELLOW BIRD LANGE AND VICTORIA STANDING BEAR CONROY (SICANGU/OGLALA). Marie Lange is pictured here with her grandmother Victoria Conroy and their sunka at center. Victoria was the daughter of George Standing Bear and she married Frank Conroy. Their children were Julia Conroy (b. about 1870), Harry Conroy (b. about 1870), Walter Conroy, and Lena Conroy. Harry and Hazel Conroy were the parents of Marie Yellow Bird Lange, Jean Hammond, Virginia Fire Thunder Rameriz, and Colleen Seamans. Harry's first wife was from the Fire Thunder family. (Photograph courtesy of Marie Lange.)

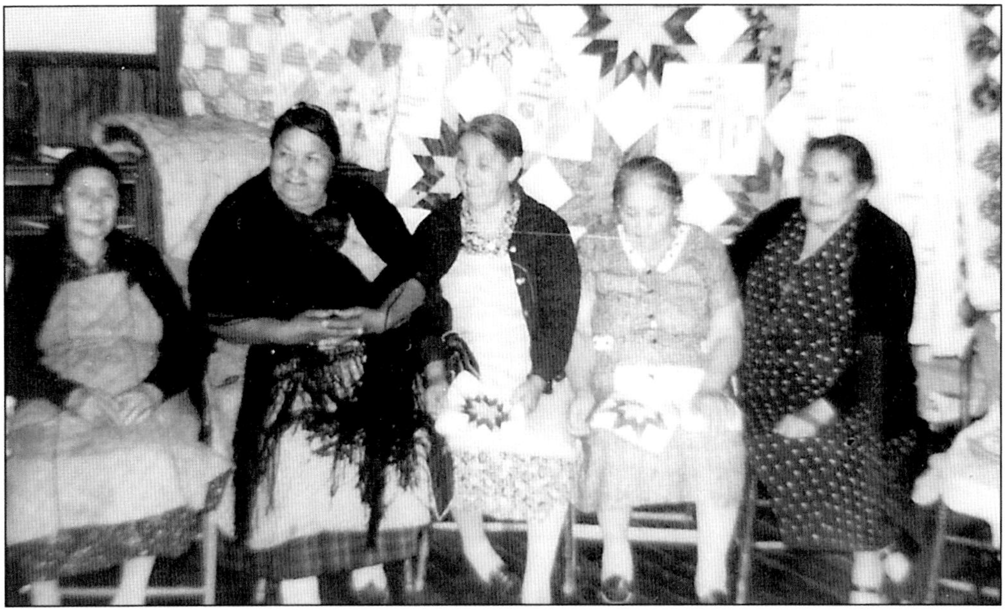

From Left to Right: Rachel Roubideaux, Lucy Little Money, Emma Wright, Nancy Lambert, and Harriet Ross. This photograph was taken in 1938. These ladies are with the Winyan Omniciye of Calvary Episcopal Church in Okreek, South Dakota. It is a meeting group for women. (Photograph courtesy of Virginia Driving Hawk Sneve.)

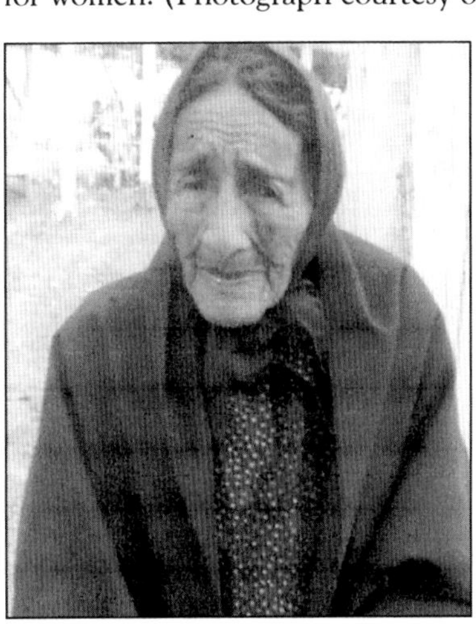

Katherine Roubideaux-Blue Thunder (Sicangu). This photograph is undated. Katie lived almost to the age of 101. The parents of Katie were Louis Roubideaux (b. 1852) and Adelia Blunt Arrow (b. 1867). She was a sister of M. Blanche Roubideaux Marshall. The children of Louis and Adelia were: Katie (b. 1890), Eliza (b.1895), Martha (b. 1897), Louis Jr. (b. 1900), and Sylvester (b. 1902). Katie Roubideaux was also married to Henry Knocks Off Two in 1909. Henry was born in 1888 at Rosebud. (Photograph courtesy of Rose Two Strike Stenstrom.)

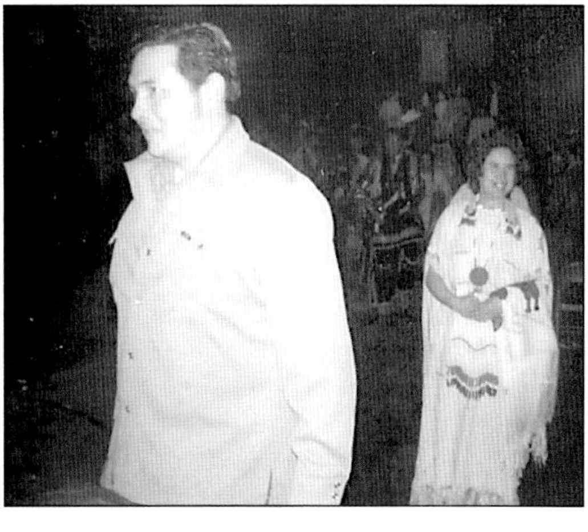

Edward Driving Hawk and Carmen Driving Hawk (Sicangu). Photograph taken on February 14, 1976. This event was the inauguration of Edward Driving Hawk as Tribal Chairman of the Rosebud Sioux Tribe. Carmen Driving Hawk is behind him. They are at Ben Reifel Hall in Mission, South Dakota. Ed lived in the Ring Thunder Community. (Photograph courtesy of Virginia Driving Hawk Sneve.)

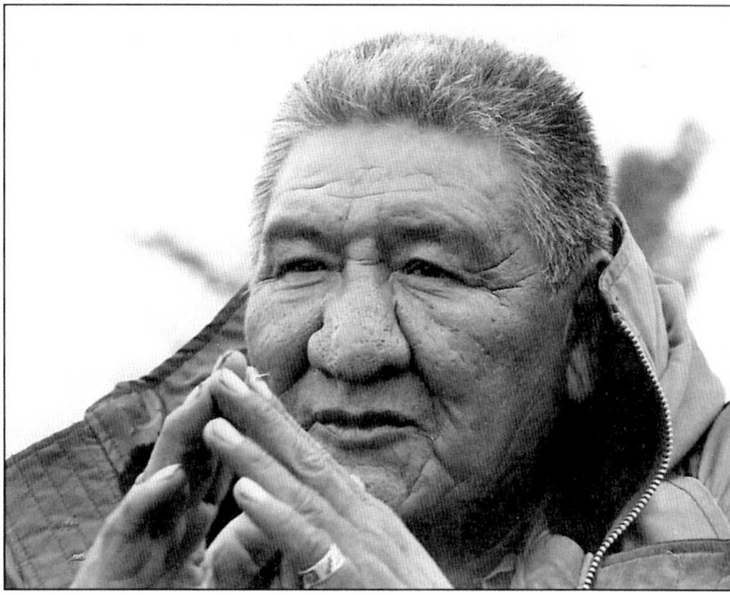

CHIEF BILL EAGLE FEATHER (SICANGU). This photograph is undated. Bill was active in Lakota ceremonies. He was born in 1914 at Rosebud, South Dakota. Bill's grandfather was a German immigrant named Joseph Peter Schweigman who married Millie Pino, a full-blood Lakota. They had four children, one of whom was Bill's father. Bill's mother was Annie Eagle Feather and his father was Chief of Police of the Rosebud Reservation, but died in 1922. Annie then married John Good Elk from St. Francis. Bill attended St. Francis Catholic School and then married Hazel Fleury in 1936. Hazel was from Crow Creek Reservation and the couple lived in California, Pine Ridge, Pierre, and then returned home to Rosebud. Bill participated in his second Sun Dance at Crow Dog's Paradise in 1957 and continued each year to participate in at least one Sun Dance per year. In 1960, Bill received the title of Chief of the Sioux Nation Sun Dance, Incorporated. That same year in addition to becoming a chief he was made a holy man by Lame Deer and Chief Fools Crow. He has now passed on and is buried at Sharp Butte. (Photograph courtesy of Ed McGaa.)

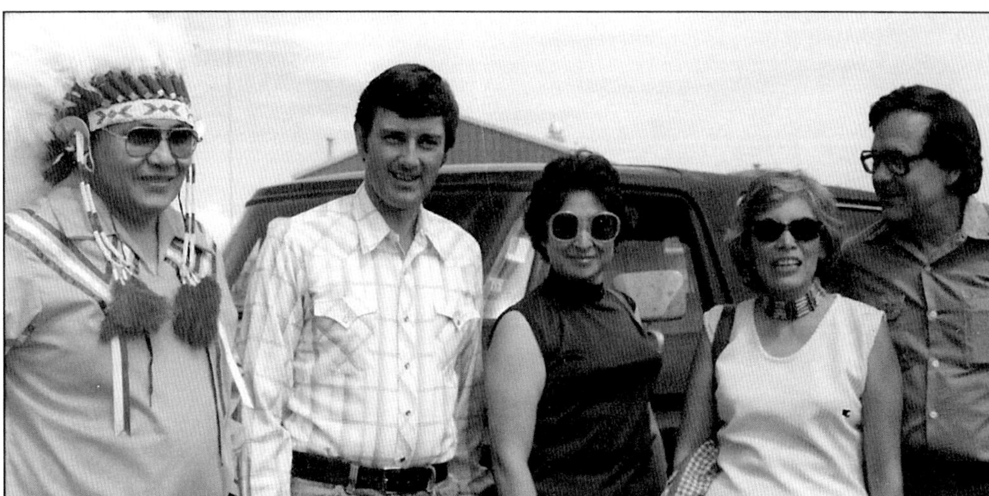

THE 1978 ROSEBUD FAIR. Pictured are, from left to right, Tribal Chairman Edward Driving Hawk, South Dakota Congressman Larry Pressler, Carmen Driving Hawk, Virginia Driving Hawk Sneve, and Vance Sneve. The photograph was taken in 1978 at the Rosebud Fair. (Photograph courtesy of Virginia Driving Hawk Sneve.)

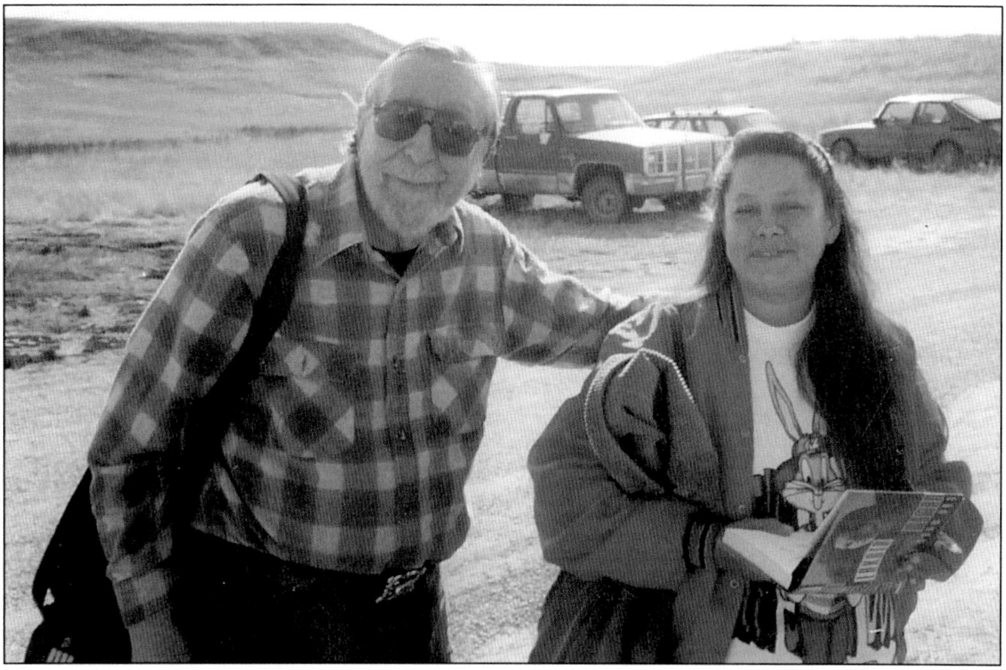

RICHARD ERDOES AND MARY CROW DOG (SICANGU). This photograph was taken at Triple 7 Ranch, South Dakota. Richard Erdoes and Mary Crow Dog are authors of the book *Lakota Woman*. The picture was taken on the set of the filming of the movie *Lakota Woman*. The movie was about the 1973 Wounded Knee takeover and Mary Crow Dog's involvement in those events. Richard and Mary served as technical advisors for the movie. They are signing a book for the author, who was also in the movie and had two movie extra parts in the film. Mary was the wife of Leonard Crow Dog and Richard Erdoes has written several Native American books. (Photograph courtesy of Donovin Sprague.)

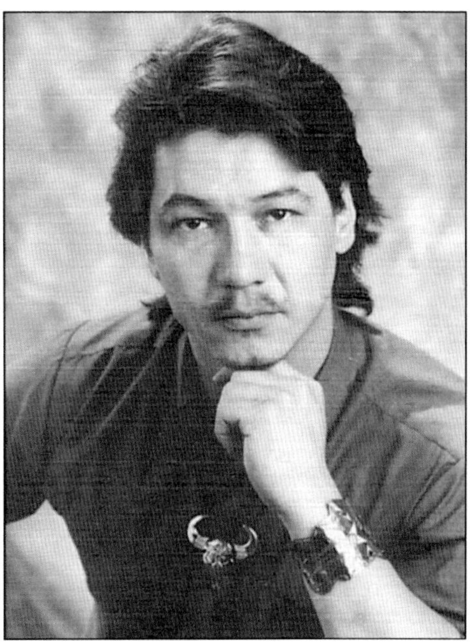

TIM WHIRLWIND SOLDIER (SICANGU). This photograph is undated. Tim Whirlwind Soldier is known for his silver and in-lay jewelry. His family is descended from Wanagi Pa (Ghost Head or Skull). They resided on the Rosebud Reservation until the 1950s. Tim was raised by his aunt, Evelyn Andrews, and he attended high school at Todd County High School at Mission, South Dakota, and in Page, Arizona. Following high school he moved back to Rosebud Reservation and also attended Sinte Gleska University. Paul Szabo introduced Tim to silversmithing in 1980. (Photograph courtesy of Prairie Edge, Rapid City, South Dakota.)

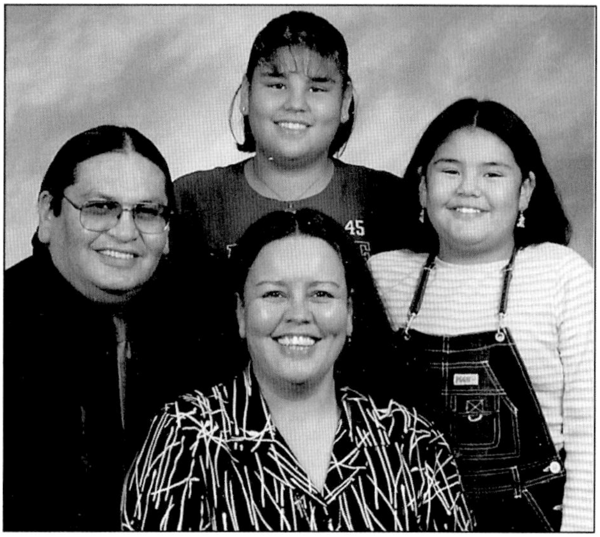

THE BLACK LANCE FAMILY. Pictured are, from left to right, Lorenzo Black Lance "Anuka Sun Wambli," Jolene Black Lance "Pte Ska Win," Anuka Sun Wambli (Good Eagle Woman), and at top Wambli He Ke Kta (Eagle Looks Back Woman) Black Lance. This photograph was taken in 2002. Lorenzo Black Lance is a well known Sicangu artist, born on the Yankton Sioux Reservation. His ancestors go back to Spotted Tail and he has taught Native American Studies for 20 years in grades K-12 and on the college level. He has done documentaries for countries such as Germany, Switzerland, and Poland. Lorenzo has given lectures all over the United States. The parents of Lorenzo Black Lance are William Black Lance (Sicangu) and Mary Julia Jandreau (Ihanktonwan "Yankton"). William's parents were Louis and Delia Eagle Little Tail. The Black Lance name for this family started being used in about the early 1950s. Wife Jolene Black Lance is the daughter of Charles Peterson II (Sisseton) and Cheryl Ducheneaux (Cheyenne River). Their daughter Anuka Sun Wambli is 10 years old and Wambli Ha Ke Kta is 14. (Photograph courtesy of Lorenzo Black Lance.)

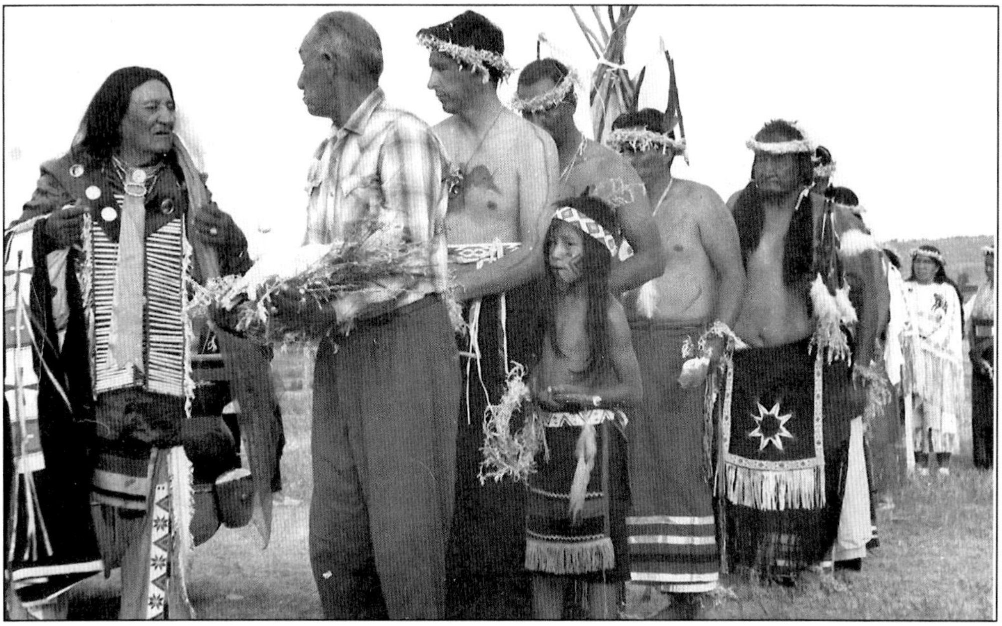

CHIEF FRANK FOOLS CROW (OGLALA), GEORGE GAP, ED MCGAA (OGLALA) AND OTHERS. This photograph is undated. This ceremony was conducted by Fools Crow at Pine Ridge Reservation. Fools Crow was a renowned medicine man from Kyle, South Dakota. The author Thomas Mails interviewed Fools Crow in two books entitled *Fools Crow* and *Sundancing At Rosebud and Pine Ridge*, which recorded pictures and information about Lakota ceremony. This photograph is included for its historic value only. (Photograph courtesy of Ed McGaa.)

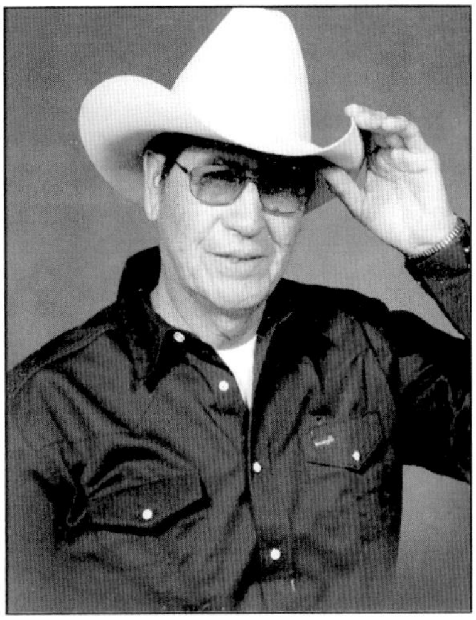

FLOYD TWO STRIKE (SICANGU). Floyd, photographed in 2004, lives at Two Strike community. His parents were Lewis Two Strike (b.1899) and Lorraine Bear Heels. His father passed away at the age of 38. Floyd married Harriet Blue Thunder, a Cheyenne River Lakota. They have eight children and one step-daughter. Floyd is a great grandson of Chief Two Strike, who was first known as White Bear when he was a boy. (Photograph courtesy of Rose Stenstrom.)

(below) **DECORY FAMILY (SICANGU/CHEYENNE RIVER SIOUX).** Pictured here in December 2001 are, from left to right: (back row) Sam DeCory Jr. and Dawson DeCory; (front row) Jace DeCory and Sam DeCory Sr., with their sunkas Tasha and Joe. This photograph was taken on Spearfish Creek a favorite camp of the Lakota. William "Samuel" DeCory Sr. was born at Two Strike Community. His father was also known as Sam DeCory and his mother was Ada Schweighman. Sam and Jace are well-known for preserving Lakota culture through dance and ceremony. Sam served in both the U.S. Marine Corps (Korea) and U.S. Army (Vietnam; four tours). He received five purple hearts for wounds, Combat Infantry Badge, several bronze and silver stars, Distinguished Service Cross, Army Master Jump Wings with one gold star denoting combat jump, USMC Force Recon Wings, Expert Rifleman and Pistol, and other Vietnam-era service medals. He served in the Green Beret and as a Drill Sergeant in Viet Nam, and was briefly a prisoner of war. Jace is an instructor in American Indian Studies at Black Hills State University. Sam had a B.A. from Black Hills State University and a M.Ed. in Counseling and Guidance from South Dakota State University. Sam was an outstanding Sicangu warrior and journeyed to the spirit world in 2002. Jace and Sam sponsored the Lakota Oyate Wacipi for many years, which honored veterans and elders. (Photograph courtesy of Jace DeCory.)

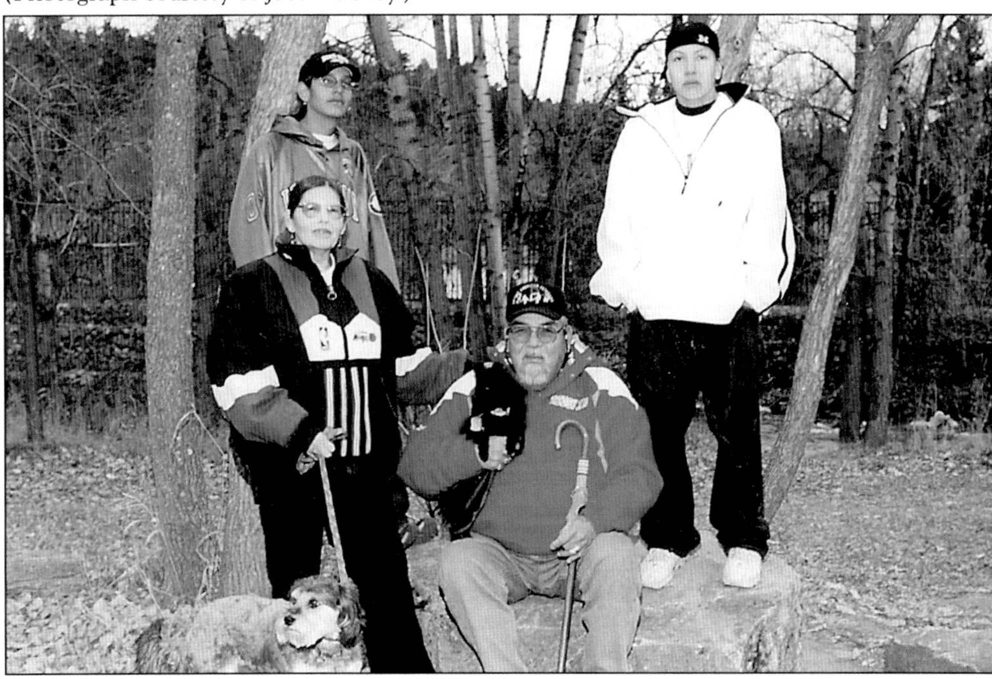

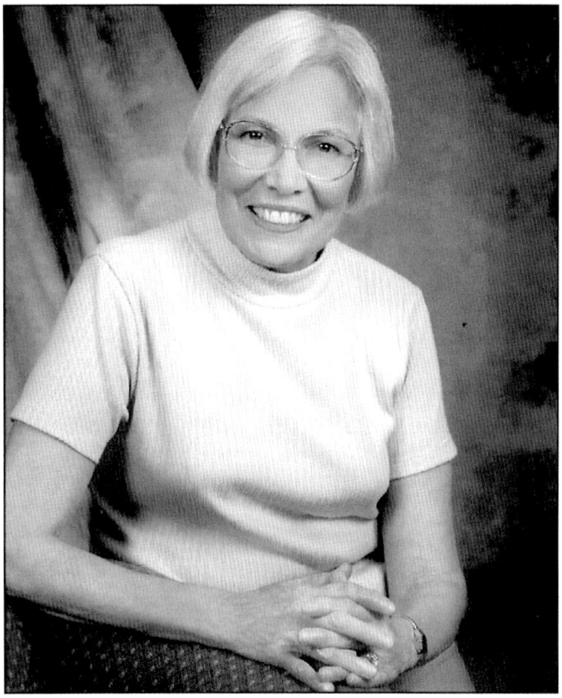

VIRGINIA DRIVING HAWK SNEVE (SICANGU). Virginia Driving Hawk was born and raised on the Rosebud Reservation. Her parents were James Driving Hawk and Rose Ross Posey, and her brother is Edward Driving Hawk. James was a minister of the local Episcopal Church and her mother was active in the community. She attend Bureau of Indian Affairs Day schools there and graduated from St. Mary's High School in Springfield, South Dakota. She received a B.S. and M.Ed. Degrees from South Dakota State University. She has taught high school and served as a counselor. She was also an associate instructor at Oglala Lakota College in Rapid City. Her first book was published in 1972 and she has added 4 books for adults, 15 books for children, and numerous short stories, articles and poems. She is married to Vance Sneve and they have three children. In 1996 Virginia received the Human Rights Award from the South Dakota State Counselors Assn. and Illustrator Human and Civil Rights Award from the National Education Assn. Her paternal grandmother, Flora Clairmont-Driving Hawk (b. 1887; d. 1977) was a storyteller of Lakota legends. Her maternal great-grandmother, Hannah Howe Frazier, also entertained Virginia with Lakota stories and history. (Photograph courtesy of Virginia Driving Hawk Sneve.)

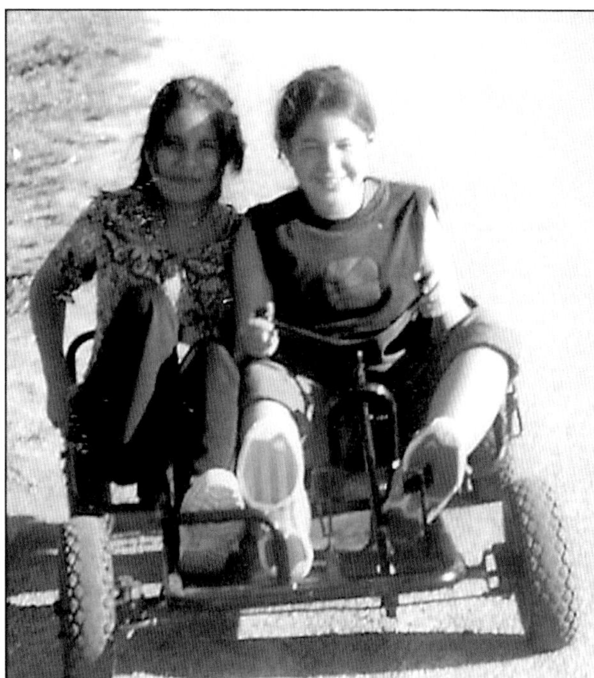

KAITLIN LEANAUGH (RIGHT) AND MONIQUE FLOOD (LEFT). This photograph was taken in 2004. These 5th grade girls enjoy a go-cart ride in the Antelope Community. The reservation provides a great atmosphere for youth growing up. (Photograph courtesy of Donovin Sprague.)

Index

BIBLIOGRAPHY

Agate Fossil Beds National Monument Museum-James Cook Collection.

Anderson and Hamilton. 1971. *The Sioux Of The Rosebud*. Norman and London: University of Oklahoma Press.

Bettelyoun, Susan Bordeaux and Josephine Waggoner. 1988. *With My Own Eyes*. Lincoln and London: University of Nebraska Press.

Big Missouri Winter Count 1890-1902. (Interpretation from Harry Blue Thunder).

Carlisle Indian School Records, Carlisle, Pennsylvania.

Driving Hawk Sneve, Virginia. 1995. *Completing The Circle*. Lincoln and London: University of Nebraska Press.

Hampton Institute School Records, Hampton, Virginia

History Book Committee of Kadoka Centennial Committee.1989. *Jackson Washabaugh County History 2. 1889-1989*. Pierre, SD.: State Publishing Co.

Lame Deer, John (Fire) and Richard Erdoes. 1972. *Lame Deer, Seeker Of Visions*. New York: Simon and Schuster.

Lewis and Clark Journals.

Little Bighorn National Monument Archive Records.

Mails, Thomas E. 1978. *Sundancing At Rosebud and Pine Ridge*. Sioux Falls, SD: Center for Western Studies, Augustana College.

Mellette County, SD Historical Society. *Mellette County 1911 to 1986*

Napesni, Ollie. 2003. *Salt Camp*. Vancouver: Leading Education/Trafford Publishing. Rosebud Census of 1875.

Seegrist, Nellie. 1981. *Lakeview Settlement, Rosebud Sioux Reservation, Todd County, SD 1910-1980*

Sprague, Donovin. 2004. *Pine Ridge Reservation*. Chicago: Arcadia Publishing.

Tripp County Historical Committee. *Tripp County, SD 1909-1984*

Weinberg, Marjorie. 2004. *The Real Rosebud*. Lincoln, NE: University of Nebraska Press.